D1601090

GESTURAL
POLITICS

GESTURAL POLITICS

Stereotype and Parody in Joyce

CHRISTY L. BURNS

State University
of New York
Press

Published by
State University of New York Press, Albany

Production by Susan Geraghty
Marketing by Patrick Durocher

Printed in the United States of America

For information, address State University of New York
Press, State University Plaza, Albany, N.Y., 12246

Library of Congress Cataloging-in-Publication Data

Burns, Christy L.
    Gestural politics : stereotype and parody in Joyce / Christy L. Burns.
        p.   cm.
    Includes bibliographical references and index.
    ISBN 0-7914-4613-1 (alk. paper) — ISBN 0-7914-4614-X (pbk. : alk. paper)
        1. Joyce, James, 1882–1941—Political and social views. 2. Politics and
literature—Ireland—History—20th century. 3. Literature and
society—Ireland—History—20th century. 4. Joyce, James,
1882–1941—Knowledge—Psychology. 5. Stereotype (Psychology) in
    literature. 6. Parody
in literature. I. Title.

PR6019.O9 Z535 2000
823'.912—dc21   99-045915

10 9 8 7 6 5 4 3 2 1

CONTENTS

ACKNOWLEDGMENTS

A voice in *Finnegans Wake* commands us to "Forget, Remember!" Yet I owe thanks to more people than I could possibly recall here, so long this book has taken to see its way to completion. From its earliest stages, I have had much support and advice from Richard Macksey, Hugh Kenner, Werner Hamacher, and Neil Hertz. At the College of William and Mary, many colleagues have read portions and offered helpful guidance: Nancy Gray, Kim Wheatley, Susan Chast, Chris MacGowan, and Ken Price. The Zürich James Joyce Foundation, under the benevolent direction of Fritz Senn, granted me a scholarship that allowed me to spend a semester at their archives working on this project. Special thanks to Fritz, Dan Schiff, Ruth Frehner, Antonia Fritz, Ursula Zeller, and Suzanne Bochan for all their kind help, and much gratitude to the *Finnegans Wake* reading group, which I will always remember with great fondness. Two summer grants provided by William and Mary and a semester's leave granted me by the English Department there also enabled me to revise two chapters when time would otherwise never have allowed.

The University of Michigan Press has kindly allowed me to publish here a revised version of "In the Original Sinse: The Gay Cliché and Verbal Transgression in *Finnegans Wake*," which was included in a collection, *Quare Joyce*, edited by Joseph Valente (© 1998 by The University of Michigan Press). An earlier version on lesbian sexuality was also published in the *James Joyce Quarterly*'s special issue on "Homosexuality and Joyce" (vol. 31.3, Spring 1994), and I owe them thanks as well for republication rights. *Novel: A Forum in Fiction* (vol. 31.2) published a shorter version of the Irish Nationalism chapter in its spring 1998 issue (Copyright NOVEL Corp. © 1998), and they have graciously allowed me to use that material. Nancy Cunard's estate has likewise allowed use of her unpublished comments on Joyce, which the Harry Ransom Humanities Research Center at The University of Texas at Austin made available. The Paul Klee estate, additionally, granted permission for the use of "The Timid Brute" on the book cover (© 2000 Artists Rights Society (ARS), New York/VG Bild-Kunst, Bonn).

More broadly, I have had the happy experience of intellectual exchanges with many Joyceans, who have discussed our mutual interest with much wit and insight: Vincent Cheng has always been an inspiration in his intelligence, commitment, and integrity; Joseph Valente's high energy and exceptional brilliance has gotten me through several moments of doubt; Margot Norris, Suzette Henke, Christine Van Boheemen-Saaf, John Bishop, Scott Klein, and so many others have been invaluable both in their work and kindness. Jean-Michel Rabaté, Derek Attridge, Michael Groden, and Bonnie Kime Scott provided extremely useful commentary and criticisms that helped me in the last stage of revisions. And very special thanks to my editor, James Peltz, to Susan Geraghty in production, and the State University of New York Press for seeing this project through to completion.

Finally, too many friends to mention have lent their endless support. I can name only a few: Cordelia Martinez, Beatrice Hanssen, Glenn Telfer, Loren Council, Jack Martin, Todd Jackson, Susan Derks de Sola Rodstein, Brigitta Gerl, Hiro and Lesley Amano, Sharon Marcus, and David Wittenberg. Warm thanks as well go to my family, Jean, Bill, Katie, and Carrie Burns.

CHAPTER 1

Introduction:
Parody, Aggressivity, and Stereotyping

In October of 1908, as Joyce was discussing politics in a small wineshop in Rome, he overheard one patron ask another whether "Signor Giacomo" was a socialist, to which the friend responded that Joyce was "un po' di tutto'"—"a little of everything."[1] In the intervening years, the numerous critical reconfigurations of Joyce's politics have variously borne out this wry assessment. Initially labeled a pacifist for his retreats to Switzerland during the wars and a cosmopolitan for his mockery of nationalism and the Irish Literary Revival, Joyce has more recently been reclaimed as Irish for his persistent use of Irish locale, history, and his texts' implicit critique of British colonialism.[2] Joyce's gender politics have likewise been construed at opposite extremes, with French theorist Julia Kristeva praising his later prose style as "écriture féminine" and American feminists Sandra Gilbert and Susan Gubar branding him a masculinist who parodies female speech and stereotypes women.[3] Current critics have further broached the subject of Joyce's representations of sexuality, and one of the emerging questions is whether Joyce's "perverse" textuality works toward an integration of homosexual desire or if his treatment of gays and lesbians marks the blind spot of a repression.[4] For those of us invested in feminism, queer theory, and de-essentializing approaches to Irish studies, these radicalizing readings may supply sharp new insights, and in other ways they may suppress Joyce's complex and often critical scrutiny of the aggressive nature of stereotyping. I am here proposing to re-open the question of Joyce's textual politics, focusing particularly on an ambivalent gesture in his works that moves between conscious artistic intentions and unconscious desires, between social commentary and pleasurable diversion, between ambitious universals and humorous disruption of their more arrogant claims. Joyce's parodic and experimental approach to representation creates this space of interrogation, where the limits of bodily gestures and material sensations are tested against the drive to capture meaning in its most embracing and political form. In the space of this conflict, Joyce's parody, humor, and meanings emerge.

My goal is not to elide questions about stereotypes in Joyce's writing; indeed, I will often be acknowledging their presence. When I began this work, I had hoped to find that stereotypes dissipated under the influence of Joyce's *écriture féminine* and his punning play on the multidirectedness of meaning. Indeed, they often do, but recognizable stereotypes surface, even in *Finnegans Wake*, although they are framed by an ever-deepening awareness of their growth out of aggressive social gestures. Looking back over Joyce's writings, then, I began to identify a pattern of gestural politics. I will be suggesting here that Joyce's work repeatedly retraces a double gesture, one that both mimics the subject's turn toward stereotypes and inscribes narrative ripples and ironies that draw attention to the absurdity of such aggressive representations. The contrary critical approaches to Joyce, which either dismiss his work on the grounds of politics or brush off such concerns with a nod to aesthetics or humor, miss the crucial *conjunction* between such textual moments. Joyce's focus on particular types serves as a catalyst to his art, moving it along a series of transformative shifts. Thus, gender stereotyping culminates in *A Portrait of the Artist as a Young Man* and is challenged by the emergence of women's voices in *Ulysses*. This change may not erase stereotypes of women from Joyce's text, but it crucially breaks down the more oppositional constructs pervasive in *Portrait* and calls into question the starker codes of masculinity. In *Ulysses* as well, an ambivalence about Irish nationalism ruptures into a full critique, just as the episodes' styles disperse readerly expectations of a unitary narrative. Finally, in *Finnegans Wake*, sexuality swerves away from traditional, heterosexual confines, tracing various forms of "perversion" that echo (and perhaps drive) Joyce's disruption of verbal clichés in the text. Of course, this tale of aesthetic transformations spurred by Joyce's pressure upon cultural stereotypes only begins to sketch the nature of these shifts. His interest in stereotypes may be at times quite unconscious, revolving around alternating obsessions and resistances. Moreover, gender, sexual, and nationalist types extend throughout his works, so that no single moment of crisis can be easily defined. I will be arguing here that Joyce's aesthetic changes are integrally linked to his use and cross-examination of stereotypes, which in turn is blunted against bodily and material resistance, represented both in Joyce's fictional scenarios and in the vibrancy and eventual boundaries of language as his medium. Stereotypes therefore inform, quite specifically, each new aesthetic innovation, and each innovation, in turn, serves to further disrupt and call into question the very process of stereotypic definition and conventional constraints of words.

The risk of attempting to navigate both representational politics and aesthetics is that one might be lured into the trap of one or another exclusionary extreme. Critics can be half-blind to Joyce's project, ignoring either the reductions or the self-critical inflection in his work. Thus they often manage to replicate the very problems they cite, either in terms of a disengagement with aesthetic inquiry or a reductive categorization of Joyce's textual politics. The history of Joyce criticism is rich with such moments; perhaps the most persuasive was David Hayman's identification of Joyce's success with his *mastery*, as a hyper-conscious manipulation of all previous literature and culture.[5] If in the 1950s the overwhelming allusiveness and experimentalism of *Ulysses* and *Finnegans Wake* made such a vision of the author attractive, this portrait of the artist as complete master was so potently realized that its mystification has since been broadly resented. Certainly, Joyce flaunts some critical prowess in "Oxen of the Sun" and throughout his work, but this portrait of controlling omniscience ignores the more humorful Joyce, the Joyce whose close engagement with the unconscious and its infiltration of language informs such important readings as those by Jacques Derrida, Jacques Lacan, and Julia Kristeva. On the American scene, however, the portrait of the master held sway well into the 1970s, when Gilbert and Gubar attacked Joyce's place in the literary canon in *No Man's Land*. Their quick analyses of Joyce seem more informed by 1950s interpretations than actual readings of his work, but their impact on his place in modernism and, most importantly, his relation to contemporary and postmodern concerns has been astonishingly severe. Yet if their incisive challenges compelled the Joyce "Industry" to recognize stereotypes of women in Joyce's work, they themselves reified Joyce as a singular agency rather than an author whose conscious intentions are often interwoven with unconscious slips, later self-mockery, and ironic distantiations. They criticize Joyce for his "appropriation of dreams in 'Circe,' his mimicry of music in 'the Sirens,' his usurpation of the Mass (and the Black Mass) in 'Telemachus' and elsewhere, his parodying of female speech in 'Nausicaa' and 'Penelope.'" They claim that Joyce usurps the "mother tongue," condenses it in his "spell of power," and turns it into "hard" male discourse (259–260). If Gilbert and Gubar condemn Joyce's parody without analysis, their pronouncements still reveal a double-edged concern: first, the suspicion of mastery in general; and second, specific anger against mastery when it is focused on the female. Mastery takes many forms, one of the most recognizable being the act of categorization and stereotyping; as Joyce's work readily foregrounds the question of how these structuring actions relate to judgment, Gilbert's and Gubar's charges against him are not without precedent.[6] Often, however, Joyce's "mimicry," "appropriation," and "parody" are complex processes of stylistic self-revision and social critique, which may hinge upon a resistance to the very caricatures Gilbert and Gubar so clearly see. I am not arguing that *Ulysses* is free from stereotypes of women; on the contrary, I will be exploring the extent and influence of such stereotypes. But the very polarity that creates such clichés in Joyce's writing is conspicuously replicated in such reductions of his work.

At another extreme, Joyce's tendency to undermine objective point-of-view, in combination with the multivocity of his narrative styles, has been frequently invoked to blanket all concern about textual politics. This turn toward *pure* aesthetic explanation is as diffuse and self-blind as the wistful construct of the text it provides. Indeed, Joyce's status in the literary canon has been centrally contested on both sides of the "politics of modernism" debates, perhaps more on account of early institutional interpretations of Joyce than for what he himself has written. New Critical readings that would lay claim to the superiority of Joyce's aesthetics seem (still) to lift Joyce out of any political reach, and political readings that seek to radically claim or purge him from the list of acceptable and currently compelling authors too hastily overlook the social engagement implicit within his aesthetic choices. These debates about Joyce echo an even larger schism between Marxist critics, who are concerned about the impact of avant-garde literature on political consciousness. Narratological experiments that create critical distance have been viewed by Georg Lukàcs and others as undermining the clear realism of social crises, whereas, for Walter Benjamin (et al.), the avant-garde enables its readers and viewers to locate a *positive* distantiation that allows for more complex and critical understandings of political and social situations.[7] While my own sentiments tilt toward the latter position, I do not believe that even the most radical narratological experiment can eradicate the concerns that have sometimes been raised about many modernists' politics, particularly where stereotypes are at stake. I see a crucial interplay between Joyce's aesthetics and his textual politics, which I am proposing turns upon important questions now being raised about the negative impact of misrecognition in literary and social representations. A fresh study of Joyce's writing thus becomes imperative to this new development in textual politics, which compels analysis from within the very text being critiqued.

If mine is then a serious project, humor will be its constant tease. In previous analyses of Joyce's parody, his humor has been invoked as if to set him beyond politics and critical scrutiny, a gesture that has perhaps caused many feminist readers to feel ambivalence toward his writings. Even as writers like Zack Bowen and Robert Bell have elucidated the humor and the liberating effects of Joyce's parody, modernist critics have yet to come fully to terms with the complicated politics of parodic narratives that oscillate between unconscious subscription and conscious retraction of social stereotypes.[8] And analysis of humor, more generally, has yet to close the door on the problematic question of social implications. In an essay on jokes published in 1905, Freud suggested that humor functions as an exchange between the teller and the receiver, with its comic success depending on the exclusion and mockery of some other. A joke can invoke "a public of its own," using laughter to effect "a far-reaching psychical conformity."[9] Humor that transgresses in one quarter may just as readily reify exclusionary limits in another. Henri Bergson, five years before Freud, noted that various forms of slapstick allow an audience to release their own fear of falling outside of social boundaries, so that the laugh we give in answer to a pratfall or oafish behavior implicitly punishes or gently warns the fool of his impending exile.[10] Joyce replays Dublin humor both in exculpatory jokes like the mockery of Herzog the Jew in the "Hades" episode of *Ulysses*, and also in his long-standing debt to pantomime, now thoroughly documented by Cheryl Herr. While humor's integral role in Joyce's aesthetic practice may often subvert such negative gestures of fixation and angry sobriety, we still have no intensive analyses of the calibrated relations between humors in Joyce's writing, which is, as Freud and Bergson observed, a very unstable element in any scenario or exchange. By integrating the effect stereotypes have on Joyce's experimental art—and keeping sight of his multilayered approach to humor—I hope to reclaim the significance of his writing both for our understanding of textual politics and in terms of the link between aesthetics and typologies.

In such a large, single-author industry as Joyce's legacy now commands, critical debates about politics have often been taken personally by critics on behalf of Joyce, as a figure of the biographical imaginary. There is a temptation to identify with Stephen Dedalus or Leopold Bloom, Molly Bloom or Gerty MacDowell—and even with the author himself. Yet, as critics have long noted, Joyce erases himself from his writings through a progressive self-parody, a form of Romantic irony that allows him to slowly separate himself from autobiographical identification of the strictest form.[11] It is my sense that, haunted as Joyce was by subjective alienation—his keen awareness of the split within the self—he put pressure on the limits of representation, turning toward multiple subjective variations and thus demonstrating the ways in which narratives are complex echoes of the subject's struggle toward critical self-consciousness. In this sense, Joyce's examination of the process of stereotyping might give us an important model for those interested, well beyond the literary study of Joyce's work, in the very links between different forms of consciousness and representational aggressions.

When Joyce's work delivers up stereotypes through the thoughts of Stephen Dedalus or, in the "Cyclops" episode, through those of The Citizen, it also mocks the unstable psyches that give rise to such reductions. So at the conclusion of *Portrait*, Joyce leaves his readers with an image of the artist as potential aggressor and rebel, both. This emerges toward the novel's end, after Stephen Dedalus has encountered E.C., the former subject of his erotic fantasies, romantic hopes, and poetic identifications. He recalls her asking him, "was I writing poems? About whom? I asked her. This confused her more and I felt sorry and mean. Turned off that valve at once and opened the spiritual-heroic refrigerating apparatus, invented and patented in all countries by Dante Alighieri. Talked rapidly of myself and my plans. In the midst of it unluckily I made a sudden gesture of a revolutionary nature. I must have looked like a fellow throwing a handful of peas into the air. People began to look at us."[12] Stephen's comical gesture arises from a burst of energy, through which his body obeys an unconscious signal emanating from the friction of desire and discomfort in his mind. Within the narratological *mise en abîme* of framings (the bodily gesture, Stephen's memory of it, Joyce's composition, etc.), we can see both the violence of the gesture, as a kind of signal to aggression even as he regrets his mean query toward E.C., and we can also observe a softly ironic commentary and corrective. *Portrait* as a novel pursues the subjective development of narrative consciousness to the supposed crystallization of Stephen's identity, so that Joyce gives us a character who goes through a series of oppositional, often defensive gestures, oscillating between a split within himself. The significance of Joyce's style, however, lies in the prismatic effects a layering commentary lends it, which accrue as we read. One can identify with Stephen's outrage, while experiencing his discomfort with the emerging aggression, and laugh at the comical scrutiny he gives his sudden gesture. Finally, one can simultaneously hear Joyce's own faint laughter, and perhaps sympathy, at the portrait he has just created.

Critics may embrace this protean form of perspective, but always it seems to exclude the possibility of launching a fully thoughtful critique of the textual politics of *Ulysses*, *Portrait*, or *Finnegans Wake*. Protracted discussions of Joyce's ironic relations to Stephen may assure us of his gradual disaffection for Stephen's inflexibility, but the text that remains unquestionably includes stereotypes of women and parochial authority that may be palpably experienced by particular readers. Herein lies the tug of curiosity, the critical puzzle that has yet to be dealt serious analysis. Joyce may be ironic and Stephen even *self-ironic*, but can the text not still effect aggressive portraiture and stereotyping? Must we then dismiss Joyce from a canon of taught and valued texts—or can we not still gain from reading the dialogue about such caricatures within Joyce's writing? In that Joyce's later works, *Ulysses* and *Finnegans Wake*, chart the loosening of aggressivity's hold on Joyce's aesthetic practice, the *representational* politics he has left us plays out a tense dialogue between reactive gestures and a diverse proliferation of images and words that comically overwhelms the binaristic lock. Stereotypes may never disappear in Joyce's writing, but as a kind of processural bend, a map of aggressive consciousness, they are challenged and the psyche that generates them repeatedly mocked and explored. The very gesture toward mastery that is implicit in stereotypic pronouncements is thus undermined even as Joyce textually creates it.

Given the inevitable failure of attempts to identify a single, consolidated "Joyce" position with a particular, set politics, the problem of the political in Joyce's works needs to be understood more explicitly in terms of his parody, so as to engage more fully questions about Joyce's tendency to reflect a politics in his own representational forms. I will be assessing Joyce's parodic inflection of stereotypes as it informs his changing aesthetic practice, linking the periodic employment of certain types with a shift in his narrative experiments. My approach may be termed "political" in its interpretation of the relations between representational effects and society's drive to stereotype various groups in the course of marshaling its own definition. Such forms of negative typing have been the focus of recent critical attention, particularly by Charles Taylor who, in his commentary on the politics of recognition, has forcefully argued that, "our identity is partly shaped by recognition or its absence, often by the *mis*recognition of others, and so a person or group of people can suffer real damage, real distortion, if the people or society around them mirror back to them a confining or demeaning or contemptible picture of themselves."[13] Art can certainly contribute and give voice to acts of social aggression, and while this realization has been central in the 1990s, it was already a concern of Joyce's own. One can see this in his response to the Irish Revival, to censorship, and, finally, in his reaction to social judgment and his constant replay of anxieties about political and personal betrayal. As Joyce's particular defenses chafe against his vested critique of social aggressivity, his parodic gestures slide from those that more ardently reify negative types to those that playfully dissipate such aggressive portraiture. I will therefore be describing Joyce's textual politics in terms of the relative measure of aggressivity or affection present within the gesture of representation itself.

In Joyce's writing, stereotypes erupt at moments when a subject's thoughts are destabilized and aggressivity breaks loose. In psychoanalytic terms, aggressivity arises when a subject views him- or herself in tense opposition to a particular figure or society at large. While Jacques

Lacan distinguishes the word from its more explicit and conscious manifestation, aggression, he insists that aggressivity is one of the crucial elements in the structure of all subjectivity and, when heightened to an
intense degree, "its [aggressivity's] effects are more far-reaching than
any act of brutality."[14] The difficult knots that make up and sometimes
trouble a subject's attempts to draw together the "imago" or the matri-
ces of images that form his or her sense of identity will necessarily give
rise to a tension and anger that is transferred onto some other, who, if
s/he fails to deflect the image, will become the target of antagonism and
reduction. While aggressivity rarely erupts into true acts of violence,
Lacan observes its manifestation in abrupt anger, attempts to intimidate,
reproaches, and lies; its most concentrated rise occurs in the case of
paranoiacs, who find themselves threatened by the multiplicity of
impulses within their thoughts and so consolidate their identity by transferring their own negative traits onto some chosen Other. A kind of
structural gesture arises here, a dichotomizing force that can become
characteristic of a paranoiac's mind. The perspectives of such patients
are, for Lacan, strangely given to stereotypic thought, in that their "perspective of mirages [has] . . . something stereotypical about them that
suspends the workings of the ego/object dialectic."[15] Aggressivity in
extreme will allow the subject a "formal fixation" that extends his or
her sense of power and world.

　　While aggressivity can transmute into aggression and, at historical
junctures, take the form of collective drives toward social stereotyping,
it is important to keep in view Lacan's observation that it is present in
all forms of identification. In the "mirror stage," where a child first
gains an awareness of his or her self as "an ideal unity, a salutary
imago," s/he experiences the contrary but determining emotions of narcissistic identification and aggressive competitiveness. "It is," Lacan
explains, "in this erotic relation, in which the human individual fixes
upon himself an image that alienates him from himself, that are to be
found the energy and the form on which this organization of the passions that he will call his ego is based."[16] Using St. Augustine's comments, as a clarifying example, Lacan quotes his reflections on envy: "I
have seen with my own eyes and known very well an infant in the grip
of jealousy: he could not yet speak, and already he observed his foster-
brother, pale and with an envenomed stare."[17] In the act of narcissistic
identification with the other child, the infant simultaneously becomes
aware that both compete for the same affection, and so the identification that could be brotherly is tainted by its necessary differentiation,
which, according to Lacan, sparks further competitiveness. In paranoia
and more oppositional forms of identity, the narcissistic echo in the
other is muffled and differences are therefore enlarged, so that the anx-

iety that arises from attempts to repress translates into concern for control of personal boundaries. The subject's anxiety peaks, gets inverted, and is then transferred onto a drive to control the other. In this process, representations of the aggressor's selected target are tightly fixed and heavily insisted on, so that the subject can attain a fantasy of *self*-control. From this gesture of aggressive fixing of identities, stereotypes emerge. In *Gestural Politics*, I will be assessing several textual gestures, ranging from the benignly narcissistic babel that leaves words and meaning indistinct, to other more paranoid-aggressive oppositions and attacks. These gestures are more than psychological trajectories; in Joyce's work they are imbedded in the letters, the language, and the processural shifts in the texts, as much as they are embodied along the limbs of Stephen Dedalus, when he hurls up an overly strident arm. Their presence does not mean that Joyce himself was paranoid, much as Richard Ellmann's biography at times hints at some slight possibilities.[18] Instead, I would argue that such impulses are, per Lacan, endemic to any psyche, particularly one exposed to significant splits and shifts in culture and world politics, and that Joyce critically appropriated the cultural paranoia around him and questioned it with laughter in his texts.

Whether seriously aggressive or softly punning, such paranoid (and alternately narcissistic) gestures are a potential model for parody in Joyce's work. In fragments of *Stephen Hero* and in *Ulysses*, we are given glimpses of an art of gesture, which serves to combine materiality with meaning, body with spirit, sense with essence. These gestures are forms of parody, more than traditional marriages of meaning and matter, for they take a norm (a recognizable gesture) and distortively pass it through the artistic body and mind. While "gesture" has not often been invoked as a key term in Joyce's work, it re-emerges crucially in *Finnegans Wake*, after Joyce discovers the theories of Marcel Jousse later in his career. I will unpack this gestural aesthetics more fully in chapters 2 and 6; suffice it for now to say that parody finds a *physical* model in Joyce. It serves as a kind of bodily (or lettered, material) appropriation, echoing an accretion that changes the self progressively. As Leopold Bloom seems to accrue into a character throughout the day of June 16th—one who in his fantasy packs pigs feet and dreams of rich, silk hose—so too the text of *Ulysses* turns ever more furiously on its own "body," drawing on previous moments of aggression and replaying them with humorous distortions.

Parody serves both as complicitor and cross-examiner in the use of stereotypes. Reifying a negative portrait may target its source; defracting such a portrait might likewise dissipate its control. Stephen as arrogant rebel is one such target; another might be Molly, first as eroticized object and later as resistantly vocal medium. Parody thus lies at the interstices of mastery and non-mastery. As in *Spurs*, where Derrida himself is caught between reifications of Nietzsche's misogyny and deconstructive resistances, parody might be defined as an unstable representation that itself never fully masters any law or object. Like the pun, it announces the impossibility of definitive interpretation and likewise of any full, intentional artistic control. This is not to say that one can no longer read, but that one cannot use reading as a vehicle to mastery. And so Derrida finds that "to use parody or the simulacrum as a weapon in the service of truth or castration would be in fact to reconstitute religion. . . . No, somewhere parody always supposes a naivety withdrawing [making contiguous] into an unconscious, a vertiginous non-mastery. Parody supposes a loss of consciousness, for were it to be absolutely calculated, it would become a confession or a law table."[19] Joyce's parody is neither fully confession nor law, though both models of discourse inform his social and personal parodies. In fact, one thing to stress in Derrida's formulation of parody is the flow between social (legal) and personal (confessional) states, so that no radical distinctions can be made. Prior to recent postmodern reconsiderations of parody, this has raised a palpable problem for political agency.

Indeed, parody is now the central term in formulations of postmodern political agency, which have invoked it with increasing alacrity to describe how the subject mediates his or her relation to forces of social normativity. This is no arbitrary development, since the word's prefix *para-* emphasizes the mark of contiguity between a parody's own product and that of some previously received text. This etymological consistency, combined with parody's long history of alternating political acceptance and censorship, makes the term highly appropriate for describing the gesture of mediation between self and social forces.[20] Parody operates as an unstable act that builds out of the way consciousness is constructed, weighing on the question of how that consciousness is related to social normativity and how it is engaged by representational acts. Therefore in the 1980s, Mikhail Bakhtin's work on heteroglossia and the admixture of dialects and genres in literature was used to support the view that parody challenges forces of cultural normativity. Bakhtin argues that the novel, as the site of parody, dialogizes other genres, permeating them with humor, irony, and elements of self-parody, so that its effects remain indeterminate and contrary to any form of establishmentarianism.[21] Subsequently, in the early 1990s, Judith Butler took up Michel Foucault's notion of a historically constructed subject to ask where parody might be an act of subversive appropriation of the gender types and behavioral expectations society imposes on men and women.

In *Gender Trouble*, Butler uses parody as a kind of performativity of gender codes, which repeats a normative code always with the infusion of a critically subversive difference. "In a sense," she writes, "all signification takes place within the orbit of the compulsion to repeat; 'agency,' then, is to be located within the possibility of a variation on that repetition. If the rules governing signification not only restrict, but enable the assertion of alternative domains of cultural intelligibility, i.e., new possibilities for gender that contest the rigid codes of hierarchical binarisms, then it is only *within* the practices of repetitive signifying that a subversion of identity becomes possible."[22] Parody therefore can open up the binary—or transgress it—allowing a proliferation and admixture of possible gender identifications. In her most recent book, *The Psychic Life of Power*, Butler scrutinizes the psychoanalytic drives that constitute the subject through subordination. This work is both interesting and troubling. She insists that the dilemma of being mastered (or mastering) lies at the constitutive core of subjectivity, so that "it is not simply that one requires the recognition of the other and that a form of recognition is conferred through subordination, but rather that one is dependent on power for one's very formation, that that formation is impossible without dependency, and that the posture of the adult subject consists precisely in the denial and reenactment of this dependency."[23] While I share Butler's earlier sense that subjectivity is a mesh of norms and counternormative gestures and I admire her subtle description of how early constitutive grief can be complexly denied and repeated in one's consciousness and actions, her model of parody as subversive performativity tilts at times toward individual will or self-remaking even as she discusses dependency. In this more recent project, she explicitly brings Nietzsche in to describe the way "the subject is the effect of power in recoil," expanding so much on a notion of self-redetermination that she insists that a subject answers the social name given it, even when it is insulted and *mis*recognized: "Called by an injurious name, I come into social being, and because I have a certain inevitable attachment to my existence, because a certain narcissism takes hold of any term that confers existence, I am led to embrace the terms that injure me because they constitute me socially."[24] Here she takes Hegel's Master-Slave model quite closely, adapting a one-to-one causality instead of a layering of naming that comes from loving affirmation as much as a sometimes contradictory injury from other, multiple sources. She also undermines, implicitly, critics who call for social attention to misnaming and negative cultural imagining. In my work, the impact of misrecognition is not a matter of appropriation, but, arising as it often does in social spheres beyond the familial or immediate intersubjective exchange, it can have more unresistable, damaging effects on a subject's unconscious. Moreover, my own concern for textual questions and the preventions of such misrecognitions in interpretation takes my notions of gesture and parody in a very different direction from Butler's. Leaning more toward Derrida's notion of the mime, as a trace of parodic appropriation or personal style, I treat parody as a reflection of unconscious and conscious oscillations on the very body of words, which in Joyce are broken and rewritten, shaped as interruptions of definitive crystallizations. In *Finnegans Wake*, naming is often an aggressive gesture that word play and humor can derail, so that an alternative *literary* strategy emerges in Joyce's transmutation of parody. Such parodic gestures occur at moments when the object of the attack refuses to consolidate his or her identity and *appear* as such.

The question of where agency lies in this mixture of being-made and making is not one to be easily, or even ultimately, resolved. It is very much the problem of demarcating the movement from the unconscious to the conscious level of control; while this movement in pragmatic terms exists, it can never be precisely identified and caught at the moment of full crystallization—nor can one guarantee that it will not slip back. Parody, which functions as re-interpretation, reappears always at the center of such problems. No wonder Joyce's texts so readily become the battleground of interpretive tension. In his work, parody emerges first as a gesture that is so intertwined within the artist's subjectivity as to be barely distinct from his own body. Joyce's initial foray into parodic modes begins even within his most realistic text, the autobiographical fragments we have of *Stephen Hero*. In the chapter that follows, on the "art of gesture," I will be developing this notion of parody as mimic gesture, drawing this out of an analysis of Joyce's aesthetic practice as it emerges in distinction from Stephen Dedalus' comments on art. In *Stephen Hero*, Stephen humorously describes his interest in an art of gesture, a process of incorporating a pregiven text into bodily movements, drawing on models of eurhythmics and pantomime.[25] However, Stephen's is no ordinary mime in the sense of acting out one of the stock plots of pantomime; rather, it is movement *as* style, identified by its rhythmic aspect as Stephen beats out the measure of a song with his arms. Meaning-as-movement rather than syntax gradually emerges as a central aesthetic and political notion in Joyce's work. It begins as this physically incorporated rhythm and becomes crucial to Joyce's writing as it marks an oscillation between identity and disidentity, even as it is pressed underground in Stephen's thoughts when he later shifts toward asceticism and denial of the body. Eventually, in "Circe," it re-emerges as desiring, physical gesture that disrupts the balance and stasis of the early aesthetics. Joyce's initial formulation of gesture and the continuing influence of mime lends him a model for the integration of influence, one that both acknowledges a pregiven pattern or rhythm while allowing for the importance of stylistic alteration.

As stylistic gesture, parody is not "mere" style, nor is it something that can be strictly measured with reference to some fixed norm. It is rather that which defines itself in dialogue with its various contexts and, most importantly, with its own process of becoming. And "becoming" in Joyce's work unfolds through a series of resistances, rebellions, and betrayals that create neither mere text or words, but a whole world that is constantly redefined and given back to itself in the artist's representation. When Leopold Bloom's penpal Martha mistakenly types that she fears a naughty "world" instead of "word," her error might ironically point toward an anxiety Joyce often parodied: the fear that words might slide her into another world, signaling the all too dangerous efficacy of language foregrounded in *Ulysses*.[26] This is humorously brought to the fore in the "Aeolus" episode, when Professor MacHugh laconically warns: "We mustn't be led away by words, by sounds of words. We think of Rome, imperial, imperious, imperative" (U 7.484–486).

Joyce's formulation of "the Word" is associated with his representations of women, who appear first as silent muses to artistic (and erotic) inspiration, and later transform into women who babble their desire into the pool of words that make up *Finnegans Wake*. In my third chapter, *"The word is my Wife": Control of the Feminine*, I explore the ways in which female desire threatens by virtue of its uncontrollable nature and dangerous influence. Joyce's representations of women are forever reproducing the problem of controlling this desire, and the primary focal point of desire operating within Joyce's aesthetic practice is a hetero-erotics circulating around the figure of woman. Whereas female characters are given a measure of agency and voice in the early realist stories of *Dubliners*, in Joyce's first truly parodic work, *Portrait*, women are placed in the position of the silent, distant muse to male creation. In this chapter, I trace female voices from *Portrait* to *Ulysses*, as they emerge through ventriloquization and eventually open toward an articulation of erotic desires that flows into *Finnegans Wake*. Joyce achieves this release as he parodies the anxiety of cuckoldry that motivates the reduction of women to troublesome others, relegating them to the status of objects to be controlled. This control of the desired female object works in direct relation to the control of the word in Joyce's prose. In *Finnegans Wake*, Shaun, the moral papist, announces to the rainbow girls that "the word is my Wife, to exponse and expound, to vend and to velnerate, and may the curlews crown our nuptias! Till Breath us depart!"[27] This echoes an earlier claim of Stephen's, with regard to Shakespeare and Ann Hathaway in the "Scylla and Charybdis" episode, when Stephen argues that the artistic desire to control words runs parallel to the necessity of controlling women's sexual appetites. Joyce inverts this claim about the power of cuckoldry in his own work, slowly abandoning the representation of women as silent, erotic muses and experimenting with the ventriloquization of their desires in *Ulysses*. This ventriloquization plays out a dual gesture of fulfilling what might be assessed as Joyce's own erotic desires while also, in a countergesture, slowly releasing the women in his texts to a discourse of desire. As Joyce plays out this shift, so his language becomes more sensate and his text more radically accretive and voluminous in its cross-catalogue of allusions and word-play. The playfulness of words and the decentering of typological categories is explicitly linked to women's articulation of erotic desires in *Finnegans Wake*, where Anna Livia Plurabell serves as a model both for sexually desiring woman and for the author, penning letters and speaking a steady babble of desire and affection.

In *Finnegans Wake*, transgressive desires provoke a radical move toward metonymic, sensate associations, so that sensate meaning threatens to eclipse the rational, conceptual form of meaning usually gleaned from language. In my fourth chapter, on lesbian and gay clichés in Joyce's work, I explore his use of Freudian and Victorian stereotypes of the narcissist-lesbian and paranoid-homosexual, arguing that he invokes these clichés only to disrupt their "original sinse" through his language, and that he further uses a variety of transgressive forms of desire to shift representation away from a more fixed form of mimesis. Narcissism and paranoia share a central reaction to doubling, which functions as a magnet to the one and a repulsion to the other. As this doubling also defines the structure of mimesis, Joyce works these forms of consciousness into the style and shape of *Finnegans Wake*, implicating them in the relative extremes of self-love and outward aggression that pervade the exchanges within the text. In "The Mime of Mick, Nick and the Maggies," Joyce develops a model of associative desire through an allusion to *Remembrance of Things Past*, where Proust likens the girls of Balbec beach to a rainbow of attributes that peak his desire most when interpreted like colors in associative play. For both Joyce and Proust, lesbian sexuality provides a new model of verbal association, where sameness is invoked only to fissure erotically into a play of complementary differences. Sameness eventually loses its link to lesbian sexuality in *Finnegans Wake*, so that narcissism becomes a broader mode of textual meaning that employs sensual suggestion. These suggestions may not communicate rationally, in so far as they offer mostly laughter and pleasurable word-play, but *as such* they signal Joyce's reinclusion of the sensate aspects of his linguistic medium. In contrast to the *jouissance* of lesbian language in the *Wake*, male homoerotic encounters are held in check, and their very potential, arising often in the parapraxes of male-male exchanges, can give rise to abrupt escalations of aggression. Particularly when twins or doubles encounter the possibility of their "nar-

cissistic" mirroring, the clichéd associations of that image with homosexuality seems to necessitate an abrupt turn toward virulent activity
that functions as a repression of such desire. In the "Burrus and
Caseous" tale told by Shaun, two co-conspirators endeavor to negotiate
their proximity by first attacking the father ("sisar" or Caesar) and secondly by triangulating their desire through "Margareen." When this
fails, a form of paranoiac fear and struggle for control appears to moti-
vate an aggressive move to separate the two (and implicitly Shem from
Shaun) by denigrating one of the pair. Joyce's two divergent uses of the
lesbian and gay "clichés" that invoke narcissistic models are then split
between ameliorative forms of association (*jouissance*) and aggressive
resistances that give rise to aggressivity and stereotyping. Joyce's textual
practice, in the *Wake*, moves between these poles, using them as a kind
of model of extremes (radical categorization and equally radical release)
that interpretations of the book must variously negotiate in their own
methodology.

Joyce's use of paranoid structures repeatedly parodies the anxiety
about one's ability to control boundaries, and this model extends
beyond issues of sexuality into a more general perspective on a subject's
anxious relation to his social context and for the motivating anxiety for
radical nationalism. Indeed, psychoanalysis has been applied with relative success to the link between nationalism and aggression. Klaus
Theweleit and Homi Bhabha have each examined the links between
aggressive forms of nationalism and erotic desires. While Theweleit's
work focuses mostly on fascism and the construction of the soldier,
Bhabha's work addresses the link between national identity and stereotyping most explicitly, arguing that stereotypes are not set forth as ster-
ile, conceptual forms but are linked to and even created from the pull of
taboo desires.[28] If Lacan emphasizes the aggressivity of stereotyping as a
drive toward fixity, Bhabha has combined his reading of Lacan with an
interpretation of stereotype as fetishistic discourse to emphasize its relation to desire. Interpreting stereotypes in postcolonial discourse, Bhabha
finds that cultures with a particularly mixed identity and history construct stereotypes in order to suppress elements of racial and sexual difference that thwart the drive toward national purification. Understanding the practice of stereotyping in terms of Freud's notion of fetishism,
Bhabha most significantly discovers that stereotypes are always *productive*. That is, they bring with them an instability that requires repeated
replay, eliciting simultaneously the anxiety of an insufficient suppression
of otherness *and* the pleasure of replaying erotic identification and desire
for that other. And so stories about the Negro or Irish must be constantly retold, being "differently gratifying and terrifying each time."[29] It
is this link between stereotyping and erotic pleasure that emerges most

insistently in Joyce's work, hinging his parodic experiments on a refusal and invocation of a range of forbidden desires.

If paranoia is used initially to ally sexuality with textual aggression in *Finnegans Wake*, it more generally defines the desire for nationalistic cohesion throughout Joyce's work. In my fifth chapter, "In the Wake of the Nation: Joyce's Response to Irish Nationalism," I trace the tensions within Joyce's thoughts on Irishness and his representations of Irish nationalism. I argue that current analyses of Joyce's relation to his own Irishness need to take into account the dual consciousness that so defines his own sense of his nationality. I weave this argument through analyses of *Dubliners*, *Portrait*, the "Cyclops" episode of *Ulysses*, and finally in its culminative realization in *Finnegans Wake*. Joyce defines the desire for nationalistic cohesion as a form of paranoia, which focuses both negatively on "foreignness" and with a destructive cele-bration on its own seamless identity. This is most obvious in the "Cyclops" episode, where paranoia structures a defensive form of self-constitution based on radical exclusion of the Other. In this episode, the extremism of the paranoiac, who sees himself (or his nation) as perse-cuted and pitted against a rapidly expanding Other, is linked to anti-semitism and a radical drive for cultural homogeneity. And yet if the "Citizen" is a dark portrait of Ireland's most degenerate patriots, Leopold Bloom is hardly more than *mock* heroic, with his feeble response to the question, "What is a nation?" When Bloom claims that a nation is "the same people living in the same place" or "also living in different places," Joyce is provocatively calling for a more elaborate response to the problem of nationalism. I suggest that this response emerges in his reinscription of Irish history in *Finnegans Wake*, where he calls into question the erection of boundaries and the geographic localization that are used to define nationalism. Moving away from this set notion of national identity, Joyce studies gossip and hearsay, the street pub exchanges that can constitute a community. In denying the benign construction of imagined communities, Joyce reveals the violence implicit in the reach toward a metadiscourse or broader claims about the law and the right of social judgment. He creates a community of speakers whose identities shift and re-emerge, neither approaching a utopic peace nor collapsing into the valorization of violent exchange. In his complex critique of nationalist extremes, Joyce therefore builds a new concept of interaction between culture and individual subjects that calls into question the nature of group identity and ideological sub-scription.

This interrogation of group identity leads to the development of a cosmopolitan consciousness in *Finnegans Wake*, where perspective is always doubly bound by its immediate locale (Dublin) and more worldly reach. In its textual gestures, the *Wake* evades the politics of domination once supported by philosophies like Giambattista Vico's *New Science* and Carl Jung's archetypes, and so leaves behind cosmopolitanism's shadow, the Enlightenment's insistence on the benign nature of cross-cultural exchange (which in many ways enabled imperialism's worst forms of domination). As it has currently been reformulated, cosmopolitanism defines a consciousness that values difference while also understanding the complexity of mediation across cultural boundaries. In the last chapter, on "Rhythmic Identification and Cosmopolitan Consciousness in *Finnegans Wake*," I will be suggesting that Joyce's fascination with cultural clashes and the subject's struggle for differentiation leads him into a "worldview" that belies any normative categorization or archetypal stricture. Previous readings of *Finnegans Wake* have too often relied on Vico and Jung as explanatory theorists, without turning a wary eye toward the mastery implicit in their philosophies. What Joyce takes from their writings is not the drive toward mastery, but an emphasis on language and cultural memory, as well as a fleeting web of associative links that he then presses away from universalization. With the Earwicker family, Joyce reduces names and identities to mere threads running through the text, traced by ever-thinning references. The name is reduced to mere initials, barely recognizable in verbal rearrangements and textual acrostics, until finally Joyce defines it by the sigla, small marks that serve as place-holders for identity. Without these threads, the text would fold into a narcissistic circle, refusing to communicate or deliver itself up to interpretation. Were these definitional traces too strict and categories too rigid, the text would only replicate the aggressive nature of crystallizing identities that Joyce so persistently parodies. In Shaun's repeated condemnation of his brother Shem, and in Earwicker's own social branding, Joyce repeatedly replays scenarios of aggressive societal accelerations of gossip that focus on fixing the morality and nature of each person's identity. Joyce's parody of both narcissistic self-enrapture and paranoid-aggressive gestures moves the text beyond oscillating extremes, in its historical and psychological scenarios. Gesture emerges as a fusion between the body and language. Following up on his early interest in dance, mime, and eurhythmics, Joyce studied the work of Marcel Jousse, whose theories of Christological pantomime emphasize the important early connection between language and its physical embodiment in gesture. For Joyce, gestures are both textual oscillations between aggression and narcissism, and also *alphabetic* and *linguistic* gestures that reveal the materiality of language as a medium. His parodic method thus locates the interstices between concept and sensation in words, which emerge at the crux of resistance to (and deliverance up to) societal assessments, be they moralistic or loving in their interpolations.[30] Stereotypes are present as the central target of parody, to be mocked and replayed as long as this separation persists in the word. Where Joyce effects sensate play within language, the text moves away from its repeated scenarios of scapegoating and aggression, drifting into Anna Livia's final soliloquy, in which she asks HCE to "Remember!" (FW 626.8), telling him of their past and "lilting on all the time" (FW 627.21), offering at once to be his "aural eyeness" (FW 623.18) and then later exclaiming that he is "but a puny" (FW 627.24). As her words trail off, their tonal inflections step like stairs down into silence, effecting the meaning and materializing the effects of the book's closure: "A way a lone a last a loved a long the"

Ultimately I hope to have demonstrated in my analysis of Joyce that, if stereotyping is always provisionally scripted into parody, the variance of force within textual gestures that move from rigid binarisms to more associative patterns defines a politics that is embedded in our under-standings of gender, sexuality, and social identity. And in Joyce, the very determinants of how these gestures emerge are embedded in the way we attend to the mutually conceptual and material nature of the word. What unfolds in the following chapters is an analysis of Joyce's aesthetic practice as it plays off of the relative violence of textual gestures, which range between starkly polarized representations and fluid combinations of contrary attributes and events. The former give rise to and spring up from aggressive forces that repeatedly press toward moralism and con-trol, whereas the latter move beyond boundaries, toward the release of tensions that create oppositional violence. Across these moments, Joyce lets laughter and linguistic gesture effect their rhythmic disruptions and alternate ameliorizations.

CHAPTER 2

The Art of Gesture:
Parody and Joyce's Aesthetic Practice

> Whenever Joyce had developed an aspect of his art as far as he
> could take it, he seems to have felt compelled to turn on himself
> and parody his own achievement. It is as if he could never allow
> himself to be committed to anything that might be called "his"
> style.
> —Clive Hart, *Structure and Motif in Finnegans Wake*

> I swear my gots how that I'm not meself at all, no jolly fear, when
> I realise bimiselves how becomingly I to be going to become.
> —FW 487.17–19

Parody plays out the traces of an interminable becoming. Thrown forward in a move to distinguish between its own and some prior text's
position, it is likewise propelled back against the impossibility of such a
severance. Constituted by repetition and differentiation, it continually
marks and remarks again an attempted division within its own textual
identity. This condition arises from structural necessity, as parody's prefix, *para-* (Greek: by the side of, beside), signifies a contiguity between
the text itself and the other it imitates, so that the two are enmeshed, neither being fully separate from nor completely identified with the other.
Parody in this way performs a kind of pararealism, never fully delivering up the thing-in-itself nor singling out the authorial perspective. It is
distortive by nature and thereby dangerously proximate to the process
of stereotyping.

Over the course of his career, Joyce played out the tensions of the
parodist's dilemma, shifting from a light, self-directed irony to an expan-
sive parody of social norms. As Clive Hart suggests, Joyce's parody
turns on a discomfort with any fixed style or identity, representing a
drive to distance from sentimental identifications and dogmatic conviction. It thus allows an accepting ambivalence toward the necessary tensions between belief/disbelief and identification/resistance that dogged
Joyce in his youth. Encounters with the fractured nature of belief are
especially marked in the early writing, not only in *Stephen Hero* and
Portrait but also in *Dubliners*, where Joyce comes closest to full sub-

scription to realism. Those initial stories in many ways circulate around the question of belief as religious adherence, as in "The Sisters" and "Grace"; Joyce also exerts a more subtle pressure on the issue of belief as it bears upon trusting another's intentions or character in "Eveline" and "Grace."[1] There, the question of whether or not a person measures to type serves to destabilize attempts to interpret or predict their actions; Eveline can no more trust Frank's potential as something more than a cad than the boy, in "The Sisters," can assert the difference between Father Flynn's character and the types to which he is linked by the local neighborhood assessment. This dark irony gradually expands into a broader social parody that enables Joyce to challenge those binary and moralistic structures that enforced extremes of resistance and adherence in his experience of Dublin. Without parody's ability to scramble boundaries and mock extremes, Joyce's work might well have collapsed into a paranoid form of textuality, capturing an aggression and rigidity of moral righteousness, delivering up a stiff picture animated only by two-dimensional types. Instead, Joyce moved progressively toward humor and an alternating focus and derangement of character that eschews any locatable moral pronouncement.

If Joyce's work presents no pure, objective point from which to discern a single set of politics, beliefs, or adherences, then the problem arises: how can we discuss the roles of gender, sexuality, and ethnic and national identifications in his writings? How can we seriously analyze politics in a text that seduces the mind by laughter and eroticism without ever defining the boundaries between author and other? In the absence of any objective realism from which to measure deviation and distortion, the problem of assessing the use of stereotypes in Joyce's writing would seem to be elusively irresolvable. And yet the radical oscillations inscribed within his textual process, which become most pronounced in *Finnegans Wake*, suggest an imperative to come to terms with the ways in which stereotypes alternately structure and disrupt the social order.

Joyce's first laugh was against the self, the egotistically reified "I." His work begins with a slide toward mock-portraiture in *Stephen Hero*, opening the fissure of difference between his personal and textual identities that has so constantly troubled attempts to engage the stereotypes that threaten to settle in readings of his texts. One of the primary problems of discussing Joyce's textual politics has been the question of how to treat the slide between his own and Stephen Dedalus' opinions. One might simply ignore it and focus purely on the narrative dissonance, but that Joyce's frequency of self-allusion seems to call for a more complex understanding of his relation to reference and authorship. Joyce's gesture of parodic identity is initially a mere sliver of parody, but it opens a difference between Joyce and his autobiographical character in *Stephen Hero*. He progressively ironizes his relation to that character, as if he were an overly fixed memory of Joyce's former self, and this develops from *Stephen Hero* through *Portrait*. This reaches a point of crisis in the "Scylla and Charybdis" episode of *Ulysses*, where Stephen's failed attempt at a parodic performance of biographical reading marks a turn away from parody as ironic self-critique in Joyce. Afterwards, what emerges is a trajectory split between the ironic and satiric impulses, which are mutually related to parody. For parody slides between an undecidable split root that points both to the ironic, self-questioning mode through its Greek linkage to *parodia* and the mock-heroic poem, and to the satiric mode, *parodos*, which refers to imitative songs sung in Greek satyr plays.[2] When parody is more ironic, it plays on the fissured intentions and ambiguous sympathies of its own author, whereas satiric parody launches itself more clearly as an intervention in the social arena. Nonetheless, parody always contains some degree of both these aspects, being at times more sympathetic and then, at other moments, lethally aggressive.[3] Yet it never turns on its target without some accompanying turn upon itself, an aspect that distinguishes it from other forms of satire.

By insistently parodying that with which he identified, Joyce put himself in the odd position of judging what was both part of himself and also somehow grown estranged. As a "biografiend" (FW 55.06), he applied this development of aesthetic practice to his art, so that his creation and ironization of Stephen Dedalus allowed him to explore representation as a form of becoming and, in a sense, *not* becoming; that is, by miming his former beliefs and dilemmas, Joyce transformed them partially into type and partially into an individuated "portrait" of sympathetic memory of a former self. He thus embraced the ambivalence within identity and disidentity between author and text, and this fissure widened as he developed the narrative dissonances of *Ulysses* and the splintered characterology of *Finnegans Wake*. The trace that links all of Joyce's texts in this change is the *gestural politics* of his engagement with (dis)identity and representational modes, the relative degrees of identification and differentiation that determine the slide between benign portraiture and agonistic caricature that Joyce increasingly treated with critical awareness. Rather than defining "politics" as a belief construct or consolidated position, then, I interpret it in terms of the degrees of violence and fixation encoded in those representational gestures that potentially lead to stereotyping. The act of freezing analysis of a person's or text's "beliefs" may be the greatest violence of all for Joyce, so that an analysis of his textual politics must operate through scrutiny of his parodic approach to representation. And if parody has emerged as a key term in recent debates about politics and agency, it is due primarily to its conceptual location at the interstices between the self and its constitutive influences. A gesture of mediation, it arises as a textual paradox that, when applied to notions of socially constructed subjectivity, reveals a subject arising from and simultaneously turning to interact with its social context.

I choose "gesture" as a way to approach Joyce's changing parodic style both because it is his own term—derived initially from a brief (and humorous) aesthetic discussion in *Stephen Hero* and then returning in late *Ulysses* on into *Finnegans Wake*—and also because it brings the concept of "parody," so often treated as a text-to-text reference, closer to the questions of physical embodiment, sexual desire, and, curiously, to the problem of stereotype and cliché, all of which are central concerns in Joyce's writing. Joyce never elaborated "the art of gesture" in an explicit aesthetics, as he did the distinction between kinetic desire and static, epiphanic experience. Rather, the term is offered suggestively and emerges, when Stephen mimes it, at the node of the senses, casting Joyce's verbal art in terms of the visual and aural experiences given by mime and music. It goes underground as Stephen becomes more rigid in his approach to representation in *Portrait*. As it is suppressed by Stephen, however, gesture is taken up in Joyce's own aesthetic practice, where parodic oscillations continuously expand. Gesture then resurfaces in fragmentary references in *Ulysses* and in *Finnegans Wake*, and Joyce continues to integrate it into his stylistic process on an almost unconscious level, using its stage model as a structural understanding of his allusive art. Joyce figures gesture as mime, dance, and eurhythmics—all processes that depend on the physical incorporation of a text into one's own "self." He also eventually draws on the linguistic theories of Marcel Jousse, whose interest in ritualistic recitations of the Mass combined with a conviction that language needed to be wedded to the body to communicate most forcefully. "Gesture," in Joyce's work, thus defines parody as a model for the integration of influence, and yet the emphasis on incorporating the body into this gestural art progressively associates it with the problems of the limits of representation and its relation to desire, corporeality, and more general aspects of societal exchange.

RHYTHMIC (DIS)IDENTIFICATIONS

The art of gesture is offered but lightly in *Stephen Hero*; it is held forth less as a serious aesthetics than as comedic suggestion:

—There should be an art of gesture, said Stephen one night to Cranly.
—Yes?
—Of course I don't mean art of gesture in the sense that the elocution professor understands the word. For him a gesture is an emphasis. I mean a rhythm. You know the song, "Come unto these yellow sands?"
—No.
—This is it, said the youth making a graceful anapaestic gesture with each arm. That's the rhythm, do you see?
—Yes.
—I would like to go out into Grafton St some day and make gestures in the middle of the street.
—I'd like to see that. (SH 184)

What is this art of gesture that Stephen shows his ironic interlocutor? Surely he has the look of a mime, snaking out rhythms along his arms. Stephen would seem an odd conductor of music, standing in the middle of Grafton Street on a busy day. If Joyce later indulges in extensive appropriations of street mime, here Stephen calls for a *stylistic* mime, not some "pantomime" as the silent art of storytelling.[4] There is no story, only the movement. Meaning-as-movement rather than syntax is a notion that will gradually emerge in Joyce's work, becoming a "changeably meaning" mass of language in *Finnegans Wake* (FW 118.27). In *Stephen Hero*, the meaning invoked is closely tied to rhythm, deriving from an art of gesture that would be a physical adaptation of the sensate properties of music. Much as the dramatic has been emphasized in Joyce's aesthetics, the lyric aspect of prose is here crucial. With the image of a rhythm incorporated through the body—and also translated into the materiality of language that brings with it scansion and sound—comes the lyric combination of music, dance, and recitation to rhythmic accompaniment. In the Paris notebook on aesthetics, written in 1903, Joyce identifies three basic conditions of art:

the lyrical, the epical and the dramatic. That art is lyrical whereby the artist sets forth the image in immediate relation to himself; that art is epical whereby the artist sets forth the image in mediate relation to himself and to others; that art is dramatic whereby the artist sets forth the image in immediate relation to others.[5]

At the juncture in which the art of gesture first appears, Joyce is setting out an image that bears an immediate relation to himself, and only later in portions of *Portrait* and more fully in *Ulysses* do the epical and dramatic aspects of his work more often overwhelm the lyrical. Yet by the time Joyce begins *Finnegans Wake*, the lyric has again taken over, invading the language and the very textual construction, not only in the sense of self-reference, which is highly mediated and distorted in the *Wake*, but more importantly in its relative dismissal of mimesis in favor of the lyric's two central aspects: the emotional impact and its sensate (rhythmic and mouth-rounding) effects. In his discussion of the lyric, J. F. W. Johnson speculates that

> the first "lyrical" poems came into being when men discovered the pleasure that arises from combining words in a coherent, meaningful sequence with the almost physical process of uttering rhythmical and tonal sounds to convey feelings. The instinctive human tendency to croon or hum or intone as an expression of emotional mood is evidenced in the child's babbling; and the socialization of this tendency in primitive cultures by the chanting or singing of nonsense syllables to emphasize tribal rites is a well documented phenomenon.[6]

Joyce repeatedly returns to this focus on the sensuous link between words and meaning in *Dubliners*, *Portrait*, and through all his fictional works. Various influences in his environment and intellectual training may have sparked Joyce's interest in the lyric; I will be examining some probable sources, such as eurhythmics, symbolist poetics, and mime, in order to better clarify what is less than explicit in Joyce's scattered postulates of aesthetic principle. He was, as mentioned earlier, inspired by the prominence of street mime in Dublin at the turn-of-the-century, but he arguably also derives much of his gestural conception from an emerging approach to music pedagogy.

When Stephen works his body into a gestural music, he appears to be experimenting with a form of eurhythmics, a method of teaching musical awareness with the help of rhythmic bodily movements. This art was developed around the turn of the century in Great Britain and on the Continent through the writings and teaching of Swiss educator Émile Jaques-Dalcroze. Jaques-Dalcroze developed his technique while teaching harmony at the Geneva Conservatory, beginning in 1892, and published his theories in and around 1897.[7] He saw the body as the medium to the mind, and as such a crucial component of any learning process. He protested that children were being taught to play music and sing before they were taught how to *listen* to and appreciate the art, and he therefore proposed that eurhythmic exercises be used to develop a deeper rhythmic understanding, which would be absorbed not only on a conscious level but also embedded on a "psycho-physical" level. Previously, plastic movement had been used as an accompaniment to music, as with dance; Jaques-Dalcroze was proposing that it be treated as an innately important *expression* of musical understanding.[8] He argued that rhythmic development affected the whole of a child's educational potential, and in a lecture delivered in Leipzig in 1911, he claimed that "lessons in rhythmic gymnastics help children in their other lessons, for they develop the powers of observation, of analysing, of understanding, and of memory, thus making them more orderly and precise."[9]

In emphasizing the "psycho-physical development" of a child, Jaques-Dalcroze was offering a corrective to what he saw as the current educational practice of addressing only "the conscious powers" of pupils. He suggested, instead, that "all that part of education by rhythm which aims at penetration of the subconscious mind is entrusted to a more powerful influence than word and sight: to *music*, a pre-eminently rhythmic art, both exciting and soothing, which acts not only on the nervous sensibility but also direct on the feelings."[10] Eurhythmics thus draws on and develops associative forms of memory as well. Most interesting, for my purposes here, is Jaques-Dalcroze's sense that eurhythmics creates a balance between the unconscious and conscious modes, between the irrational instinct the body supplies and the structured endeavor to control such impulses. "Rhythm," he writes, "is an element of an irrational nature. Metre exists and is maintained only through reasoning: it develops the powers of control. To vibrate *without metre*, then to express oneself *in metre*: such is the province of man and of the perfect artist."[11] Jaques-Dalcroze's model of a balanced interrelation between conscious and unconscious flows of the mind—as a kind of gesture that entails both—fits with an understanding of Joyce's parody that includes both his will-to-parody and also his more unconscious desires and resistances.

Joyce wrote *Stephen Hero* between 1901 and 1906, with his humorous invocation of an art of gesture being written, as editors guess, sometime in 1906, after he had lived on the Continent nearly two years.[12] Jaques-Dalcroze was expelled from the Swiss Conservatory in 1904, an incident that might have caught Joyce's attention and sympathy.[13] While there is no absolute confirmation that Joyce was alluding to Jaques-Dalcroze's method in *Stephen Hero*, two things hint at its possibility. First, he almost certainly had heard of this form of eurhythmics by the time he wrote *Finnegans Wake*, and he makes a pun on the word in Issy's response to question 10, in which the children are asked, "What bitter's love but yurning, what' sour lovemutch but a bref burning till shee that drawes dothe smoake retourne?" (FW 143.29–30). In Issy's response, she teasingly boasts: "And my waiting twenty classbirds, sitting on their stiles! Let me finger their eurhythmytic. And you'll see if I'm selfthought. They're all of them out to please" (FW 147.07–9). Joyce puns on bodily rhythm, arithmetic, and sexual desire at once. Secondly, Stephen's anapestic gestures along his arms mimic the very first of Dalcroze's exercises: to have students beat time with arm movements.[14] Joyce may have known of eurhythmics eventually through Lucia's experimental dance lessons. Otherwise, combining his interest in music with familiar forms of pantomime, he may have been alluding to similar practices.[15] If this eurhythmic form of parody does not fully develop until *Finnegans Wake*, where Joyce meets a newer version of it in the work of Marcel Jousse, here Stephen appears to be using the basic notion of embodying music with physical gestures.

Stephen barely alludes to the song, taking only its elemental rhythm and running it through his own medium, the body, without explanation or verbal thematics. He mimes the sensual aspects of the song rather than its theme, perhaps conveying a mood, but without sound or words. Two aspects of this art seem relevant to Joyce's parody: the emphasis on *sensate* aspects of the medium—the body or letters of the word—and the implicit formulation of allusion as a kind of incorporation of the other within one's "own" gesture, a process of integration that, in its *clinamen*, calls into question the very attempt to distinguish between what is one's own and some other's style. In Joyce's works, parody's *clinamen*— its mark of differentiation—is often subtle, and its sympathies are equally difficult to discern. As with ventriloquized monologue, one cannot judge precisely when an author is positively identifying with the voice s/he writes and when putting on show the faults of the "speaking" agent.[16] Joyce's presentation of stereotypes can be judged only in terms of the *clinamen* of his style, a *clinamen* that is not, per Harold Bloom's use, a willful revision of some other author; rather, as the term is developed in the work of Jacques Derrida, it would be a gesture that plays between necessity and chance, freedom and indeterminism.[17] It is also, like parody, a movement between the conscious and unconscious, the desire to control and the impulse to repeat. In this it is much like the gestural art described by Jousse in his work on the "rhythmo-catechistic" milieu of Palestine at the time of Christ in which Jousse found a doubled form. He observed that as the Priest's audience repeats liturgy, it both replays the "stereotype" and "cliché" of the verbal form, while it also, in its gestural enactment, creates a new improvisation, a new series of meanings and gestures (*Les Rabbis d'Israel*, xxv and passim). In my last chapter on the critical reconsideration of stereotyping in *Finnegans Wake*, I will be addressing Jousse's influence on the gestural aesthetics and politics of that text. However, since Joyce did not encounter Jousse's work until the late 1920s, I am here more concerned with other models of earlier influence, which could all have fed into Joyce's own particular theories about the embodiment of the word and gestural textualities. Initially, Joyce uses something akin to eurhythmics, probably influenced by the predominance of street mime in Dublin at the time. This physical form of language, in Joyce, troubles the line between conscious, artistic control and unconscious repetition. "Gesture" is not so much a willful rewriting as a revision constantly sliding back into the possibility that forms it, then subtly pulling away, in a kind of rhythmic variation that only partially appropriates the image, motion, or sound being played by the artist.

Gesture is therefore not some *thing* added onto a preestablished meaning, but a processural notion. Not surprisingly, Stephen distinguishes his art of gesture from a simpler mode of elocutionary gesture, where formalized arm movements accompanied recitations of poetry. *Bell's Standard Elocutionist*, published through Belfast in 1871, gives a portrait of elocution as Joyce might have known it, describing in a section on bodily gestures an art quite opposite that of Stephen's, rigidly codifying bodily poise, foot placement, and other forms of posture. The authors prescribe the manner in which arm gestures should lend emphasis to dramatic recitations and insist that "no motion should be made without a reason for it; and whatever attitude or position any action leads to, should be maintained until a new motive either dictates a new movement, or allows the gesture appropriately to subside. Impulsive jerks and meaningless or indefinite shifts of the head, hands, arms, or feet, should be carefully avoided."[18] There are no rhythms allowed in this form of gesture; one must hold each position and avoid "meaningless" repetition or shifts. The meaningless gestures Bell leaves aside seem to have had meaning for Joyce, for that which is not codified can be perhaps more evocative, and evocation was of greater importance to Joyce than "emphasis." "I don't mean art of gesture in the sense that the elocution professor understands the word," Stephen says, "for him a gesture is an emphasis. I mean a rhythm."

Stephen's aesthetics of rhythm extends beyond this anapaestic gesture in *Stephen Hero*, reappearing in the theory of art that he describes in *A Portrait of the Artist as a Young Man*. In *Stephen Hero*, Stephen speaks of epiphany as a moment in either art or nature, in which the *quidditas* of a thing leaps forth and is recognized, when "the relation of the parts is exquisite, when the parts are adjusted to a special point" (SH 213). Defined as symmetry, the relation between the parts of a thing will maintain a steady, equilibrious rhythm. This is made explicit in *Portrait* in Stephen's analysis of Aquinas' claim, "Three things are needed for beauty, wholeness, harmony and radiance" (P 212).[19] However, this formula takes Stephen's aesthetics away from sensate combinations between ideas and bodies and turns toward a static, elative moment of apperception. This occurs in Stephen's discourse on aesthetics, directed to Lynch. First, in Stephen's formulation of the artistic consciousness, he remarks that the artist perceives an object initially in its wholeness and separate from, but related to, its context; this Stephen calls *integritas*. Next, the mind will "pass from point to point, led by its formal lines," thus apprehending it "as balanced part against part within its limits." At this stage of apperception, called *consonantia*, Stephen notes that "you feel the rhythm of its structure" (P 212). Rhythm allows the object to retain its complexity, leaving it irreducible if still equilibriously contained. If Stephen takes this formulation from Coleridge, then it is rhythm cut off from desire, as well. In Coleridge's *Essay on the Principles of Genial Criticism*, he writes that "the sense of Beauty subsists in simultaneous intuition of the relation of parts, each to each, and of all to the whole: exciting an immediate and absolute complacency, without intervenience, therefore of any interest sensual or intellectual."[20] If Stephen is considering Coleridge here, he at least translates "complacency" into Walter Pater's more ecstatically vibrant epiphany.[21] In both instances, however, art maintains equilibrium within the system.

Claritas Stephen defines again through the lens of a Romantic idealism, so that it shifts form and materiality, becoming pure ideal and essence. Stephen speculates that Aquinas, in his mention of *claritas*, refers to "symbolism or idealism, the supreme quality of beauty being a light from some other world, the idea of which matter is but the shadow, the reality of which it is but the symbol." *Claritas* is that "which would make the esthetic image a universal one" as it is made to "outshine its proper conditions" (P 213). Stephen thus takes the Aristotelianism of Aquinas toward Plato's more abstracted idealism, where the shadows hint at the essence beyond materiality and world. As a result, rhythm drops out. *Rhuthmos* operates as form or schema in Aristotle's *Metaphysics*, associated as it is with the notion of order (*taxis*) and position (*thesis*).[22] It is a movement contained within the constraints of form. But whereas Aristotle refuses to separate the final form from its material actualities, Coleridge, following Plato, looks for the essential idea, the universal, that lurks somewhere beyond materiality.[23] In Stephen's theory, as the object is apprehended in its relational rhythms, its *quidditas* leaps forth, attaching it by implication to some larger category of meaning, a category that will retain its structure as a fixed universal. Rhythm thus *dies out* at the moment of aesthetic grasping, until the visionary experience is again dissipated and the moment has passed.

But what happens to Stephen's art of gesture, his appropriation of the anapaestic rhythm of song in *Stephen Hero*? And how might it be relevant to Joyce's own aesthetics? Stephen's theories in *Portrait* seem to have been formulated by Joyce, for himself, in the Pola and Paris notebooks (1903–4), just as he was beginning to write *Portrait*. As mentioned before, Joyce demarcates the genres of lyric, epic, and drama, and also defines a notion of epiphanic art associated with beauty (CW 141–48). These jottings show that he already had developed the psychological tilt used in *Portrait*, arguing that art is "human disposition of sensible matter for an aesthetic end" (CW 146). Joyce was noticeably concerned with "proper" and "improper" art as well. The former promotes static sensations that appeal to the intellect, while the latter (which Stephen calls "kinetic") inspires desire. Morality, then, is determined by equilibrium.

Disequilibriuos art, as it calls on pleasure and moves its audience away from judgment, preempts the intellectual stasis that would raise it above desire. I suspect the chief influence that shifted Joyce out of a moral account of art was the expansion of a psychological and ever more subjective emphasis in his writing, leading him deeper into the unconscious and the fissuring parodies of *Ulysses* and *Finnegans Wake*. This emphasis is added to *Portrait*, while the aesthetics still resists its implication. That is, the very subjective nature of the narrative undermines (or mocks) the universality of the claims Stephen launches. When Stephen argues that art is "the human disposition of sensible or intelligible matter for an esthetic end" (P 207), he implies that *claritas*—perception of the thing's essence—can only be achieved through the *artist's* perspective. This move is modeled in the passage above from *Stephen Hero*, where music must travel through the artist's body. The role of the mime is not simple apperception, however. S/he must by implication create an effect, transferring perception through his body—literally as Stephen might stand out on Grafton Street recreating music through rhythmic gestures. The rhythmic dance carries with it a piece of the artist's self, the *style* of the gesture made, a fleeting signature inscribed within the mimetic process. Yet can *claritas* then "make the esthetic image a universal one" as it is made to "outshine its proper conditions" (P 213)?

I am suggesting that, while this stasis is the implication of Stephen's *Portrait* aesthetics, Joyce's narrative dissonances and gradual disidentification with Stephen disrupt this very position. In later *Ulysses* and *Finnegans Wake*, Joyce critiques controlling perspectives like Stephen's and, earlier, his own. The moment of aesthetic grasping, which serves as a reduction of perspective's rhythmically complex elements, reemerges as a motif at moments of aggression within Joyce's plots. Bloom resists affixing a type (whore, intruder) to Molly or Boylan after a long day's struggle with thoughts of their appointment, while Stephen, true to his aesthetics, is busy labeling enemies (Buck, Haines, et al.). Binaristic aggressions are undone by oscillations between positionalities in Joyce's work, although they repeatedly re-emerge in a range of scenarios in *Finnegans Wake.* The contiguity between language and materiality, however, repeatedly pulls language away from a categorical abstraction not dissimilar to stereotypes, so that particularity or the Real (per Lacan) disrupts many of the gestures of reductive assimilation.

Joyce's oscillation between the transcendence of materiality, in Stephen's development in *Portrait,* and his own repeated return to verbal embodiment may have arisen from Joyce's early interest in the writings of Stéphane Mallarmé. Indeed, Stephen's formulation of *consonatia,* in which the perception will "pass from point to point," echoes not only Coleridge but also seems to take up Arthur Symons' summary of Mallarmé: "the poet, who has seen the thing from the beginning, still sees the relation of point to point."[24] Mallarmé's gestural art uses mime explicitly as a model in prose poems like "Mimique," and his realization of aesthetic experience through materiality was remarked by Symons, who was largely responsible for that author's influence on modernists like Joyce around the turn of the century.[25] David Hayman has argued that Joyce studied Mallarmé both early and late in his career, although the question of how Joyce eventually interpolated Mallarmé's ideas is an opaque one, and, in general, the extent and nature of Mallarmé's influence on Joyce has remained at issue.[26] Ellmann and others have noted that Joyce copied down Symons' translation of one passage in *The Symbolist Movement in Literature,* suggesting that Joyce's main familiarity with Mallarmé was heavily, if not exclusively, mediated by Symons' interpretations. The passage they focus on is one in which Mallarmé calls for verse that evokes only "the horror of the forest, or the silent thunder afloat in the leaves; not the intrinsic dense wood of the trees."[27] This would seem to emphasize an evocative art, one that reaches beyond realism and materiality and points more toward emotional and sensate impact. But Symons interprets this more as an insistence on the separation between materiality and meaning. Mallarmé is supposed to be searching for a sensation that is, at first, "no more than a rhythm, absolutely without words," and this rhythm is the "executive soul" that guides the artist's perception. Instead of pursuing the nature of this rhythm, Symons turns to identify the Symbolist movement as a "revolt against exteriority, against rhetoric, against a materialistic tradition," and claims that the Symbolists had faith "against the evidence of the senses, against the negations of materialistic science."[28] The question is whether, as Hayman has also suggested, this particular art is a struggle to *leave behind* material conditions—other citations, allusions, the medium itself—or whether Joyce takes in and gradually develops the ambiguity in Mallarmé's play between abstractions and contexts.[29] Certainly Joyce gained several elements from Symons' summary: an empha-

sis on evocation, the notion of the invisible artificer, as well as some figurations of women as key aesthetic objects.[30] Perhaps most kindred was
Mallarmé's desire to see literature transformed by musical influence.
Symons quotes him at length on this ideal moment when music "rejoins
verse":

> We are now precisely at the moment of seeking, before that breaking
> up of the large rhythms of literature, and their scattering in articulate,
> almost instrumental, nervous waves, an art which shall complete the
> transposition, in the Book, of the symphony, or simply recapture our
> own: for, it is not in elementary sonorities of brass, strings, wood,
> unquestionably, but in the intellectual word at its utmost, that, fully
> and evidently, we should find, drawing to itself all the correspondences
> of the universe, the supreme Music.[31]

This musical elevation of literature dreams the dream of *Finnegans
Wake*, which Joyce moved toward only as he develops his notion of gestural art. I would suggest here that, even were he only familiar with
Symons' summary, Joyce seems to have worked to unravel the tension
within that summary, between polarizing meaning/matter or finding
some aesthetic experience "beyond" such philosophically insistent distinctions. Stephen, in *Portrait*, acts out the separation of body and soul,
spirit and flesh, while the text's own implicit aesthetic shifts—particularly in *Ulysses*—toward a merging between linguistic embodiment and
artistic significance (or meaning).

This interpretation would pursue Joyce's work more along the lines
of Mallarmé's own, for in the latter's work writing is not a fight for position but a gesture that elides the polarization that would take place
along lines of aggressivity. In Jacques Derrida's reading of Mallarmé, the
act of mime "always plays out a difference without reference, or rather
without a referent, without any absolute exteriority, and hence, without
any inside. The Mime mimes reference. He is not an imitator; he mimes
imitation."[32] In this way, gestural writing can destabilize reference, since
it is never present *in itself* (it is a process, not a thing), and as such it
always alludes to something that can never become present. One cannot
present a process; rather, the mime performs the admixture of allusion
and identity that creates parody. Indeed, Joyce's later influence, Marcel
Jousse, also acknowledges a likeness between Mallarmé's work and his
own project of recovering the "mimographic" roots of language, where
writing is directly related to gestural presentation.[33] Mallarmé's is therefore a different version of mimesis, one that dismisses the classical
notion that art and nature are innately separate and that material sub-
stances are alien to the ideas they mimetically point toward. Now there
are no ideas but in movements and gestures, the actions of mime. The
text, as a collection of words, must display its own struggle between

desire and accomplishment, between performance and memory, between symbolic gestures and real or naturalistic enactments. This aesthetics points to the twin directions in parodic styles like Joyce's, which press on the impossibility inscribed within the drive to purify symbols or meanings and to separate verbal definitions from visual and punnical aspects. A gestural emphasis in Joyce's work would thus reverse the reading Hayman attached to Joyce, arguing that for him art was a struggle for mastery, a desire to make language his own.[34]

Mallarmé's model of a processural mime seems to be one of the strands integrated into Joyce's complex parody of autobiography and his gradual development of a gestural art. This aesthetic practice, in Joyce, rhythmically acts out the conscious self while disrupting signatures with the body and its more unconscious style, leaving an oscillating identity often defined by differences. In its appropriation of mime, this gestural art takes less the stock plots or caricatures of that practice, struggling instead between stereotype and a critical unraveling of such containments. While a resistance to stereotyping may not be the impetus of Joyce's work with gestural language, it is a progressive outcome. In *Portrait*, gesture operates more explicitly in the preconceptual stage, where Stephen cannot yet understand violence and separation and so moves toward aggressivity as he incorporates moral binarisms and moves away from his initial, childlike perception of language in its relation to sensate experience.

MEANING AND MATERIALITY

Stephen's foray into the world constructed by language, in *Portrait*, provides a double image of the complex relations between the erotic, sensate aspects of language and its more formal, categorical nature. Stephen's initial syntax is rife with "to be" equations and simple verbs in active construct, so that we get sentences that establish simple interpretive categories and distinctions:

> When you wet the bed first it is warm then it gets cold. His mother put on the oilsheet. That had a queer smell. (P 7)

> Uncle Charles and Dante clapped. They were older than his father and mother but uncle Charles was older than Dante. (P 8)

Stephen learns through binary oppositions (warm/cold, nice/not so nice, queer/familiar) and through relative comparative measures (older than). He has set categorical meanings that can be clarified by oppositional knowledge or expanded in comparison. Puns, of course, trouble his sense of equivalences and clear-cut, categorical definition:

> His hands were bluish with cold. He kept his hands in the sidepockets
> of his belted grey suit. That was a belt round his pocket. And belt was
> also to give a fellow a belt. . . . That was not a nice expression. (P 9)

What Joyce so realistically gives here is the random observations of a
mind consumed with the need to anchor its world, fresh with new
understanding. As Stephen endeavors to navigate the world of Clongowes, he struggles with the problem of separating nice from not nice,
usually aligning those terms with pleasant and unpleasant. In a sense, he
suffers the fall from an Edenic alignment of material and language, a fall
that Joyce will replay and resurrect in *Finnegans Wake*.

More importantly, the notion of any gestural language disappears
in *Portrait*, when Stephen suffers a radical repression of the body after
the retreat on St. Francis Xavier's feast day. There, the rotting corporeality of man's state is associated insistently with sin and hell, so that
all desire not licensed by God—a seemingly antiphysical God—would
be punishable by hell fire and death. Stephen is thinking on death as
much as sin, throughout the days of prayer and admonition. As the
retreat begins, he reviews his life at Clongowes: "the wide play-
grounds, swarming with boys, the square ditch, the little cemetery off
the main avenue of limes where he had dreamed of being buried, the
firelight on the wall of the infirmary where he lay sick, the sorrowful
face of Brother Michael" (P 108–9). The boys are urged to "put away
from your minds during these few days all worldly thoughts, whether
of study or pleasure or ambition, and to give all your attention to the
state of your souls" (P 110). In this series of sermons, Joyce emphasizes the Christianic separation between physical and spiritual aspects,
a distinction provisionally overcome by the transubstantiation of
bread and wine into body and blood. If an emaciated Stephen still suffers from denial of the body in *Ulysses*, he will also playfully demonstrate his "art of gesture" at "Circe"'s opening with the image of the
loaf and jug. Here, in *Portrait*, Stephen still indulges, one last time, in
a passion for food and excess. After the first day of the religious
retreat, he eats at home with "surly appetite," but sees the "greases-
trewn plates" as an indicator of his own animalistic decay: "His soul
was fattening and congealing into a gross grease, plunging ever deeper
in its dull fear into a sombre threatening dusk, while the body that was
his stood, listless and dishonoured, gazing out of darkened eyes, help-
less, perturbed and human for a bovine god to stare upon" (P 111). It
is as if he is separate from his body—"the body that was his"—as
something he could take possession of or abandon. The next day, the
priest serves up a vision of the death of the body and the terror of judgment. As a result Stephen dreams a nightmaric vision of defecation and
animalistic decay:

> A field of stiff weeds and thistles and tufted nettle-bunches. Thick among the tufts of rank stiff growth lay battered canisters and clots and coils of solid excrement. A faint marshlight struggled upwards from all the ordure through the bristling greygreen weeds. An evil smell, faint and foul as the light, curled upwards sluggishly out of the canisters and from the stale crusted dung. (P 137)

Joyce is here a far cry from his Rabelaisian embrace of the body. Stephen's horror is with the excrement, the left-over, the body without use or intention—excess. The displeasures of material conditions press on him. Rimbaud's and Baudelaire's putrefying corpses and transgressions of the corporeal boundaries are not yet available to Stephen. Instead, he sees "goatish creatures" in images of cruelty and disgust: "They moved in slow circles, circling closer and closer to enclose, to enclose, soft language issuing from their lips, their long swishing tails besmeared with stale shite, thrusting upwards their terrific faces" (P 138). Even after Stephen disavows the pious aspect he here cleaves to, the separation between body and soul, word and meaning, maintains. Toward the end of *Portrait*, Joyce moves into diary form, and in that autobiographic genre a glimpse of gesture surfaces. Stephen, on meeting E.C., finds himself self-consciously talking "rapidly of myself and my plans" and "in the midst of it unluckily I made a sudden gesture of a revolutionary nature. I must have looked like a fellow throwing a handful of peas into the air" (P 252). Stephen's bodily gesturing gives away his hidden ill-ease and partial aggression, enacting a complex fusion and scission between mind and body, unconscious and willful self-control.

The development of a gestural aesthetic may emerge out of Joyce's response to debates about the separations between materiality and meaning being put forward in empiricist and idealist philosophies since the eighteenth century. Inheriting Descartes' dualism coupled with British empiricism's inductive approach to science, John Locke argued that we always encounter a separation between primary (essential) and secondary (externally apparent) properties of objects, being able to assess only the secondary, physical traits. Soon after Locke, David Hume reasoned against any attempt to claim knowledge of what lay beyond the known, perceivable world, insisting that "all the colours of poetry, however splendid, can never paint natural objects in such a manner as to make the description be taken for a real landskip. The most lively thought is still inferior to the dullest sensation."[35] Sensation is thus all we can know in the strictest empiricist philosophies. Interestingly enough, language becomes a central concern for such philosophical projects, so that Locke, in 1690, includes a book (long section) on the topic in *An Essay Concerning Human Understanding*, in order to deal with the duplicitous and amorphous nature of words.[36] He notices the generalizing nature of language—something Immanuel Kant will reconstructively transform into a categorical aspect of the understanding in *The Critique of Pure Reason* in 1781.[37] But Locke takes a stand reminiscent of Plato's, chiding "wit and fancy" in figurative speeches, as they "insinuate wrong *Ideas*, move the Passions, and thereby mislead the Judgment; and so indeed are perfect cheat."[38] Words are still the cloth to concepts, and their more sensate medium must not—in its secondary nature—interfere with the essential intention of the writer. After the empiricists, Kant marked a separation between what can be known through experience (*a posteriori*) and what may only be gathered within the mind (*a priori*). An idealist in some ways similar to Berkeley, he insisted on the role of perception in shaping our access to empirical sensation, so that his idealism, which appealed to Romanticists, allowed again a supremacy of the abstract over the physical.[39] The inner categories of perception may be known, according to Kant, by virtue of inner examination, and their existence is guaranteed by abstract "truth" secured beyond subjective experience. Phenomenology would diverge from this at the beginning of the twentieth-century, scrutinizing sense-experience as the avenue to a fuller understanding, rather than troubling a separation between full knowledge and sense data. Neither disallowing generalizations, like notions of duration and extension, nor reducing knowledge to pure perception, as Berkeley did, Phenomenology set aside the epistemological dualism that split body and mind, material and meaning, and explored the complex interrelations between these two aspects of understanding.[40] This occurs in a broader context, however, where language was being treated as a screen and possible obscurant to meaning, so that Joyce and many of the modernists had to turn away from dualistic epistemologies to reclaim the more vibrant aspects of their medium.

Aggressively oppositional ways of perceiving block such a fusion between meaning and materiality, and in *Ulysses* Stephen's consciousness serves as a centralizing force of resistance to gestural art. His heavy irony and almost narcissistic isolation pitches a climax in the "Scylla and Charybdis" episode, where he proposes to a circle of literary critics the argument that Shakespeare identifies with the dead father of Hamlet, rather than the active and violent son. To achieve this reading, Stephen relies heavily on biographic reading, and as his argument fails and he begins to parrot his audience's expectations more progressively, Joyce's ironic parody, based as it is in the gradual disintegration of a one-on-one autobiographical sketch with Stephen, breaks down. He moves from a contextually defined reading of Shakespeare to isolating logic, where the artist is self-created through his selection of literary progenitors. The collapse of Stephen's wit upon itself sparks a dramatic shift in Joyce's parodic style. As David Kiremidjian has noted, Joyce begins to develop his use of parody most fully after the close of "Scylla and Charybdis"; Joyce even signed and dated the final draft of this episode, particularly marking it as the close of the first half of *Ulysses*.[41] Moreover, those who have worked through Joyce's compositional notes point to the close of this episode as the place where Joyce leaves behind his simpler narrative and parodic strategies and moves toward a wilder, more dis-equilibrious style. Michael Groden remarks an "uneasiness" with style after "Scylla and Charybdis," noting an edgy shifting about of technique. He speculates that Joyce began to feel constrained by interior monologue, and consequently incorporated shifting perspectives, aggressive narrators, and the parody of styles from episodes ten to fourteen ("Wandering Rocks" to "Oxen of the Sun"), experimenting with ever more radically new styles in the last four episodes.[42] Indeed, the narration, marked by free indirect discourse, gradually breaks into dramatic and poetic genres, allowing the textual form to reflect the episode's internal actions. As Stephen plays up to his audience, so he becomes a character (a ham-let) in his own play. In the next chapter I will explore how the content of Stephen's own argument—his branding of Ann Hathaway with infamy for supposedly cuckolding Shakespeare—challenges his own notion of willful and artistic control. Here, it is most crucial to note that it is the juncture at which Joyce switches from a more autobiographical focus toward a broader social engagement, and as his parody shifts so too does the art of gesture re-emerge.

One can see now how the overdetermination of binaristic constructions—especially those of materiality and meaning—laid the conditions for Joyce's struggle to redefine literary modes of meaning. One gesture that Joyce employed to counter such dualities was the appropriation of the Annunciation, where woman's womb becomes the fleshy place of divine or otherworldly inspiration and creative spirit. If this appropriation threatens to disembody woman, abstracting her from specified corporeality and translating her image into that of pure transformative force, it was at the very least an attempt to return language to the context of embodiment. Yet Joyce's most significant shift toward a gestural art that both fused meaning and matter and also challenged the aggressive process of stereotyping that arises from polarizations occurred as he treated women not as mothers so much as seductive agents of desire, moving beyond the artist's conscious control. So while the "Oxen of the Sun" episode stages an exhaustive parody of the "birth of language" in close proximity to the birth- (and potentially death-) throes of a mother in labor, "Circe" is the episode that finally does transform language and Joyce's literary approach through its circulation around the threat and lure of women's erotic power. It also takes desire toward a confrontation with the very abstraction of women's images, implicit in Joyce's use of symbolism in *Portrait*. While I will return to give more extensive address to this problem of abstraction in the next chapter, on "Control of the Feminine," here I would like to address "Circe" in its play on seduction, where the imagination can recreate materiality as well as be itself transformed by the sensate lure of object and flesh. It is also no coincidence that this episode returns to a model of stage art and, in it, Stephen again articulates his theory of gesture.

"CIRCE" AND THE AESTHETICS OF DESIRE

In "Circe," the art of gesture returns in the full force of its physical manifestation of desire. While in the National Library Stephen condemns Ann Hathaway for her seductive will and unfaithfulness, here he swerves toward Dublin's red light district in search of a sacredly profane encounter—with the woman one *pays* to be unfaithful. He swaggers into nighttown reciting the introit of the Mass: "*Vidi aquam egredientem de templo a latere dextro. Alleluia . . . Et omnes ad quos pervenit aqua ista*" (U 15.77–84). "I saw water coming out of the temple on the right side . . . and all those to whom the water come shall be saved." Stephen may be substituting, in his mind, another liquid of salvation as he swerves past various ladies of the evening. As he approaches the divine place of "rhythm," Bella Cohen's brothel, he drunkenly expounds a more decadent version of his *Portrait* aesthetics to Lynch: "So that gesture, not music not odour, would be a universal language, the gift of tongues rendering visible not the lay sense but the first entelechy, the structural rhythm" (U 15.105–7). The "universal language" is that of love, but tinged with a certain sexual "rhythm." Suddenly the antikinetic artist is interested in a more bawdy interpretation of his art. "Pornosophical philotheology," Lynch calls it. In defense of his sexual agenda, Stephen argues that "[W]e have shrewridden Shakespeare and henpecked Socrates. Even the allwise Stagyrite was bitted, bridled and mounted by a light of love. . . . Anyway, who wants two gestures to illustrate a loaf and a jug? This movement illustrates the loaf and jug of bread or wine in Omar" (U 15.111–17). Stephen then "slowly holds out his hands, his head going back till both hands are a span from his breast, down turned, in planes intersecting, the fingers about to part, the left being higher" (U 15.124–27). Stephen's Mass becomes a kind of drama, a mimic enactment of the meeting of wine and bread, blood and body, spirit and matter. Be it sexual and laced with infidelity and uncertainty, love transfigures and likewise transubstantiates. At the same time, as Ewa Ziarek suggests, Stephen's suspicion that paternity "may be a legal fiction" (U 9.844) leads Joyce to question the metaphorical constraints of language, so that Stephen figures the female womb as a "matrix of language" wherein the succession (or intention to pass on meaning) is forever vulnerable to uncertainty.[43] "Circe" marks a tension between Stephen's desire to achieve artistic transfiguration and his inability to surrender a drive for totalizing control. Yet this chapter of the textual unconscious underscores the absurdity of Stephen's insistence on control. Desire becomes the drive that compels change, rather than will, so that the unconscious takes over in the chapter of transformations. Jean-Michel Rabaté observes the odd relations between gestures and the textual unconscious in this episode, suggesting that "voices are linked to gestures in a wild pantomime that generates the most delirious of hallucinations, while the themes developed by this staggering gesticulation body forth myriads of symptoms all produced by an unconscious, a very peculiar textual unconscious that can only be attributed to the preceding chapters of the novel."[44] Pausing over Stephen's association of "gesture" with a "universal language," Rabaté suggests that the episode epitomizes the performative power of language, and so "*Act* would thus perhaps be a better term than *gesture* here."[45] And yet if "act" would emphasize the potency of Joyce's language, *gesture* might also suggest the more extended temporal relation, dependant on repetition and a more integral definition through the body.

Character and meaning are transformed in their Circean manner when the surface power of language ceases to be inconsequential but becomes the very essence and truth of that medium. Nowhere is narrative more dense than in the episode that appears to function without narrative, with narrative operating from within the stage directions, which are anything but direct. Witness the opening set-up of "Circe":

(The Mabbot street entrance of nighttown, before which stretches an uncobbled tramsiding set with skeleton tracks, red and green will-o'-the-wisps and danger signals. Rows of grimy houses with gaping doors. Rare lamps with faint rainbow fans. Round Rabaiotti's halted ice gondola stunted men and women squabble. They grab wafers between which are wedged lumps of coral and copper snow. Sucking, they scatter slowly, children. The swancomb of the gondola, high-reared, forges on through the murk, white and blue under a lighthouse. Whistles call and answer.)(U 15.1–9)

The scene begins simply enough, with a description of the street and train tracks nearby, but soon contraries emerge and the directions become more suggestive than realistic. Are the "rare lamps" exotic or merely few in number? Are they—one assumes—in the "grimy houses" or out on the street corners? Before one can root around for details, the scene's description shifts toward even looser associative patterns.

"Stunted men and women" turn out to be "children," an unusually poetic switch in a genre of text that should deliver cut-and-dry descriptions of the setting. Their ices also are not realistically identified, but described by appearance as "wafers between which are wedged lumps of coral and copper snow." Appearances are everything here and illusions only are identified as reality.[46] After illusions commandeer perspective, however, fantasy takes over and things are not even "what they seem." As Hugh Kenner observes, metaphors have become actual, with all their allusive possibilities becoming real and visible. He suggests that many of the strange moments in "Circe" are not hallucinations, but rather an odd method of placing all figures and analogies "on the plane of the visible and audible."[47] Soon bells will be calling "Haltyaltyaltyall" (U 15.181), an odd onomatopoeia that indicates the message within the sound (stop!). As Bloom says, "everything speaks in its own way" (U 7.177), but here it speaks specifically to an interpretive perspective. Bloom hears "halt!" and stops. If this is similar to Joyce's spelling out of a cat's meow or a machine's "sllt," Joyce's words extend now away from phonetic realism toward an emphasis on how the ear bends a sound toward its relevant message. Eventually wreaths of smoke will be reciting, "Sweet are the sweets. Sweets of sin" (U 15.655), and kisses will warble "Icky licky micky sticky for Leo" (U 15.1272). When the soap Bloom has shifted between pockets all day sings, "We're a capital couple are Bloom and I / He brightens the earth. I polish the sky" (U 15.338–39), the material "speaks" an image the audience might well apply to Bloom's stage character, given his characteristic tick all day of shifting the soap between pockets.

When Joyce abruptly moves from the genre of fiction to that of drama, he puts on stage many of the aspects of his work with parody. He allows poetic descriptors to turn into realistic description, and thereby teases the reader's slight ability to separate fact from fantasm. As Paddy Dignam rises from the grave, changing into various versions of dogs (beagle, dachshund—U 15.1204f.), the scene is both real, in that it is being performed on stage and can be "witnessed," and unreal, in that it only takes place as a part of a textual nightmare. The line between the "truth" as reality and falsifying distortions is wavy in nighttown. Perspective folds in on itself, and Joyce laughingly makes fantasy more real and reality less interesting.[48] The *surface* of language here at least briefly gains significance equal to its "inner meaning," and the arbitrary associations brought about by metaphor and turns-of-phrase control the directions of character fantasies and identifications. As this occurs, *Ulysses*'s artist— Stephen Dedalus—experiences a radical loosening of definitional boundaries where language is linked to identity, so that every word or image may trigger memory of the past and future imaginings.

Stephen has been trying to ward off the echo of Simon Dedalus' prohibition against mixing with members of the lower classes: "stable with those halfcastes," mutters his father's image, "Wouldn't let them within the bawl of an ass. Head up! Keep our flag flying!" (U 15.3947–48). Stephen recalls his father's class prejudices and his drive for upper-class purity of breeding, perhaps present in those dogs—half-breeds and mutts—roaming around nighttown. As Stephen waltzes with one of the prostitutes in Bella Cohen's establishment, the Pianola sings, "Though she's a factory lass/And wears no fancy clothes," and he hears his father gasp, "Think of your mother's people!" (U 15.4137). Associating "mother" with "death," Stephen remarks out loud, "Dance of death," recalling (among other things mentioned in stage notes) the decay of his own family's finances. He thinks of his sister: "Dilly with snowcake no fancy clothes" (U 15.4147–48).

Stephen's chief anxiety, however, has circled around a resistance to the body as brought to his mind in the image of May Goulding Dedalus, who now "rises stark through the floor, in leper grey," with her face "worn and noseless" (U 15.4157–59). As Mulligan's own specter remarks, she is "beastly dead." Stephen may be pulling away from aestheticism, but he is repulsed by naturalism. If she once was, as her ghost claims, "the beautiful May Goulding," beauty has fallen into physical stench and repulsive aspect. When the ghost tells Stephen that "all must go through it," the reference quickly switches, by virtue of the speaker's symbolism to Stephen. She may be speaking of death, but the significance changes to meaning marriage and love. "All must go through it, Stephen. More women than men in the world. You too. Time will come" (U 15.4182–84). If Stephen desires love—sexual and more—the stench of the corpse still reminds him of death, and implicitly invokes the religious retreat. When he asks his mother for "[t]he word known to all men" (U 15.4193), instead of love Stephen gets guilt and moralism. "Years and years I loved you, O my son!" she cries out, only to reveal her remorse at his refusal to pray for her soul. "Repent!" she shouts, "O, the fire of hell!" Stephen withdraws toward the razor-edged art of the *dio boia*, and shouts, "With me all or not at all. *Non serviam*!" (U 15.4227–29). With a sweep, he breaks the chandelier, screaming "Nothung!" (U 15.4242). His gesture is violence, but not transformative violence. Stephen's anxieties are not purged or reworked in "Circe"; they are merely staged at a climax of intensity. He runs out into the street, gets into a fight unwittingly, and passes out after being punched by a soldier.

If Stephen retains a propensity for defensive resistances and dichotomous extremes—which are even more brutally parodied in the ignorance and aggression of Private Carr at the episode's end—I am suggesting that the episode as a whole contrasts such aggressive forms of perception with a loosely associative form of identity that can emerge only after desire is released from fixed moral constructions. Bloom's imaginary encounter with Bella/Bello provides an opening for such a reworking of desire, especially as it is fantastically scripted onto (and through) the body. And just as Bloom experiences renewal after a parodic reversal of roles, language undergoes a transformation by twisting objects inside out.

As the purveyor of bodily-minded consciousness, Leopold Bloom enters "Circe" as a split embodiment of two opposite types. In waking consciousness Bloom is a complex composite of possible selves, but when defensive, as he is in nighttown, he falls into the traps of self-stereotyping. Bloom's entrance to nighttown mocks this tendency, so that his initial reflection is marked at extremes as he walks "on stage":

> From Gillen's hairdresser's window a composite portrait shows him gallant Nelson's image. A *concave mirror* at the side presents to him lovelorn longlost lugubru Booloohoom. Grave Gladstone sees him level, *Bloom for Bloom*. He passes, struck by the stare of truculent Wellington, but in the *convex mirror* grin unstruck the bonham eyes and fatchuck cheekchops of jollypoldy the rixdix doldy. (U 15.143–49 my italics)

Bloom is alternately blue "Booloohoom" and then elative "jollypoldy the rixdix doldy," reflected in the extreme opposites of concave and convex mirrors. In between, he is seen "Bloom for Bloom" by Gladstone, a politician known for his even-tempered perception.[49] Yet where in "Circe" is the pure mimesis of Gladstone's vision? We get nothing informative, no list of picturable attributes—only pure identity, "Bloom for Bloom" that tells the reader nothing.

Bloom enters nighttown oscillating between guilt and desire, tacitly following Stephen but also engaged in pursuit of sensual experience. Not yet willing to think openly about sex, Bloom has displaced that desire into an interest in food. Packed with provisions, he comes in "flushed, panting, cramming bread and chocolate into a sidepocket" (U 15.142–43). He will later duck into "Olhausen's, the porkbutcher's" for a packet of pig's crubeen and a sheep's trotter. For both Bloom and Stephen, nighttown is a place of the repressed. Stephen has denied his sensual side (excepting, of course, drink), only to hurl himself toward Bella Cohen's at the evening's close. Bloom on the other hand has been consistently aware of his body and sensual needs all day, but he has persistently resisted any broader moralist reflections. In nighttown, both characters meet with the sides of their natures that have been pushed under.

The realm of nighttown is therefore the place of conscience for Bloom, especially as that conscience relates to social assessment of his character. Pockets stuffed with pig's feet, he encounters the specter of his dead father who rises, like a stage Jew, to lecture him on money: "Second halfcrown waste money today. I told you not to go with drunken goy ever. So you catch no money" (U 15.253–54). Here the more radically changeable nature of the setting begins to work, with stereotypes as the crucial link in this vaudevillian parody. Bloom's outfit is immediately transformed into "youth's smart blue Oxford suit" as he answers his father. Just as quickly, his mother appears, a stage Irish-Catholic, crying "O blessed Redeemer, what have they done to him! . . . Sacred Heart of Mary, where were you at all at all?" (U 15.287–89). Soon Molly appears in Eastern garb—a concubine or prostitute. Camels follow her, picking and offering mango fruit. All of Bloom's anxieties emerge. He remembers Molly's facial lotion forgotten at the pharmacy; he encounters a bespoiled Gerty MacDowell who accuses him of rape by desire; and he is espied in this shady part of town by a respectable Mrs. Breen, his former sweetheart. (As he reminisces with her about their courtship, she ironically responds "Yes, yes, yes, yes, yes, yes, yes" and then "fades from his side" U 15.576–77.) Already, Bloom is reenacting the more moralistic aspects of Dublin pantomimes, which often included moral lessons for the benefit of the children who attended them.[50]

Joyce works with pantomime throughout *Ulysses*, most explicitly in "Circe," to reveal the process of self-constitution through typological associations, and he uses mime centrally in "The Mime of the Mick, Nick, and the Maggies" in *Finnegans Wake*.[51] Turn-of-the-century pantomime in Dublin replayed certain basic, repeated scenarios, focusing most often on that of two lovers who rebel against parental authority in their struggle to be united. The roles were usually taken from the harlequinade, the key figures of which were Harlequin, Columbine, Pantaloon, and the Clown (Pierrot).[52] While Hayman, in the 1960s, argued that Joyce takes stock character models directly from mime, Herr instead suggests than his texts "encounter, critique, and transform" these stereotypes.[53] Certainly, Joyce seems to play on these various characters; Hayman convincingly traces a triangular parallel between Bloom-Molly-Blazes and Stephen-Muse-Mulligan, which echoes the traditional love triangle of the cuckold Pierrot, the unfaithful Columbine, and the wily Harlequin who steals her favors away.[54] However, Joyce does not literally adopt the plots and biases, and it is still unclear as to whether his characters are stock types. Certainly, in "Circe" he plays out the reductive potential of stage mime and broadly comical pantomime and slap stick. And yet the threat of these stereotypes is allowed to pursue—that is to say "dog"—the characters.

Dogged by memories (and by a series of changeable dogs), Bloom soon faces a full jury, being accused, as he is, of being "a wellknown dynamitard, forger, bigamist, bawd and cuckold and a public nuisance to the citizens of Dublin" (U 15.1158–60). He is the forerunner of HCE, who faces long tirades of accusation substantiated by gossip in *Finnegans Wake*. Soon, however, Bloom is interrupted in his initial nightmare of defense by Zoe Higgins, a "real" person rather than a projection of Bloom's worried mind. She directs him toward Stephen, steals his talisman potato, and tries to earn a buck off of him. But when he chides her for wanting a smoke, she sets off his imagination by challenging him to "Make a stump speech out of it" (U 15.1353). Bloom is immediately transformed into a politician dressed in "workman's corduroy overalls." He delivers a rousing speech, complete with the promise of a "new Bloomusalem in the Nova Hibernia of the future" (U 15.1544–45). This is immediately constructed on stage "with crystal roof, built in the shape of a huge pork kidney, containing forty thousand rooms." Bloom is praised by Paddy Leonard as a "Stage Irishman!" (U 15.1729), as he sings humorous songs and shows all "that he is wearing green socks" (U 15.1521). Even the Citizen praises him, "choked with emotion." Soon, of course, he must fall like Parnell and is again accused and disparaged by all. Bloom's rapid rises and falls hinge on light associations with his positive or negative characteristics that quickly transform him into stereotypes. In this episode, Joyce is already beginning the broad parodies of *Finnegans Wake*, where society's discomfort with the indiscernible slivers of difference within gesture creates an abrupt need to press characterizations to stereotypic extremes. Bloom is either celebrated or abhorred. When he tells a stale joke, for instance, he is immediately accused of being a plagiarist (U 15.1734). The fixation of these types enables the general populace (of Bloom's guilty conscience) to judge Bloom adamantly. In this, Joyce pursues a link between social moralism and "individual" conscience, which trangresses any distinction between the inner/individual identity and outer/social values.

It was Wyndham Lewis who first argued that *Ulysses* was an erudite parade of stereotypes, "clichés of character," as Lewis called them. He thought Joyce had cast Bloom as a "stage Jew," Mulligan as the "stage Irishman," Haines as the "stage Anglo-Saxon," and worst of all Stephen, as "the Poet."[55] Lewis might well have had "Circe" in mind, more than any of the other episodes. Certainly the characters there play roles and identify with a range of types, but they are in part *self*-cast. It is, as Kenner has noticed, simply the case that Stephen enjoys *acting the part* of the skeptical intellectual, and "Circe" makes explicit the act of assuming a role.[56] Yet as Bloom's trials demonstrate, one can never successfully "self" cast, but needs to have access to (and indeed may not ever escape from) types that are socially constructed and thereby contextually enabled. Stephen is part self-cast and set-up as cynical intellect, much as Bloom taps into his potential for heroic and degenerative proportions.

Along with strictly prohibitive structures, stereotypes loom large in the realm of the unconscious. Their extremism may be a form of parody, but it can also signal paranoia. The returning emphasis on stereotypic identifications suggests a simple reach for solid and pure identifications. This can backfire, as it does for Bloom. Shortly after "the keeper of the Kildare street museum" appears with the statues of "several naked goddesses"—one imagines much like the reproduction Bloom was seen studying earlier in the day from rear perspective—Bloom is accused by Father Farley of being "an agnostic, and anythingarian seeking to overthrow our holy faith" (U 15.1712–13). As in Parnell's case, sexual desire brings about the fall. Soon Bloom will be rigidly identified with all of his faults, even those that are mere rumor. Public hysteria blows categories wildly out of proportion, and so Bloom is "the white bull mentioned in the Apocalypse," "a worshipper of the Scarlet Woman," or simply "Caliban!" (U 15.1757–60). As Bloom acts out the sufferance of the link between morality and desire, each desire is pressed to its "good" or "bad" extreme and praised or condemned. Such extremism only intensifies the desire it denies, as desire is defined in relation to lack. More crucially, when that lack is the "lack of being," according to Lacan, it moves beyond any form of representation; "It is only ever represented as a reflection on a veil."[57]

The rhythmic relation to the body, which was dismissed along with kinetic desire in the *Portrait* aesthetics, re-emerges, just as Joyce turns more directly toward a theatrical model; in "Circe," characters mime a range of possible selves, transmuted variously by the succession of one to another contingent aspects that serially take hold as absolutes. The imagination slides such particular possibilities into radical types, fixing on stereotypes (Jew, Catholic, cuckold, hero, corrupt politician, etc.), while the body is alternately present as perfumed with alluring smells and then corpselike with rank and mold, inspiring the oscillations of desire and repulsion that gradually shake the borders of the typological consciousness. In "Circe," the textual consciousness returns to Aristotle, who argued against the Platonic notion that form rises forth unrevised in material embodiments. Rather, for Aristotle, form may "impregnate" material and give off various manifestations, which claim in that transformation their own particularity. Where Plato's tokens are yoked back in reference always to the formal essence from which they derive, Aristotle's physical manifestations are not *subjected* to an abstract type, but more specifically are a deviation and particular extension of it.[58] Joyce's extension of Aristotle emphasizes the ways in which embodiment (the body and/or materiality) presses on the boundaries of categories themselves, so that in *Finnegans Wake* a slip of the alphabet removes a word from definitional conformity and a "character" from socially determined fixity. Within the nighttown episode, the strange loosening of identifications and increasingly arbitrary associative movement of thought points toward the early drafts of *Finnegans Wake* in 1923, where the (anti)grammatical principles take over and the problem of how characters, words, and letters are to be associated emerges as a question of relative gestures that must be interpreted.

As in *Finnegans Wake*, desire and its accompanying anxiety in "Circe" erect dichotomous extremes and typological stringencies, all of which must be worked through as Joyce reaches for a more radical art of materiality. Materiality is, in a sense, Lacan's Real, the materiality that can interrupt the spiraling of the imaginary. Appropriately, nighttown is the site of this revision, as it is the body that disrupts social convention and its attempts to etch meaning onto materiality. The opposition between materiality and language breaks down, revealing the ways in which the body and the materiality of words can undermine the very construction of meaning that they also enable. As Judith Butler notes, "it is not that one cannot get outside of language in order to grasp materiality in and of itself; rather, every effort to refer to materiality takes place through a signifying process which, in its phenomenality, is always already material. In this sense, then, language and materiality are not opposed, for language both is and refers to that which is material, and what is material never fully escapes from the process by which it is signified."[59] More particularly, the propulsion/revulsion of desires that circulate around the female body in this episode call forth a range of oppositions that eventually result in a violence not only against another opposite, but against the construction of opposition itself.

Bloom's series of trial scenarios reaches a climax as Bella Cohen enters the scene, and his attention is riveted by her assertive fan. The fan taps insistently, "We have met. You are mine. It is fate" (U 15.2775). Bella's appeal is her insistence on attaining full authority—to judge, order, and control. These aspects of her personality masculinize Bella, so that as she gains in authority her sex literally (or figuratively in force, as the episode seems to have no literal space) changes into a man. As she commands him to re-lace her shoes, he is seduced by her power:

BLOOM

(*mumbles*) Awaiting your further orders we remain, gentlemen, . . .

BELLO

(*with a hard basilisk stare, in a baritone voice*) Hound of dishonour!

BLOOM

(*infatuated*) Empress!

BELLO

(*his heavy cheekchops sagging*) Adorer of the adulterous rump!

BLOOM

(*plaintively*) Hugeness!

BELLO

Dungdevourer!

BLOOM

(*with sinews semiflexed*) Magmagnificence! (U 15.2832–45)

As Bello's magnitude masculinizes him/her, Bloom's adoration and depre-
cation feminizes him into a "her." The scene climaxes initially with Bello
squatting on Bloom's upturned face and quenching a cigar in his/her ear.
But the real climax takes place in terms of guilt. Moralism and sexual
transgression mix, as Bella/Bello tells "ducky dear" s/he just wishes to
"administer correction . . . for your own good" (U 15.2882–86). S/he
urges him to confess, a practice more familiar to Stephen than to Bloom.
"What was the most revolting piece of obscenity in all your career of
crime?" Bello asks. "Go the whole hog. Puke it out! Be candid for once"
(U 15.3042–44). He confesses incoherently, is punished, and then must
take a scolding for all his errors and shortcomings. Bloom is eventually
crucified, and resurrects to the memory of the nymph's picture over his
bed and his kinetic interpretation of her as art. Meanwhile, in real time
Bloom has rejected Bella Cohen disdainfully (U 15.3480+). Yet Bloom
seems to derive some fruitful energy from the imaginary confrontation, so
that his anxieties about (not) controlling Molly are turned upside down,
as he plays an absurd version of the female supplicant.[60]
    If the imagination can travel forward associatively, loosening the grip
of moralism and oppositional fixity, it would seem that the body or "the
real" of materiality would still be founding its direction and inspiration.
And yet this is the most unique aspect of Joyce's work in "Circe"; even the
body is not stable. Bella transforms into Bello Cohen, and Bloom's body
changes to that of a woman. Gender and sex are no longer distinct, as perception (of Bella's moustache, for instance) can trigger the awareness of
male attributes of the female-sexed body. As Butler notes, the body is
"sexed" through a normative notion of male versus female anatomy, hier-
archizing our sense of which parts of the body are more crucial determinants.[61] In "Circe," the body is not a fixed locus of authority, much as the

external world is no longer the mimetic origin of Joyce's art. The "real" is instead reconfigured by the imagination and desire, suggesting that Joyce may press beyond anxious relations to the seductive appeal and the corruptibility of the body. While Stephen's resistance to the body and the decay (away from intention and spirit) prevents the play of associative desire, Bloom's encounter with Bella/Bello seems to suggest a movement beyond the stymied relationship in his own world, blocked by the death of Ruby. Bloom's sadomasochistic fantasy maps the unfolding of his contradictory desire to be both subjected and in control, charting on an erotic terrain the problem of social interaction that he has faced all day. Once unlocked, the imaginative scenario allows Bloom some relief, as it enables him to transform potentially outward-directed aggression into an inward pleasure. Stephen's relation to the body, however, remains rooted in opposition, so that stereotypes continue to drive him toward the climax of violence, shattering the lamp and expressive potential toward the episode's end.

This scene is, as Sandra Gilbert argues, "grotesque parody," but not, as she would have it, of "masculinized female mastery."[62] Joyce uses a reversal of gender roles to loosen the identification of such roles with the body in its sexual determination. He is playing out the tensions between the seductive allure of the body and (1) the domination that arrives with such pleasure and (2) the threat of corruption and decay, which Stephen more immediately experiences with the vision of his mother's ghost. Moralism, which has provided a problem for Bloom's attempts to break free from stereotypes of Molly (and, consequently, of himself), floats free from social fixity and is transformed into sadomasochism, as Bella/Bello takes over as the voice of social disapproval. This shift, or "perversity," allows Joyce's parody to break free from more fixed, agonistic versions of parody and to move toward associative chains of contiguous ideas. Rather than being blocked and accelerated by moralism, desire now moves toward associative expansion.

After the transformation by Bella/Bello, Bloom looks into a mirror and the face of Shakespeare appears:

LYNCH

(*points*) The mirror up to nature. (*he laughs*) Hu hu hu hu hu! (*Stephen and Bloom gaze in the mirror. The face of William Shakespeare, beardless, appears there, rigid in facial paralysis, crowned by the reflection of the reindeer antlered hatrack in the hall.*)

SHAKESPEARE

(*in dignified ventriloquy*) 'Tis the loud laugh bespeaks the vacant mind. (*to Bloom*) Thou thoughtest as how thou wastest invisible. Gaze. (*he crows with a black capon's laugh*) Iagogo! How my Oldfellow chokit his Thursdaymornun. Iagogogo! (U 15.3819–29)

As unreliable as Bloom's initial mirror in this episode, this mirror shows Bloom's "nature" as a cuckold and money-saver. He is Iago in that he will try to advise Stephen to take care of his money as, earlier in *Ulysses*, Deasy did, invoking that character: "Put but money in thy purse" (U 2.239–40). But as cuckold (crowned by the hall hatrack, the appropriate horns of the cuckold), Bloom/Shakespeare is likewise paralyzed.[63] In this he is loosely associated with Stephen, who has been attempting to escape creative paralysis by likening himself to Shakespeare. Dan Schwarz argues that this scene demonstrates the "shared vision" of Stephen and Bloom, representing a moment of fusion of consciousness.[64] More likely still, there is an ironic overlap of their consciousnesses, since Bloom does not know that Stephen has proven Shakespeare a Jew. Bloom and Stephen do not necessarily *merge*, but are linked by mutual association with Shakespeare, each identifying with a different aspect of cultural figure who so readily expands to absorb the values of each period of English history since the seventeenth century. For his part, Stephen has been trying in "Scylla and Charybdis" to draw a portrait of himself similar to Shakespeare-the-revenge artist. Thus, Shakespeare's visage later mutters, "Weda seca whokilla farst" in "paralytic rage" (U 15.3853). Rather than a symbolic fusion of Bloom and Stephen, the reader witnesses, in the mirror scene, the looseness of associations. Soon Shakespeare's face is "refeatured" by the now bearded face of Martin Cunningham. Cunningham is considered, both by the narrator of "Grace" and by Bloom, to have a face like Shakespeare's (D 157), so that Shakespeare functions as a cultural catch-all, standing in for whatever positive values define character at the moment. This association also expands in Bloom's mind. After some kindness to Bloom in "Hades," Cunningham is described in Bloom's thoughts as a "sympathetic human man" and "intelligent" with a face "like Shakespeare's face." Also, like Shakespeare, Cunningham seems to have married a shrew, "that awful drunkard of a wife of his. Setting up house for her time after time and then pawning the furniture on him every Saturday almost." (U 6.344–51). Immediately after Shakespeare "becomes" Cunningham, Mrs. Cunningham enters the scene singing "they call me the jewel of Asia!" a bawdy song Simon Dedalus heard her singing one night when drunk, according to Bloom's memory in "Hades." Stephen, Bloom, and Cunningham can therefore all be said to be "like Shakespeare" in the fantasy underworld of "Circe," even while they all differ from each other. Joyce thus pursues the breakdown of (auto)biographic identifications that could be charted on simple one-to-one correspondences; now, he foreshadows the characterology of *Finnegans Wake*, where broad typological constructs are shifted by virtue of associative chains through which various "characters" transmute.

As woman, Circe turns men and objects inside out, revealing not only the darkness of inner fears but also the weight of costume and arbitrary appearances. This transformative process of twisting insides out necessarily plays on the literalization of metaphor and the "speaking" significance of physical objects, so that in "Circe" the sensual aspects of things are oddly literalized. Metaphor becomes real, and the distinctions between fantasy/reality and thought/action are broken down. Symbols, like lamps or Shakespeare's visage, are held forth and shattered and material is no longer dumb, but speaks. Lynch's cap pronounces opinions—"Ba! It is because it is. Woman's reason. Jewgreek is greekjew. Extremes meet. Death is the highest form of life. Ba!" (U 15.2097–98)— and fans assess Bloom: "Married, I see" (U 15.2755). It is as if representation were turning upon itself and what emerges is a disintegration of the split between mute appearance and articulate meaning.

This transformation of language into a more loosely associative medium—freer from conscious will than unconscious desire—arrives only in and through a rampant parody of societal aggressions that take the explicit form of stereotyping. If Joyce's language can take up gestural art in its embodiment of the instability of seduction-by-suggestion, this loosening of control is counterbalanced by the images of aggressive gestures. Joyce's deconstructive approach to stereotyping, as he turns toward *Finnegans Wake*, continues to replay these extreme examples in plot conflicts while the language materializes the oscillating referentiality that denies controllable fixation of identity and definitional boundaries. This is how the critical reconsideration that is so important in Joyce's work comes about, through the repeated encounter with—rather than avoidance of—the problem of stereotyping and polarizing of identities. By erasing an objective position where these opinions and aggressions can be identified with the author, Joyce avoids the explicit identification politics the characters aggressively replay, and by posing their parlay at mocking extremes he points to a heightened awareness of their absurdity. Nonetheless, as Joyce moves toward this complex critical focus on stereotyping as a process and gestural art as an alternative, he constantly recapitulates to learned forms of desire. His representations of women, most importantly, change over the course of his career, so that the silent muse begins to speak not mere moralism, as with Stephen's mother, but to articulate an uncontrollable flow of desire and dream. One of the chief focuses of debates about Joyce's textual politics has been his representations of women, particularly in the works prior to *Finnegans Wake*. I will therefore begin my exploration of three instances of how Joyce deals with specific stereotypes by approaching his most often discussed and debated control of the feminine.

CHAPTER 3

"The word is my Wife":
Control of the Feminine

In *Finnegans Wake*, Shaun preaches the necessity of controlling one's wife and word:

> My unchanging Word is sacred. The word is my Wife, to expose and expound, to vend and to velnerate, and may the curlews crown our nuptias! Till Breath us depart! Wamen. Beware would you change with my years. Be as young as your grandmother! The ring man in the rong shop but the rite words by the rote order! (FW 167.28–33)

Preaching to the rainbow girls, Shaun insistently informs them that "the word is my Wife" to think upon (ponse) and to strike (pound), to sell (vend) and to worship—*or* wound (Latin: venerate/vulnerare)[1]—till breath (or death) tears them apart. In the dream play of *Finnegans Wake*, one slips into the recognition of what this drive to control suppresses: that when "breath us depart" Shaun will no longer be able to control his progeny, either of the mind or the body. The husband/artist worries that he might find "the ring man in the rong shop" and, like Leopold Bloom, wind up a cuckold. So if "wamen" (Middle English: wame)[2] is the womb to men's word, Joyce's parody simultaneously replays and mocks the drive to control woman's sexual fidelity, engaging in the impossible effort to make certain of one's offspring, both familial and literary.

In Joyce's writing, women are often in a troubled relation to the artist's unconscious. In *Portrait* they are moralists who oppress Stephen, or women who can only be controlled when silenced and abstracted. In *Ulysses*, where they begin to tease the erotic in "Circe," "Nausicaa," and "Penelope," the text jumbles and gradually reclaims its alphabetic and tonal embodiment—its sensate replication of sounds, visual tricks, and the physicality of its own medium. And as Joyce's textuality moves toward an ever more thorough acceptance of the materiality of its own medium—in puns and in word-play—so too are the women in his texts freed to speak desires and exceed typological containments. This change creates a relatively new form of textual gesture in *Finnegans Wake*, where Issy's and Anna Livia's words turn away from aggression and toward a soft babbling play on sensate verbal pleasure, even as Joyce continues alternately to parody the control of the feminine, as in Shaun's sermon above.

Joyce's interest in the drive to control women's desires was always more than a thematic concern; the figures of women in his works are repeatedly used as catalysts to stylistic change. It is, as Luce Irigaray has noted, that the silencing and metaphorical figuration of women enables certain philosophical projects and the creation of a metadiscourse, which woman's plurality and her plurivocity necessarily disrupt.[3] In Shaun's lecture, Joyce mockingly models the ways in which a gestural politics may turn aggressive and controlling in its moralistic containment, and he specifically parodies marital constraint of women, paralleling them with the endeavor to control language. If Joyce's art of gesture works to connect language and bodily gesture, here he takes critical (if also comical) distance from the implications of the "Oxen of the Sun" episode in *Ulysses*, where the "womb to word" metaphor is stretched to offense, as the rowdy literati and medicals parodically represent the "birth" of the English language while Mina Purefoy gives physical birth nearby, after three days of what has been apparently a painful stretch of labor. The politics of both erotic and maternal repression are often signalled by an aggressive, even hostile, attempt to control women as metaphors of the envied, creative womb. Earlier, I discussed Gilbert and Gubar's attack on Joyce for appropriating the "mother tongue" and overmastering the feminine; while I there objected to their hasty analyses, it is important here to note the various moments where such concerns would seem naturally to be raised. Yet if Joyce is not a radical feminist (on any account), radical *écriture* becomes his achievement. These two seemingly opposite aspects of Joyce's work *do* come together in the mediation of his aesthetic, as it transforms from volitional to a more fluctuating mode informed by the unconscious. His work moreover cycles back through self- and social analyses in terms of gender, reflecting ever more critically and integrally as he moves toward *Finnegans Wake*. Neither American nor French feminists of the 1970s fully address all the elements of the feminine in Joyce's writing, but a postmodern feminist perspective might, were it to balance the text's more fixed and fluid moments, and Joyce's parodic use of unconscious and conscious images.

I will here be suggesting that, over the course of his career, Joyce moved away from a partially complicitous parody of Stephen's vision of pure and "virginal" symbols of objectified women. Women—and words—progressively give voice to desire and resistance to the Symbolist containments bent upon their figures. As women become subjective agents in Joyce's work, his use of symbols likewise changes, so that they become less fixed and operate more as suggestive traces that run through the experiential variations of meaning and non-meaning. The link between women and words is transformed in Joyce's writing as he disengages from an early, aggressive impulse to control the feminine and turns contrarily to parody such impulses. In terms of his use of French Symbolism and Mallarmé's influence, Joyce chooses the figure of woman for that of parody, just as Mallarmé cast her as a figure for aesthetic inspiration. And yet in Lacan, in Nietzsche, and such figures that Derrida draws on in *Spurs*, this treatment of woman as the figure of parody can function as a dangerous location of her role.[4] Mallarmé's *Mimique* draws in part on Paul Margueritte's booklet, *Pierrot Murderer of his Wife*, in which the mime mimes a murder of the woman he loves.[5] She must die in orgasmic laughter, in return for her infidelity—a parody that makes her a figure of love and anger, of virtue and unfaithfulness. Joyce relinquishes such aggression thematically in *Ulysses*, when Bloom reflects on revenge broadly but rejects it immediately (U 17.2220 and passim). However, his aesthetic use of women does not truly shift away from controlling containments until the midpoint of that book, where the textual processes themselves shift and loosen into more radically sensate and formally open experiments. Textual gestures become more extreme and also more detrimental to the control and stasis earlier associated with masculine attempts to fix and stabilize the feminine. However, if by *Finnegans Wake*, Joyce arrives at a kind of "écriture féminine," this occurs only because he insistently represents, transforms, and ventriloquizes women as progressively desiring agents. I will be exploring the politics of such representations across his work, culminating in a dialectical reading of Joyce's stylistic experiments and thematic repetitions in *Finnegans Wake*.

Joyce's work has enjoyed a notoriously split reception among feminists. We have, on the one hand, charged that Joyce gives glimpses of misogyny too often in his works, and on the other, from French feminists like Julia Kristeva and Hélène Cixous, we have come to understand Joyce's linguistic experiments as *écriture féminine*, which employs a semiotic replication of the unconscious in a manner that babbles, flows, and disrupts the (masculine) control of the Symbolic. In *Desire in Language*, Kristeva explores the rhythmic heterogeneity of language, which appears first in infants as "rhythms and intonations anterior to the first phonemes, morphemes, lexemes, and sentences."[6] This may later recur in psychotic discourse, where meanings are lost in madness, but it can elsewhere produce "in poetic language 'musical' but also nonsense effects that destroy not only accepted beliefs and significations, but, in radical experiments, syntax itself, that guarantee of thetic consciousness."[7] In this destruction of all pregivens and dogma, heterogeneous rhythm might be solely liberating in its effects. In *Finnegans Wake*, as Anna Livia flows out to sea thinking "First we feel. Then we fall" (FW 627.11) allowing memories to co-mingle with dreams, Joyce's language moves through an ebb and flow of meaning, sometimes tugging on prior references or clear remarks, while at other moments merely playing on sound and erasing any definable sense. All is not reference in language, in that it would direct our attention away from the word itself; some things culminate in its alphabetic body, or in the mouth that speaks it and the ear that hears. So ALP claims, "You will always call me Leafiest, won't you dowling? Wordherfhull Ohldhbhoy!" (FW 624.22–23). She may be loveliest, leafiest, and "fhull" of wonderful words for her oldboy, but her words are also inhabited by breathy misspeaks, which destabilize any full lock on meaning. These are not only puns that arise from phonic misspellings, but also soundings that point to the embodiment of words, the "dowling" that connotes an accent on "darling," and the extra breath in "Ohldhbhoy!" that makes the term specific to her voice, her word, and the particularity of its visual anomaly on the page.

Were such gestures of liberation from meaning's tighter grasp all paramount in the *Wake*, it would be a purely benign text, devoid of conflict, insult, and war. Nothing, however, could be further from the truth. The *Wake* is constantly bursting with fights, accusations, and aggressions. These paranoid-aggressive outbursts are often masculinized, while Joyce's return of the word to womb, body, and materiality occurs most often through the feminine. The text lisps softly at times, with Issy's or Anna's more seductive and ameliorative prose. Such *écriture féminine* may, as Suzette Henke suggests, demonstrate "the 'she-truth' of female *jouissance* and the ultimate limit of any discourse articulated by man."[8] At the very least, Joyce remakes language in a way that undermines and even attacks the ideological codes of patriarchy, both in his subversion of masterful language and in his refusal of the splice between meaning and embodiment.

Although many readers of the *Finnegans Wake* may agree that Joyce's avant-garde linguistic experiment liberates language from the rule of the Symbolic, this does not guarantee that, within the complex thematics of the text, sexual politics have found liberation altogether. Those who find Gerty MacDowell's wistful marmalade insultingly insipid will likewise find Issy's flirty lisps—albeit laced with greater sexual savvy—somewhat contained within a male erotic imaginary. Indeed, at moments one might picture Joyce, or his audience apparent, salivating over the objectified portrait of a less-than-mature women with only a coy fantasy of control over men, sexuality, and societal judgment. And those who have found Joyce's blithe comment that Molly Bloom was "der [sic] Fleisch der stets bejaht," will not be freed from such erasures of female consciousness by the marriage of flesh and word in the women of *Finnegans Wake*.[9] Anna Livia may either be liberated into sexuality— or trapped in her own embodiment. This quandary of feminist politics, in terms of its treatment of the erotic and language, is deeply troubled and challenged in Joyce's writing. He allows women sexual prowess without negative assessment progressively as he develops his linguistic-material experiments, but these portraits of desiring women still function in some part as erotic titillation for the male-centered imagination. Women might be merely allowed to *play* at mastery, only when their narratives and imaginations are overmastered by male authors. And so we might ask, what difference does it make that this text was written by a man? And how might the literary reception have differed if Djuna Barnes or Gertrude Stein had penned these words?

I would like to suggest that, even within the limitations of such speculative history and unquantifiable probabilities, Joyce engages in what is both a dangerous game and a progressively reflective poetics as he grows to favor the feminine in its alliance with words. The efficaciousness of language, at first denied women in much of Joyce's writing, becomes analogous with the very force of women. Here Joyce risks feminizing himself and parodying masculinity, pursing as he does a femininely configured associative process that promises to undermine polarization, competitions, and outbursts of aggression.[10] Joyce's work requires of the reader a constant vigilance, taking up the avant-garde distantiation from art, which demands a repeated rupture of any overly sentimental identification with one voice or character in the text. One needs to be consistently alert to the changing ways in which Joyce represents women, as well, for his figuration of them shifts at crucial moments where his aesthetic moves toward a more seductive (and less aggressive) gestural politics. Women are the central figures for this in Joyce's writing, initially contained by male artists like Stephen, and then progressively released to be aesthetic and linguistic agents in themselves. They become *bodies* that fuse with words, creating a more gestural language associated with *écriture féminine*—one that persistently contests abstraction and dematerialization, which would otherwise enable stereotypes to crystallize.

PORTRAIT: AN EROTICS OF SUPPRESSION

When Joyce's experimentation with parody began, women were either censored for articulating strong opinions or held silent, in a distance, as erotic and imaginative inspiration. *A Portrait of the Artist as a Young Man* presents a starkly split perspective on women. Women like Dante may be forcefully active, refusing Parnell political authority on the grounds of moralistic censure, while *within* the tale women's figures are often passively caught in Stephen's own cycle of desiring obsession and refusal. The extremity of his perspective seems particularly appropriate to the adolescent struggle with control, which is so often in conflict with desire. Between such obsession and denial, Joyce endeavors to find a modernist aesthetic beyond moralisms, an aesthetic that recovers from the loss of objective, universalized notions of value by loosening the adamantly split, absolute modes of valuation. Consequently, this drive elicits an interpretive dilemma: if Joyce's aesthetic practice is posed as a challenge to the harsh strictures of home, church, and state, how can one assess the social impact of his representations of women? How can we read politically in a manner that moves beyond mere censor and resistance? I am offering here a deconstructive emphasis on textual processes as one way to answer this dilemma, although the sexual politics informing deconstruction's primary texts here (Mallarmé, Nietzsche, Lacan) must also be taken into account as I construct a somewhat deviant approach, reclaiming materiality to do so.

In taking seriously Joyce's resistance to moralism, I would like to firmly emphasize that one need not polarize against feminism. On the contrary, the flippant dismissal of feminist politics as "mere moralism" arises from a too-thin understanding of contemporary analysis of the social impact of representational modes on gender development, and the collapse of woman into moralistic censor is itself a representation that works to silence women's voices. My tactic will be to examine both textual thematics and linguistic gestures (narcissistic vs. paranoid constructs) to assess the political impact of Joyce's work on his readers and implicitly within his aesthetic. And as for moralism itself, Joyce imposes that role on women as he turns toward Symbolism. As Susan Stanford Friedman has observed, he revises the image of May D(a)edalus between *Stephen Hero* and *Portrait*, so that the woman who supported and even shared Stephen's interest in continental literature becomes the censor and the "castrator" in the sense of upholding morals in the face of desire, art, and the expansion both offer.[11] *Portrait* thus makes a rough beginning, as Joyce comes to understand desire and its relation to moralism, society, and his own medium, words.

In his construction of *Portrait*, Joyce appears to have been drawn toward French Symbolism's figuration of woman as the *clou* to artistic invention, a crucial hinge within the art of creatively reconfiguring representation. French Symbolists, on Mary Ann Caw's analysis, "had particular designs on the transparent woman, who served up the sign, con-

veying it with fidelity, patience, and absolute personal silence. She herself is patiently ruled out. To Mallarmé, for example, the ballerina as she
danced was neither woman nor dancer, she was the conveyer of the
sign. . . . She is only emblem, unindividualized metaphor. . . . She is the
direct instrument of the idea, her legs doing the idea's writing, not her
own. She isn't given the real to act in or out."[12] In *Portrait*, Joyce seems
to appropriate just such an approach, as Stephen's artistic imagination
develops around abstracted images of women. Critics have long noted
that Stephen's ardent splitting of women into celebrated and deprecated
extremes reduces women to stereotypes in either gesture.[13] E.C. (Emma
Clery) is the most explicit model for such reduction, being not only cast
on the virgin/whore dichotomy most broadly, but somewhat humorously as well split between "bird" and "bat" in Stephen's mind. As a
winged figure, she excites imaginative inspiration and, alternately, sexual desire and dread. Even as he longs for her, Stephen presses her image
back and distances it in a gesture of self-defense. Thus, over the course
of a few days, he thinks of her first as a gentle bird and then as a "batlike soul" representative of all Irish women:

> And if he had judged her harshly? If her life were a simple rosary of
> hours, her life simple and strange as a bird's life, gay in the morning,
> restless all day, tired at sundown? Her heart simple and wilful as a
> bird's heart? (P 235)

> she was a figure of the womanhood of her country, a batlike soul wak-
> ing to the consciousness of itself in darkness and secrecy and loneli-
> ness. . . . (P 239–41)

Emma is initially a bird, augur of future good faith for Stephen, but she
is soon transformed into a "batlike soul," a figure of vampiric tenden-
cies that later haunts Stephen's dreams in *Ulysses*.[14] By virtue of
Stephen's extremes—his desire to worship an ideal and his aggressive
rejection of anything less—he polarizes his perceptions of women into
two radical opposites: the elevated symbol and the deprecated stereotype. Both positions delineate the possible definition of "woman" in a
deterministic containment. Joyce opens Stephen's entry into authorship
through the erasure of Emma Clery's more fleshy and thoughtful reality,
as well, reducing her to the initials E.C. in much of the book. It is as if
the abstraction and *fixing* of woman enables Stephen to change and the
text to transform.

Change occurs for Stephen only through the fixing of an unchangeable feminine image. As a boy, Stephen begins reaching toward symbols
and ideals by imagining women as lovers who might transform him into
a man. This occurs in response to a negative change, the slow decline of
his family's finances, during which he turns to fantasy (and *literature*)

and is mobilized by symbolic systems that resist change through time or linguistic interpolation, first in *The Count of Monte Cristo*. In having Stephen turn to literature, Joyce implicitly presents a portrait of the seductive impact of literature's use of women, even as its influence is carried forward through *Portrait* and into *Ulysses*. Not only does Stephen indulge in escapism through reading, but the book he is drawn to is explicitly about inner darkness and separation from the world. Deprived of his wealth and imprisoned in a tower, as the Stephen of *Ulysses* will be, Cristo loses and eventually regains the devotion of Mercedes, whose image stirs "a strange unrest" in Stephen's blood. As Woman, she becomes a fantasy of light beyond a dark world, a place of escape and a locus of longed-for constancy. Love becomes for Stephen the moment where this fantasy world and the real world around him will someday fuse:

> He wanted to meet in the real world the unsubstantial image which his soul so constantly beheld. He did not know where to seek it or how: but a premonition which led him on told him that this image would, without any overt act of his, encounter him. . . . They would be alone, surrounded by darkness and silence: and in that moment of supreme tenderness he would be transfigured. He would fade into something impalpable under her eyes and then in a moment, he would be transfigured. Weakness and timidity and inexperience would fall from him in that magic moment. (P 67)

If female seduction will later be demonized by Stephen in "Scylla and Charybdis," here it is the process that enables transformation and the fusion of literary consciousness with the real-world context. The difference, perhaps, is that Stephen has not yet encountered a woman in the flesh who will replace his particular demands with desires of her own. At this early stage in *Portrait*, the "unsubstantial" image of woman seems to remain intact for Stephen as pure image even as it appears in the real world. Such an image will encounter him with a "supreme" tenderness that will "transfigure" him. This transfiguration is change, but a change that does not move him forward or back so much as allow him to be more tightly recontained within himself. That is, this woman appears to be one who will be fully complicitous with his very intentions—like a *word* that would fully realize all the artist's meaning. Embraced by this preconscious fidelity, Stephen will become "impalpable," losing not only the capacity for pain but also "weakness and timidity and inexperience." The moment is "magic" in that it will purify him and restore the confidence that is lost to him after all the changes at home. These abstracted sexual scenarios allow Stephen to believe that his own identity, when confirmed in the eyes of a woman, will not slip into a painful reflection of his declining home environment. He is, in that sense, using symbolic woman as the figure that can anchor his masculinity and ensure his maturation.

This woman, like words, corresponds exactly to Stephen's expectations. At this early stage, it might well be said that Joyce's intended aesthetic, within Stephen, reflects a reading of Mallarmé that separates the chaff of language from the clean core of authorial intention. Humorously enough, however, Stephen's first magic moment with a real woman is an encounter with a prostitute. This woman does make him feel "strong and fearless and sure of himself." When she requests a kiss, he "surrenders" himself to her and falls into a half-swoon with his eyes closed, "conscious of nothing in the world but the dark pressure of her softly parting lips," through which he experiences "an unknown and timid pressure, darker than the swoon of sin, softer than sound or odour" (P 108).[15] The prostitute is professionally engaged in predicting men's needs and desires, so Stephen still encounters less resistance from reality. Later, in his exchanges with Emma, he has little control unless she is fantasy.

Before we set too strict a delimitation between real women and fantastic constructs, it seems important to notice that women are never "real" outside of literature or social construction for Joyce; within his writing, inevitably, all will be literary constructs, fabrications taken from spliced impressions of women he knew and women he imagined. But further still, the internal and external fields of reality (historical reality versus literary) cannot be so firmly delineated, as gender perceptions shape the way women are viewed and how they construct themselves in the "real," extratextual world. What one can assess in Joyce's works is the gestural aspect, the ways in which representations of women are either held fixed in a distance, which echoes in those moments an overanxious authorial control of words, or where they are given a certain fluidity and erotic, verbal embodiment in the text. We can analyze and describe the degrees of difference between such figurations, and also remark the more obvious effect these differences have on Joyce's textual experiments as they emerge around such changes.

With Emma, Stephen faces greater resistance to his imaginary construction; in *Stephen Hero*, she gives an outright refusal of his "one-night-of-love" proposal (SH 198). Thus in *Portrait* Stephen takes recourse to an erotic abstraction of her; it does, however, stay open to a subtle dialogue between her control and his *within* his thoughts. While writing his villanelle to her image, he is able to seduce himself into a partial identification with her desires and partially, then, to loosen the bind of the dichotomy. Emma becomes the "temptress" of his villanelle, inspiration both to wet dreams and poetry (P 223), and it is her "strange wilful heart" that inspires the first verses (P 117). Eventually within this constraint, otherness, willfulness, and opposition focus Stephen in a way that allows him to write. It gives him an audience, the resolution of which is to join himself with Emma in addressing the poem implicitly to himself and explicitly to her: "Are you not weary of ardent ways. . . ." "Weary! Weary!" Stephen thinks, "He too was weary of ardent ways" (P 241). Stephen can find a way to identify with his opposite, to substitute himself for the other, and his symbols thus become a part of his self, reflecting even in their reduction his battle with moralism, codes or intentions that oppose his maturing desires. So even at their most seductive, silenced images of women draw Stephen toward contiguous association and subtle parody, as he plays out masculine/feminine oscillations within himself. And yet the Other is not yet realized here as a subject, for Stephen only identifies across the oppositional boundaries when he can close his eyes or, more explicitly, when he can erase the real, speaking Emma and replace her with an imaginary, silenced construct.

Stephen also complicates his dichotomized view of women by crossing one oppositional category with another, describing each experience in similar language. That is, Stephen's typifications of women are not completely straightforward, but arise through a profane mixing of degrading stereotype (whore) and celebrated archetype (Virgin Mary). Stephen's urge to profane the sacred is, implicitly, a compulsion to challenge the very categories that have constructed his consciousness, to transgress social codes and taboos; this is a process, however, that *requires* stereotypes in extreme at the basis of its pleasure. This is therefore not a transgression that ultimately transcends. Stephen describes his encounters with prostitutes in language that echoes his praise of and surrender to the Virgin Mary. He even remarks his own "lewd" pleasure in transposing these figurations (P 105). This pleasure, however, is displaced or forced underground into his unconscious when, as mentioned before, a priest threatens him and his classmates with the fires of hell if they do not "put away from your minds . . . all worldly thoughts" (P 118). Stephen then begins to repress his sensual side and afterward experiences women (and words) with an esthete's idealized sublimation of desire. Gesture becomes less identificatory and parody recedes; dichotomies are more finally crystallized and the body more often abhorred. Therefore Stephen's later encounter with the bird-girl, though rife with sexual allusions (to her bosom, thighs, and legs), is sanitized as a vision, an augur of good future and faith (P 185-86). She looks at him without speaking, sealing his sense that this has been a symbolic encounter. While her passive disinterest makes her something of a potential narcissist, Henke notes that it is Stephen's interpretation of the scene that most clearly bespeaks narcissism: "his communication [with the girl] is a matter entirely of narcissistic projection . . . afraid of the 'waters circumfluent in space' that symbolize the fluidity of female desire, Stephen is determined to control the world of physiological process by freezing life in the sacrament of art."[16] When the "bird-girl" finally turns to meet Stephen's gaze, she encounters "the worship" of his eyes and "suffers" his gaze "without shame or wantonness." She merely pauses a moment, blushes, and turns away.[17] This is enough to make Stephen cry "Heavenly God!" with profane joy. Stephen's joy is "profane" in that it draws on the pleasure of crossing the line between symbolic abstraction and physical desire, which constituted Stephen's prior mixing of experience with both prostitutes and sacred symbols. He renames this desire, however, as purely aesthetic and abstract, denying the more desirous and erotic aspects of the experience. At the moment of Stephen's freezing of desire, he sublimates the erotic appeal of the scene into aesthetic elation. Oscillations within dichotomies thus cease and gesture or rhythm drops out.

When women abandon typological constraints, they pose a threat to the artist's self-control and also the control of his language. As they cross definitional boundaries, so too will Joyce's language leave behind more staid forms of referentiality. The link between the need to control women and the ability to control language is not explicitly voiced until *Finnegans Wake*, and is only implicit in Stephen's reading of Shakespeare's cuckoldry in *Ulysses*. But in *Portrait* words are still wedded to Stephen's developing relation to sexuality and women. He is, at the very least, troubled by unfaithful language. *Portrait* consistently defines young Stephen as struggling to understand language as a link between its meaning and its sensate properties, its aural, rhythmic, and visual effects. Stephen's growing distinction between bodies and significations is not simply a process of maturation, however; it is Joyce's depiction of the conflict between social strictures and sensate or seductive aspects of art, language, and relations to others. Consequently, when the sins of the flesh are lanced at the Easter retreat, the more sensate aspects of language are also pushed under.

In the early stages of Joyce's career, the sensuous and distracting aspects of language are more suspect than revitalizing. Within a pun, meaning is "unfaithful" or sent simultaneously in two different directions; this combines with the reduction of the name from a proper to a generic noun. So in the infirmary, Athy explains that his name is that of a town in County Kildare, but wonders what Stephen's name, Dedalus, refers to (P 23). Joyce will interrogate the alignment of subjectivity with mythological types in *Ulysses*; but here, in *Portrait*, what is foregrounded is the proper name's problematic tension between individual and type, the specific and the general. Emma Clery's name plays on the French for clear (claire) and English for clerical, marking her as a simple form of moralism, one who declines Stephen's invitation for one night of passion in *Stephen Hero*. Here, puns and hybrid words are still treated as surprising word play, only offering a disruptive suggestion in the face of categorical separations and definitional boundaries. This duplicity, of both words and women, initially troubles Stephen, and, as he grows older, his awareness of language becomes even more overwrought as it is entangled in an increasing sensitivity to England's cultural colonization of Ireland.

Emma is not clear to Stephen, just as HCE in *Finnegans Wake* is a trace that holds allusion alone. Stephen can perceive Emma's outer aspect but has no access to her "primary" meanings. Names that turn toward nouns heighten the awareness of the inherent foreignness, the implicit estrangement within language. Stephen, of course, claims his last name, "Dedalus," as a note for his destiny: the artist who will fly beyond Dublin's nets. On another front, however, Stephen is alienated from the language through which he consummates his art. As a young man, the English dominance of Ireland's language instills a sense of distrust in him. After telling the dean of his college that he is using an instrument called a "tundish"—a word the dean admits he did not know—Stephen reflects angrily on the colonization of language: "His language, so familiar and so foreign, will always be for me an acquired speech" (P 205). In his response to the otherness of England and its language, I am suggesting that Stephen appropriates the other Other of his world. He takes the vision of woman as other inside himself, construing his own relationship to poetic writing in terms of female gestation and birth: "O! In the virgin womb of the imagination the word was made flesh" (P 236). This is divine rather than human procreation, but Stephen likens his mind to the womb, just as he consistently refers to his soul as "her." Language and woman, as two troubling others in Stephen's world, are thus pressed together metaphorically.

In *Finnegans Wake*, a voice warns us that "she'll confess it by her figure and she'll deny it to your face" (FW 271.14–15). Throughout Joyce's work, woman functions as a figure for parody and punning, in her denial of the truth and her elision of philosophical endeavors to unveil or unmask her "true" identity. She is a figure of contiguity and the crux of parody, in that sense. According to Irigaray, woman's voice, identity, and desires are forever represented as doubled: "if 'she' says something, it is not, it is already no longer, identical with what she means. What she says is never identical with anything, moreover; rather, it is contiguous.

It touches (upon)."[18] *Portrait* in many ways operates as Joyce's attempt
to sort out his own relationship to symbolism, particularly with an
application to words and how they invoke symbolic forms of meaning.
Stephen endeavors to make language fully conscious, to exert control
over his word, and this mirrors the control of women and his desire for
them. Such a figuration of "woman as word" strikes a climax of crisis
at *Ulysses'* midpoint, in the "Scylla and Charybdis" episode. Not coincidentally, this episode contains Joyce's most radical parody of Stephen
as he plays out a failed unconscious form of critical parody in his reading of Shakespeare (who there "shakes a spear" at women). This alle-
gorical transformation of parody occurs as woman must again be fixed
at the pivot point of the aesthetic argument.

SEXUAL (DIS)POSSESSION IN "SCYLLA AND CHARYBDIS"

In the National Library, Stephen argues that Ann Hathaway's supposed
seduction and later cuckolding of Shakespeare marked the playwright
with the initial wound that negatively inspired his genius, thereby
acknowledging the dangers of women's sexual desires and identifying
the artist's inability to control women as a spur to the vengeful artist. As
Stephen enacts his own revenge art on willful women, the episode shifts
from simpler dialogue to comical narrative to stage production. Aes-
thetically in *Ulysses*, Joyce is less concerned with making words sensate,
as in *Finnegans Wake*, and more with construction of narratives that
draw their form from the very content of the episode's discussion. Thus,
"Scylla and Charybdis"'s narrative humorously reflects thematic concerns in Stephen's argument: tying the relevance of a name to one's own
character (so Piper pipes, etc.), and marking Stephen's need to be "on
stage" before Dublin's literary circles. This fusion between form and thematic content occurs as Stephen struggles between Plato's separation of
form from ideas and Aristotle's more integrative approach to signification. The possibility emerges for a more gestural art, one that appropriates parody into material and formal embodiments. Within this shift,
female desire and willfulness play central roles. I will be suggesting here
that Ann Hathaway's figuration, as dangerously desiring woman, is
what disrupts Stephen's previous erasure of women's voices and propels
Joyce's parodic experiment to a new level.

    Stephen argues that Shakespeare writes *Hamlet* from the depths of
a wounded heart, and he claims that, by ventriloquizing anger through
Hamlet's ghost, Shakespeare seeks to revenge himself publicly on Ann
Shakespeare for her willful seduction of him in his youth and her later
supposed infidelities. Stephen claims that Shakespeare's marriage to Ann

was no insignificant error, but a major mark, a wounding inspiration. And thus, "[a] man of genius makes no mistakes. His errors are volitional and are the portals of discovery" (U 9.228–29). Volition proves to be the very problem Stephen sees at the back of Shakespeare's writing. According to Stephen, Shakespeare works as a revenge artist, bent specifically on "branding" Ann Hathaway "with infamy" for being an actively desiring woman (U 9.677). On Stephen's account, Shakespeare had two reasons for his aggression, the first being that Ann had robbed him of his will, or authority, by her seduction, and the second, that she was later unfaithful to him:

> He chose badly? He was chosen, it seems to me. If others have their will Ann hath a way. By cock, she was to blame. She put the comether on him, sweet and twenty six. The greyeyed goddess who bends over the boy Adonis, stooping to conquer, as prologue to the swelling act, is a boldfaced Stratford wench who tumbles in a cornfield a lover younger than herself. (U 9.256–60)

In the Time Sonnets, Shakespeare plays on the pun in his own name—will or William—and here Stephen argues that will is seduced by Ann Hathaway, and the loss of control marks Shakespeare with an indelible grief. This portrait of a willful Ann enrages Stephen's audience. If Stephen reads Ann Hathaway as a wounding influence on Shakespeare, a troublesome tart who overbore him when he was young and deceived him (with his brother, no less) when he was older, the Victorians had read Ann's character as that of a patient Penelope, waiting at home in Stratford for Shakespeare's return.[19] "Do you mean to fly in the face of the tradition of three centuries?" John Eglinton responds to Stephen's slighting references to Ann (U 9.214). But Stephen persists, arguing that this initial "wounding" marks Shakespeare for life: "Belief in himself has been untimely killed. He was overborne in a cornfield first (a ryefield, I should say) and he will never be a victor in his own eyes after nor play victoriously the game of laugh and lie down. Assumed dongiovannism will not save him. No later undoing will undo the first undoing" (U 9.455–59). Stephen notes the undoing of the will by sexual physicality in the form of an actively desiring woman, who Stephen twice condemns for the danger of her seduction and also implicitly for being unfaithful to the model of virtuous woman-as-passive-recipient of male desire. As Stephen rails against the overpowering will of woman, he casts the figure of Ann Hathaway as vixen and slut, a reminder of the dangers of female sexuality. As for Shakespeare, his belief in himself seems to be linked to sexual control, as a kind of willful self-actualization linked to potential creation of others—books or babies, in Stephen's later discussion of fathers and sons. Stephen has been struggling against the guilt of resisting his mother's last request: that he pray for her.[20] Therefore, in part, his own biographical urge to fix, brand, or stereotype his mother as willful goul is displaced and reworked in his reading of Shakespeare, and the return of an *inspired* ghost, in contrast to the more menacing shadow of May Dedalus that rises from the grave in "Circe." Moreover, Stephen's repudiation of sexual exchanges in "Scylla and Charybdis" may point to the near conflation of sexual desire and deathly decay that inhabits Stephen's hallucinations in "Circe."

This resistance to corporeality and seduction gives rise to a structural aggression in Stephen's thoughts. Rigid identities are essential to his recasting of *Hamlet* as a revenge play, so that Shakespeare is to be identified with the murdered king proclaiming the infamy of an adulterous Gertrude, aligned with Ann. Every position must remained fixed. Yet even as Stephen charts William Shakespeare's struggle with "Will" or volition, he complicates the scheme of agency—to act or be acted on—when he introduces a definition of the ghost (Hamlet) who is a point of dissipation. Stephen asks, "What is a ghost?" and answers, "one who has faded into impalpability through death, through absence, through change of manners" (U 9.147–49). Stephen suggestively alludes to "ghosts" as texts that have faded in their "palpability" as the arena of their reception goes through a "change of manners." The question is whether an *absent* presence (a ghost, memory, or some such thing) can have a palpable effect. If King Hamlet *as a ghost*—and therefore *dis*-embodied—could cause nine deaths to occur, so the memory of Ann Hathaway, even at great remove, might have spurred Shakespeare to write revenge plays long after leaving Stratford. So art likewise can serve as an efficacious form of cultural memory. But in this analysis, Stephen takes death away from the corpse and relegates it to language and the imagination alone. He also implicitly divides language's meaning from its material medium. The author's will exceeds or lives beyond the shell of conveyance.

Eventually, Stephen does as Buck Mulligan earlier suggested, "[h]e proves by algebra that Hamlet's grandson is Shakespeare's grandfather and that he himself is the ghost of his own father" (U 1.555–57). This occurs as Stephen approaches his "all-in-all" thesis, which appears to allow for a broadening of the artists' self-definition but, in Stephen's case, narrows into a return to Romantic self-isolation. Stephen has been trying to escape from both Plato and the Romantic image of a passive Hamlet, and he therefore contradicts Lyster, the librarian, when he waxes enthusiastic over Goethe's characterization of the young prince as "a hesitating soul taking arms against a sea of troubles, torn by conflicting doubts" (U 9.3–4). Stephen moves instead to draw the portrait of an *active* Hamlet, one "wielding the sledded poleaxe and spitting in his palms. Nine lives are taken off for his father's one. . . . Khaki Hamlets don't hesitate to shoot" (U 9.131–33). Stephen's Hamlet would do as Stephen spurs himself to do, "He acts and is acted on" (U 9.1018–19). This model inspires the aggressive gestures I have already discussed above, with respect to Ann and others.

In response to John Eglington's resistance to a stark alignment of Shakespeare with the ghost, rather than the younger Hamlet, Stephen introduces a familiar notion of the artist:

> As we, or mother Dana, weave and unweave our bodies, Stephen said, from day to day, their molecules shuttle to and fro, so does the artist weave and unweave his image. (U 9.376–78)

Stephen now moves to a notion that the artist leaves a piece of himself in every character, a notion derived partially from Walter Pater's work and, as Ellmann has noted, from Mallarmé's essays.[21] Mallarmé argues that *Hamlet* is a psychological drama of one person who uses various characters to represent aspects of himself. Reading the book of himself, he finds Laertes as his belligerence, Polonius as his foolishness, and so on. The artist, Stephen will argue, elaborates his characters as possible selves.

One might say that Stephen abandons his aggressive model of attacking others—Danes or Women—when he introduces the "all-in-all" thesis. But then he pushes is to its furthest extreme and finds only a Berkeleyan subjectivism, where he would want a more Aristotelian notion of integration between mind and world. Berkeley extended Aristotle's use of psychologism to argue that what is perceived has real being, but what is not perceived has no being. In answer to John Locke's separation between perceivable, secondary qualities and the invisible, unchangeable primary qualities of objects—their material essences—Berkeley answered that all the objects composing our world are collections of ideas. He was an "immaterialist" whose philosophy was called "idealism."[22] As Stephen finds himself flinching at Buck Mulligan's materialism, he draws back toward the Berkeleyan side of Aristotle, but presents a parody of the psychological tilt of perception carried to extreme in its exclusion of materiality.

Read broadly, Stephen's "possible selves" thesis allows for the artist's constant integration of environment and biography into his work; but read narrowly—and Stephen's reading narrows as the episode proceeds—it takes the artist back into his isolation. He can never encounter an other to disrupt or shift his perspective. This occurs as Stephen sweeps constantly closer to Platonism and Romantic self-isolation. Joyce thus sets up the tension between differential associations and their potential collapse into sameness, a problem that haunts *Finnegans*

Wake. In "Scylla and Charybdis," the algebraic formulation awaited so long turns out to be a flipping of definitions that proves both (1) Shakespeare was not writing *Hamlet* as a tribute to his recently deceased father; and (2) the artist is his own origin. Stephen removes the artist not only from the influence of his immediate environment, but eventually also denies his relations to the literary traditions preceding him. And as William Noon has noted, Stephen succumbs to the Sabellian heresy that he had earlier disdained.[23] Sabellius held that the Father was himself his own Son, and so collapsed the differences between the three Trinitarian entities, destroying the possibilities for communication. In trying to deny overbearing influences such as May or Simon Dedalus, or Buck Mulligan, Stephen slides too far and denies all influences, of a textual or historical nature. Thus Stephen's all-in-all thesis narrows into a noose: the defense against influence becomes a wall of isolation that locks him in with his misery:

> Maeterlinck says: *If Socrates leave his house today he will find the sage seated on his doorstep. If Judas go forth tonight it is to Judas his steps will tend.* Every life is many days, day after day. We walk through ourselves, meeting robbers, ghosts, giants, old men, young men, wives, widows, brothers-in-love, but always meeting ourselves. (U 9.1042–46)[24]

When Shakespeare is claimed by Stephen as his "father," as a literary predecessor rather than a biological parent, Stephen also represses the corporeality or the material aspect of words in favor of an argument about Shakespeare's intentions. And woman ("Weib" and "Fleisch") is at last forgotten, her words erased from the configuration of artistic progenation.[25] As Stephen completes his arguments, Shakespeare is an artist who so identifies with his characters that he can be "all-in-all" and read as partially identified with any role in his plays—except perhaps those aligned with Ann. Aggressive othering is still a constitutive aspect of Stephen's aesthetic, but it is so thoroughly displaced onto Ann Hathaway that all others can become radically contiguous by association, without boundaries or aggressions. Stephen's "all-in-all" thesis therefore presents a particular kind of narcissistic reading that still depends upon one firmly drawn boundary and still therefore leads to aggression. If it is internally benign, it allows (and, indeed, insists upon) oppositional gestures toward women.

Woman here represents to Stephen the locus of seduction, not just as a physical, sexual experience, but as the dislocation of meaning, of reference, of moral distinction. Women and words are both unfaithful to Stephen's intentions with respect to them, and what is gendered feminine attracts to it a range of controlling anxieties. Seduction marks the dissolution of boundaries, an act that results in the destabilization of categories or definitional determinations without any pause for judgment or analysis. As such, it deconstructs any system of morals. Seduction is moreover opposed to analysis; it is the philosopher's enemy as much as language might seem to be. And yet if seduction is parody's (and woman's) threat, by virtue of its contiguity to what it imitates, parody also engages in a partial seduction as well as partial analysis and distance. Consequently, it resists attempts to set up an extreme opposition between it and its target; yet neither does it allow a complete conflation between the two. With parody, partial sympathy emerges along with any resistance, and this is what twists out the humor. And what can be more seductive than humor? Stephen reflects that "that at which you laugh, you will also serve," as he watches Buck seduce the library audience with ribaldry and laughter.

The very threat of seduction, which would at a minimum transgress and at worst erase the slash (/) that is the necessary structure of moralism, propels Stephen back into the dichotomy of desire and morals. The first seduction he resists in *Ulysses* is Buck's teasingly erotic friendship. Stephen may fear homosexual attachment or, at least, the imposition of the role of buffoon. He worries about his friendship with Buck and, formerly, with Cranly, even as he also worries about his mother's last demand. The woman who might betray Stephen is not real, however, but abstract and symbolic; she is his literary muse who betrays him by turning to others, favoring Buck and Haines instead. But why choose woman as the other here? For Stephen noticeably does, as he insistently forgets that Claudius was the target of King Hamlet's revenge, and that the ghost begs his son to forgive Gertrude. Desire and fear drift across scenarios for Stephen, so that betrayal is a term applied equally to his relations to Buck and his anxieties about his mother. When Stephen turns to his mother in "Circe" for "the word known to all men," it matters not if he means love, life, or even death, so much as that his desire is blocked in her answering gesture toward the threat of hell. She invokes his sin of not praying for her:

> Who saved you the night you jumped into the train at Dalkey with Paddy Lee? Who had pity for you when you were sad among the strangers? Prayer is allpowerful. Prayer for the suffering souls in the Ursuline manual and forty days' indulgence. Repent, Stephen. . . . Repent! O, the fire of hell! (U 15.4195–4212)

When Stephen rebels, it is against religion's attempt to control him through the univocal, the one, the insistent Word, identified with the keepers of religion in Joyce's writing: women. This moralism, however, simply reverses Stephen's resistance, so that he himself becomes the agent of containment and aggression.

The oscillating tensions that make up Joyce's textual gestures circulate around the perceived familial dangers and societal disruptions considered endemic to any change in women's positions. Whereas the symbolism of Mallarmé's and Joyce's own early writings contains women within simplified and silenced figures, women begin to articulate choices and desires in the latter half of *Ulysses*. Curiously enough, they are first given voice in *Dubliners*, Joyce's early experiment with realism prior to his marked focus on parody. There, the images of silenced women begin with Mangan's sister, Eveline's mutely frozen figure, and the death that silences Emily Sinico in "A Painful Case." But these figures are alternately contrasted with outspoken women, who are strong, and even manipulative mothers and wives. In Joyce's final, complex portrait of Greta Conroy in "The Dead" (drawn in 1907), the silent muse breaks in upon her husband's fantasies and rearranges his perception not only of her and their relations, but also of himself in relation to others more generally. Therefore Joyce's own replication of Symbolist uses of women in *Portrait* immediately follows his own critical relief from that practice, since he begins revising *Stephen Hero* into *Portrait* just after finishing "The Dead" in 1907.[26] Still, this use of women plays a considerable role in his changing textual practice, so that Stephen's aesthetic insistently separates the erotic from the aesthetic, even as Joyce's own writing reflects a linkage between desire and language.

In *Ulysses*, Joyce continues to work through this dichotomous approach to women as both privileged creators as well as independent desiring agents. If Ann Hathaway is aggressively deprecated and Mina Purefoy is thoughtlessly disregarded by a group of rowdy medicals, Joyce goes beyond the double gesture of mocking and replaying these erasures. He begins to experiment with giving women voice. These voices have sometimes drawn the ire of critics, and yet I am suggesting that they can be read as part of a larger trajectory away from the very gestures of containment that initially determined them. Desire, as it is being enfolded into Joyce's language, finds no place of "proper" representation, but as Joyce's art becomes more gestural in its incorporation of materiality Joyce weaves desire and sensate pleasure into his aesthetic practice, allowing that practice to become less defined by aggression and oppositional boundaries.

VENTRILOQUIZED DESIRE: GERTY, ISSY, AND MOLLY

When Joyce begins again to allow women a role in narrating their own stories, it is unfortunately with that "namby-pamby jammy marmalady drawersy" style for which he has become infamous.[27] Gerty MacDowell is the first woman to be given an extended narrative voice since *Dubliners*, where free indirect discourse provides narrative access to women's thoughts. Here, however, Joyce's narrative seems to slant decidedly toward Gerty's own self-idealized perspective:

> Gerty MacDowell who was seated near her companions, lost in thought, gazing far away into the distance was, in very truth, as fair a specimen of winsome Irish girlhood as one could wish to see. She was pronounced beautiful by all who knew her though, as folks often said, she was more a Giltrap than a MacDowell. Her figure was slight and graceful, inclining even to fragility but those iron jelloids she had been taking of late had done her a world of good. . . . The waxen pallor of her face was almost spiritual in its ivorylike purity though her rosebud mouth was a genuine Cupid's bow, Greekly perfect. (U 13.79–89)

Gerty's narrative goes on in this manner, flowing in a wavelike motion that reaches toward some imaginary romance and then pulls back into more realistic conversational bits. She is seeing herself as a silent muse, and all Joyce has done for now is to turn the insides of the object outward for us to see. The issue of her agency is already extremely troubling, if this is indeed her voice. Not surprisingly, some feminist criticism has taken as its point of attack specifically this vocalized version of a female stereotype. Undeniably, Gerty is a stereotype, a pathos-ridden version of the unrealistic virgin who converts her frustrations, sexual and social, into a sickly sweet narcissism and fantasies of future affections. Furthermore, she is not well educated and a poor reader, one who never questions the instruction handed her through the cheap romantic novels and women's journals that suffuse her consciousness with cultural stereotypes. She believes that women must be demure, must always be sweet, must never be sour, and definitely must never—even as they pose innocent-erotically—reveal a glimpse of their own sexual desires. With her consciousness structured by so many social directives, Gerty is more split between sexual desire and the appearance of purity than Stephen Dedalus. Molly Bloom, Joyce's second major experiment with female ventriloquism, will turn against such social instruction, but the heroine of the "Nausicaa" episode accepts and is burdened by a range of gender norms. Woman here is explicitly a mirror to cultural symbols and stereotypes, and not simply a passive recipient but ardently attentive to the goals (marriage, family decorum) she is directed to desire. It is as if Joyce allows the symbols (of Stephen's desires) to speak, but as they speak they can only echo the cathexis of *male* desires.

I would like to pause for a closer examination of Gerty's reflective, unreflecting consciousness—but not to disagree with those who have identified Gerty as a social stereotype that can give strong offense. Certainly, Gerty seems to be a speaking object, less than a subject, voicing the erotic language of female denial ("No I am not arousing you, yes I do") arousing, in soft porn, both her author and his intrafictional voyeur, L. Bloom. And yet to dismiss this episode in just these terms is to turn away from the deeper problem of seduction as it is implicated in symbolization, which is caught within Joyce's interest and weaves through his writings. Recall the earlier observation that Stephen softens his aggressive stereotyping of Emma when he partially identifies with her while writing the villanelle. If this does not remove her from the status of symbol, it begins to allow some form of hypothetical agency to woman. Here, Joyce allows the object agency, and Gerty exposes an elaborate tangle of displaced desires. She is both agent, as speaking desire, and object, in the dreadfully obvious impact social imprinting has had on her mind. If Gerty is a simple, stereotypical female narcissist, Joyce's parodic ventriloquism reveals both the problem of mirroring or imitative forms of reading, and more importantly, the flaws of privileging mimetic art. For without any subversive distortions encoded into her mirror of social norms, Gerty becomes a cliché, a sad reminder of women self-formed on broad social types.

Gerty is the perfect image of a young woman "smiling at the lovely reflection which the mirror gave back to her!" (U 13.162). As a figure of sweet, virginal narcissism, Gerty appears to conform to Freud's model of the woman who survives her social entrapment only by turning in on herself, loving her beauty in a circle of self-reference that will inevitably attract Freud's stereotypical male, who is irresistibly drawn toward the self-objectifying woman-as-object.[28] Heterosexual desires, both male and female, are thus variously orchestrated around the objectification of the woman-as-object and her narcissistic self-directed gaze. Yet Gerty's narcissism is not a simple inward turning, but an attempt to measure up to the "positive" image of the delicate female posed in the mirror society holds up to her. We are told that Gerty "knew how to cry nicely before the mirror. You are lovely, Gerty, it said" (U 13.192–93). If Gerty is crying "nicely" here, she seems to have learned to fake grief or—more likely, given the grief of her surroundings—to mediate her own representation of sorrow through a reference to the image her mirror gives back to her. This mirror is no simple duplication of childish dreams; rather it reflects Gerty's implicit consciousness of the broader social judgment that approves or disapproves of her behavior. More precisely, the mirror instructs her as to *how* she should present her grief, if ever she should express it before the eyes of a potential suitor. The mirror is not radically other than Gerty's mind, but her own mind is not in the least divorced from social directives that tell her to pose for the male gaze. Joyce's model of female narcissism therefore reveals the instabilities encoded within attempts to separate female self-love from desire for the other. It is neither full narcissism nor an odd, implicitly aggressive one. Rather, Gerty's narcissism opens up as a deconstruction of the stereotype of vain, female narcissism.

Freud's interpretation of female narcissism relies on the assumption that women can escape the male imaginary—the cultural constraint of a world centered on male desire—by turning inward, supposing that there is some space in a woman's consciousness free from cultural mediation. When she looks into the mirror, however, Gerty is learning to fake sadness, as well she might learn to fake pleasure, in order to appease her imaginary male voyeur. In fact, within the episode Gerty has a *real* audience, Leopold Bloom, who ironically reflects on the limitations of woman's narcissism, thinking, "Pity they can't see themselves. A dream of wellfilled hose" (U 13.792–93), implicitly questioning facile notions that women can and do see "themselves" in mirrors. As Jules David Law has argued, Bloom's thought should be read as his recognition that women cannot see themselves as *men* see them, and yet Law's position is both paradoxically true and not true.[29] For the ironic twist to contemporary readers of this book is that, of course, female critics *do* strangely occupy this specular position of Joyce, Bloom, and the male imaginary as it defines the pornographic object. As Virginia Woolf has observed, we have at our disposal innumerable books by men describing what women are, how they feel, and what thoughts they are capable of thinking.[30] The social fabrication of Woman in fact relies on this pronounced male mediation, whereby women can not help but to view themselves through some partial identification with the male gaze.[31] Much of this occurs through the influence of advertising, which encourages women to view themselves as perfectible objects. And so Gerty thinks of her face as "softlyfeatured," but with a special, mysterious cast:

> the love that might have been, that lent to her softlyfeatured face at whiles a look, tense with suppressed meaning, that imparted a strange yearning tendency to the beautiful eyes, a charm few could resist. Why have women such eyes of witchery? Gerty's were of the bluest Irish blue, set off by lustrous lashes and dark expressive brows. Time was when those brows were not so silkily seductive. It was Madame Vera Verity, directress of the Woman Beautiful page of the Princess Novelette, who had first advised her to try eyebrowleine which gave that haunting expression to the eyes, so becoming in leaders of fashion, and she had never regretted it. (U 13.104–13)

Gerty is such a weave of cultural influences, it is hard to find any core voice to call hers. She is, in that sense, a figure for *Ulysses*'s pastiche of styles and allusions. Here, the female imagination is shaped parodically, as it is identified with, while also to varying degrees contrary to, male expectations of feminine behavior. As the subject caught in the bind of viewing itself (and actively constructing itself) as object (and therefore passive), woman can only ever waiver upon the thin line of contiguity that separates subject/object, and active/passive constructs. The question for feminism is how to shift Gerty's more precise reproduction of social expectations to a parodic form that allows greater subjectivity, agency, and articulations of desires that might not just spiral back into the male sexual economy. Here, however, Gerty is fully caught by the gaze:

> She could almost see the swift answering flash of admiration in his eyes that set her tingling in every nerve. She put on her hat so that she could see from underneath the brim and swung her buckled shoe faster for her breath caught as she caught the expression in his eyes. He was eying her as a snake eyes its prey. Her woman's instinct told her that she had raised the devil in him and at the thought a burning scarlet swept from throat to brow till the lovely colour of her face became a glorious rose. (U 13.513–20)

It is as if Bloom's eyes light her up more than any physical contact, as though Gerty only wishes to be an object. Law is undeniably (if humorously) correct in implying that Gerty does not experience male erection and, in light of the social prejudice against conscious expressions of female desire, Gerty must displace her own desires for sexual pleasure into fluffy, romantic images. This displacement is encouraged and facilitated by the women's magazines and sentimental fiction with which Gerty's mind has been overfed. These texts were invested in training women in the art of posing for the male (premarital) gaze. Whether or not authored by women, they are always directed by the dominant culture's prescription that women repress their sexual desires, reject an awareness of their own sexual prowess, and treat their bodies as objectifications of male fantasy while simultaneously disguising that act, for themselves, as the impetus of romantic love. As Margot Norris has pointed out, women's desires were channelled into notions of marriage and courtship in 1904, for the sake of economic and social security. Norris establishes that, for women, the "demand for love" is formulated in terms of their need to be nurtured and to have emotional and basic physical wants met. This becomes more important for women than any struggle for recognition as a subject.[32] Gerty has been socially indoctrinated to view herself as an object and to barter her body, albeit decorously, in full view of male desire.

My point then, succinctly put, is that while Gerty MacDowell can never view her body from some distinct male perspective, she also can never view it in any way *other* than through the male gaze. That is, her self-image is instructed by a world that constantly reconnects woman's sexuality to male desire. Caught in this double-bind, Gerty can also never name her physical desires or direct her attention toward her own erotic pleasures. Were she to begin to resist the cultural clichés that have created her, however, she might in some part be able to revise the terms of her own self-awareness, twisting her identification as erotic object into a deeper level of mediated desire.

And if some revisional resistances to such construction might emerge for other figures, Gerty MacDowell seems most tightly entrapped in the need to model herself as a figure who will please and appease male desires.[33] Female narcissism is ironically then a *heterosexual* construct here, although Freud stereotypes it as homosexual. In "Nausicaa," women's consciousness of her sexuality is created in and through the male imaginary. It is as if the mirror that is woman can only reflect back to man the predetermined model of femininity. At least, this appears to be the case in Gerty's self-construction through gender norms. And although Bloom's thoughts draw on the stereotypical model of the narcissistic female when he later thinks, "best place for an ad to catch a woman's eye on a mirror" (U 13.919–20), Gerty's form of narcissism is not a simple, circular one. Rather, any self-love will be fed through an identification with the loving eye of the imaginary man who is always watching and (hopefully) approving a woman's manner. If women look often into mirrors in *Ulysses*, they are, like Stephen Dedalus, checking on how the world ("he and others" U 1.136) see them. Gerty's narcissism is therefore *not* a gesture of divorce from the social or the real; rather, it is an overly intense engagement with the expectations and gender norms posed by society. This very intensity, however, constitutes a gestural politics that effects her self-erasure.

If Gerty admitted sexual desire into her formulation, and if she had room for a more undirected pleasure, she might evade some portion of the social pressure that rests on her. There are a few moments when the possibility seems to offer itself. On one occasion, Gerty describes her pleasure in looking at a picture of another woman, who is also pictured as the object of another's (a man's) gaze. We catch Gerty dwelling on one particular image of a woman who is as adored and desired as Gerty wishes to be. In the outhouse, Gerty has pinned up a picture from the grocer's Christmas almanac:

> the picture of halcyon days where a young gentleman in the costume they used to wear then with a threecornered hat was offering a bunch of flowers to his ladylove with oldtime chivalry through her lattice window. You could see there was a story behind it. The colours were done something lovely. She was in a soft clinging white in a studied

attitude and the gentleman was in chocolate and he looked a thorough aristocrat. She often looked at them dreamily when she went there for a certain purpose and felt her own arms that were white and soft just like hers with the sleeves back and thought about those times. (U 13.334–42).

Gerty is arrested both by her desire to *be* the woman in the picture and her implicit identification, as the woman's admirer, with the male gaze represented in the picture. Through this split-desiring gaze, Gerty experiences both the pleasure of identifying with the woman's grace *and* the desire to court her through the mediating representation of the gentleman in chocolate. If, for Gerty, this is a romantic scene with a story that touches the heart, rather than arousing the body, the episode introduces the possibility of a fissure within the structure of the female gaze that threatens to dissolve oppositions between hetero- and homosexual bonds as it overlaps the space of female and male desire. And there is the faint suggestion that she might learn self-arousal from her experience with the picture, although it seems mostly to arrive through mental fantasy rather than physical experience.

Unlike Gerty, Molly knows that if she looks in the mirror, it "never gives you the expression," especially not that of sexual desire (U 18.414). While Molly's character has received its own split reception, Joyce does in her "polylogue" create a different gesture that parodically reuses and in many ways subverts the dominant gender norms in Dublin 1904. Unlike Gerty, Molly candidly acknowledges that the stakes of her displays are sexual arousal. She emphasizes the importance of her own arousal, and has even resorted to masturbation, apparently, to ensure it. (She humorously recalls trying to use a banana to this effect—U 18.803.) Like Gerty, however, her sexuality is defined through the male gaze, in that her thoughts suggest a woman whose main source of sexual pleasure is arousing her male partners. Her enjoyment of this seductive power is pronounced in her memories of how Blazes Boylan is aroused when she drops her clothes, and of how, during sex, she "made him pull out and do it on me" and then later let him finish inside her (U 18.154–57). Much of Molly's pleasure derives from provoking and controlling male desire, the very thing Stephen appears to dread. Her climactic memory of Bloom, as well, is a memory of pulling him down "so he could feel my breasts all perfume" as he waits to hear her final "yes" (U 18.1607–8). As Molly claims control over the other's desires, she becomes a distinct threat to masculinist constructions of subject/object relations, which insist on the passivity of the woman and validate only the man as actively desiring agent. The anger against Molly in the 1950's is by now well documented, and arises in part from the threat posed by this potential reversal.[34] Molly's character is an odd combination of Gerty's pent up desire released and Ann Hathaway's more aggressive seduction. Her pleasure in overturning subject/object relations mediates between these two extremes.

When female desire is finally given a place of articulation in *Ulysses*, Molly's language carries within it signs of Joyce's own shift toward an emphasis on the more sensual aspects of language. As Christine Van Boheemen-Saaf has remarked, Molly's interpretation of metempsychosis as "met him pike hoses" picks up on the sexualizing possibilities of the words, "evoking sexuality rather than spirituality."[35] In contrast to Gerty's "marmalady" clichés, Molly's interpretation of language is predetermined by her closer relation to words as sensate play; she does not visualize the word so much as hear it, and as she hears it it does not transform into abstract, aphysical meaning. Molly, as musician, hears and incorporates the cry of a train into her thoughts, body, and voice: "sweeeee theres that train far away pianissimo eeeee one more tsong" (U 18.908). Here, Molly plays on the sounds of words, emphasizing the liaison between her thoughts, her body, and the noises that come to her from the distance. Her parodic refunction of gender norms thus goes further, as her erotic body—never fully representable in linguistic terms—can teasingly threaten to emerge through the materiality of language. The relative absence of grammatical tracers and the shifting references of words signal the beginning of Joyce's more remarkable transgressions of definitional boundaries of words and grammatical constraints in *Finnegans Wake*. So, in *Ulysses*, Joyce inverts claims about the power of cuckoldry, gradually abandoning the representation of women (and words) as silent, erotic muses, while experimenting with the ventriloquization of their desires. This ventriloquization plays out a dual gesture of fulfilling what might be assessed as Joyce's own erotic desires while also, in a countergesture, slowly releasing women to a discourse of desire. As Joyce pursues this shift, his language becomes more sensate and his text more radically accretive and voluminous in its cross-catalogue of allusions and word-play.

FINNEGANS WAKE AND THE SENSATE WORD

The human body is also a process. It is not a unity but a plural totality with separate members that have no identity but constitute the place where drives are applied. This dismembered body cannot fit together again, set itself in motion, or function biologically and physiologically, unless it is included within a practice that encompasses the signifying process. . . . Outside the process, its only identity is inorganic, paralyzed, dead. Within the process, on the other hand, by confronting it, displacing its boundaries and laws, the subject in process/on trial discovers those boundaries and laws and makes them manifest in his practice of them.

The *linguistic structures* that attest to this practice of the process are radically transformed by it. These rhythmic, lexical, even syntactic changes disturb the transparency of the signifying chain and open it up to the material crucible of its production. We can read a Mallarmé or a Joyce only by starting from the signifier and moving toward the instinctual, material, and social process the text covers.

—Julia Kristeva, *Revolution in Poetic Language*

No one would contest that Joyce disturbs the transparency of language as a medium in *Finnegans Wake*. Like so many of the avant-garde championed by Kristeva, Cixous, and those interested in a more radical language, Joyce disrupts the symbolic order, the laws of clear reference and unification of meaning that otherwise govern writing. He transgresses taboos on language, encouraging puns and split references instead of repressing them, drawing attention to the musical and rhythmic aspects of words rather than pressing them toward the model of a purely neutral medium. The rhythmic gestures that Stephen Daedalus mimes in *Stephen Hero* are now encoded musically into Joyce's language. Both music and dance are pronounced aesthetic influences in the *Wake*, and the voice seems to overtake the visual in its importance. As one of the avant-garde cited for developing *écriture féminine*, Joyce allows the semiotic and contradefinitional elements of language to rise into his texts. Kristeva describes the semiotic's resistance to male, patriarchal language (Lacan's Symbolic), while Hélène Cixous explains that this style is associated with woman, both in terms of her way of entering into speech and in her refusal, psychologically, of separations and the cutting of connective relations. Being initially denied a voice, figured as silent and outside of speech, woman must hurl her body into speaking, signifying the effort of entering into language. Posited upon the radical negation of her imposed silence, such speech is an abrupt and *physical* experience. Hers is thus a compulsively *gestural* speech, insofar as the body is merged with the word's delivery. But also she will resist abstractions and categorizations, the breaks and negations that French feminism will identify with patriarchal society. In this more radical writing, which refuses the supposed separation between body and language, a *rhythm* accrues across the text, running over boundaries and denying both radical sameness and full differentiation.[36] For Kristeva, this rhythm is likened to the *chora*, an instinctual rhythm that displaces the violence of the drives, transgressing representation, memory, and the sign altogether.[37] Whether from dance or music, this rhythm is, in Joyce, more than "style"; it seizes upon a link between the unconscious, which informs the book of dreams, and the body—of humans, of words, and also the brute materiality of the signified never captured in the word but only echoed in the forced forgetting of language's own material, alphabetic form.

If Joyce's linguistic experiments coincide with this definition of radical *écriture*—even to the point of giving women, like Anna Livia or Molly Bloom, the role of extra-grammatical, flowing speech—it has still been troubling to many that Joyce is, simply put, a man. The French feminists have been quick to point out that this "style" need not be anchored in sex so much as a feminine form of writing, which men can also create. And yet they do not take into account the problematic containment of women's speaking in and through a male consciousness, figured as it is by its own culturally encoded investments in women. Indeed, while Joyce's language is wonderfully innovative and liberated from normative constraints, his images of women and verbal reflections on them, even in *Finnegans Wake*, are not necessarily equal to such innovations of style. It is my aim here to suggest that style and characterizations in the *Wake* eventually do represent a particular sexual politics, one that encompasses both liberation and recontainment, carrying—as dreams do—the limited imaginings of the past mixed with freer potential for the future. The crucial axes of this analysis move around the term "control," an act Shaun commands when he insists that "The word is my Wife" in the passage with which this chapter began.

Shaun may attempt to catch and define the rainbow girls (or Issy), but he finds these are, as they earlier assert, "not shabby little imagettes, pennydirts and dodgemyeyes you buy in the soottee stores" (FW 25.2–3). Rather, they elude his comprehension at various points in the *Wake*, so that he finds that he does not know "whose hue" (FW 227.25). His lecture to them upon the "Word as Wife" attempts to morally reclaim what he can neither physically nor conceptually grasp: the meaning (and mastery) of desire. And yet the nature of words (and wombs) interjects uncertainty and eludes such gestures toward mastery. As a voice propounds in *Finnegans Wake*, "In the buginning is the woid, in the muddle is the sound-dance and thereinofter you're in the unbewised again, vund vulsyvolsy" (FW 378.29–31). Earwicker (a bug) may be the father or "buginning" of paternity, but this is, as Stephen Dedalus has suggested, posited upon a void—or merely the "woid" or word one cannot trust to be true. Beyond the patriarch's void-suspended word is the "muddle" of sound-dance, a kind of unclear language suffused with physicality. After that, we repeatedly slip back into the unknown (unbewußt), and the cycle continues. *Finnegans Wake*'s "sound-dance" indicates not only a rhythm carried within the language, stylistically, but also as it is echoed in the many dancings, prancings, and playful gesturings enacted by Issy and Anna Livia in the text. At one point, another figure also strikes a strange dance. The "Jambs, of Delphin's Bourne" is known for "Dawncing the kniejinksky choreopiscopally like an easter sun round the colander, the vice! Taranta boontoday! You should pree him prance the polcat, you whould sniff him wops around, you should hear his piedigrotts schraying as he skimpies skirp a . . ." (FW 513.9–15). Readers of Ellmann's biography will recognize the "spider dance" of James (Jambs) Joyce,[38] here enacting a choreography almost Episcopalean (from "choreopiscopally") in its form. He is feminized by this act, as his "piedigrotts" are both flying feet and petticoats that splay as he swirls or "skimpies" his skirt (and as he skips) around. Dance is not a mere coincidental motif in the *Wake*. Isadora Duncan was engaged, during the 1920s, in moving dance away from the more formal and categorically constrictive definitions of the body in ballet. For her, each movement in dance needed to evolve from the next, as a kind of unconscious reaction that developed out of a primary movement. And this initial movement was to arise naturally from an impulse or sensation.[39] As Duncan describes it, she dreamed of finding "a first movement from which would be born a series of movements without my volition, but as the unconscious reaction of the primary movement."[40] As Mark Franko suggests, Duncan was appropriating the masculine alliance between woman and her natural body, but in so doing taking dance and the female form beyond the Victorian dictates that restricted the movements of women in daily life and tightly constrained and covered their bodies.[41] In the *Wake*, desire is what is wriggled along the limbs of Anna Livia or Issy, and sensation becomes a centrally encoded aspect of language by virtue of the ways in which it moves from word to word.

The sensate effects of women's words take over and transform Joyce's last text. As this occurs, language turns back on stereotyping and effectively deconstructs the grounds of its own constitution as materiality challenges such abstraction. Still, *Wake*-words oscillate between narcissistic self-enrapture and aggressive verbal attacks, and yet at either extreme the referentiality of language pulls it back or the punnical interruptions break the anger into humor again. This does not, however, mean that we are beyond the somewhat clichéd casting of women, for Joyce still presents us with a female character who is as self-enchanted as Gerty, but who finds a source of agency in her sexual prowess, in some partial reminder of Molly. As one of the main agents of *écriture féminine* and radically voiced desire, Issy serves as an oddly conflictual figure, both for verbal liberation and gender constraints.

Issy is a rainbow of varying attributes not to be caught, while she also parades narcissism in its attachment to an adolescent stage in female consciousness. Issy ("Is is" FW 620.32) repeatedly splits and doubles within herself. Like Gerty, she is fascinated by the image in her looking-glass and preening for the chase of future beaus. Adeline Glasheen initially characterized Earwicker and Anna Livia's daughter as "*Finnegans Wake*'s ingenue lead . . . a triumph of feminine imbecility and sexual attraction."[42] Glasheen associates Issy with Gerty, Lucia Joyce, and a range of character-fissures in *Finnegans Wake*. She has been seen as Joyce's attempt to work through his dismay over Lucia's mental illness, as Issy's narcissistic self-love fissures into Lucia's schizophrenia arguably at times.[43] She moreover is a narcissistic/schizophrenic parallel to the twins, her brothers Shem and Shaun. The mirror that is externalized in their relationship is embedded within her own mind. She talks to herself, constantly glancing at the mirror, the social image she has internalized. In a more naive version, she is associated with Nuvoletta, who falls to her death and is transformed into a single raindrop or tear, after trying in vain to attract the attentions of the Mookse and the Gripes. If one hopes to find a final transgression of stereotypes of women in the *Wake*, Issy's character is in some ways a dramatic return to the nubile girl-child seductress.

As a figuration of Issy, for example, Nuvoletta is a picture of pure, childish narcissism, full of naive ideas that tend toward a form of self-love that can only be validated by male attention:

> Nuvoletta in her lightdress, spunn of sisteen shimmers, was looking down on them, leaning over the bannistars and listening all she childishly could. . . . She was alone. All her nubied companions were asleeping with the squirrels. Their mivver, Mrs Moonan, was off in the Fuerst quarter scrubbing the backsteps of Number 28. Fuvver, that Skand, he was up in Norwood's sokaparlour, eating oceans of Voking's Blemish. Nuvoletta listened as she reflected herself, though the heavenly one with his constellatria and his emanations stood between, and she tried all she tried to make the Mookse look up at her (but *he* was fore too adiaptotously farseeing) and to make the Gripes hear how coy she could be (though he was much too schystimatically auricular about *his ens* to heed her) but it was all mild's vapour moist. Not even her feignt reflection, Nuvoluccia, could they toke their gnoses off for their minds. (FW 157.8–25)

The emphasis on her "lightdress" and its particular starry accoutrements echoes Gerty MacDowell's fascination with her own clothes and, like Gerty on Sandymount Strand, "she was alone," as her friends are otherwise engaged. Her name, moreover, invokes the "Princess Novelette" that advises Gerty in all things cosmetic (U 13.110). Nuvoletta's extended passage constantly reiterates her sense of self-observation, referring to how "she reflected herself," "her feignt reflection," and the manner in which "she sighed after herself." Her aim is to catch the attention of the Mookse and Gripes, another pair engaged in rivalrous exchange below her, but they are boyishly oblivious, and she thinks, "I see. . . . There are menner" (FW 158.5). Indeed, they are ignorant of her presence, and so: "Nuvoletta reflected for the last time in her little long life and she made up all her myriads of drifting minds in one. She cancelled all her engauzements. She climbed over the bannistars; she gave a childy cloudy cry: *Nuée! Nuée!* A lightdress fluttered. She was gone" (FW 159.6–10). At the moment she rains (*nuée* is "rain cloud" in French) she is also born (*née*) anew. She falls out of her virginal life and, when she is associated with Anna Livia (in Anna's memory), she will fall not to her corporeal death but to the death of physical innocence, as she will also "fall" into sexual relations.

Issy's is a more intensive awakening to sexual prowess. She exceeds the childish cliché while not yet being fixed and set as a "dangerously desiring woman," as Ann Hathaway was for Stephen in "Scylla and Charybdis." She excels beyond the self-deluding romanticism of Gerty MacDowell. Sheldon Brivic has argued that Issy's language subverts the categories that Gerty's leaves in place: "Issy speaks as one who has been trained to excel in playing the object of desire and finds that the most effective way to express her independence is to use her performance to shock."[44] Issy takes the girlish-erotic clichés and appropriates them, to the confusions of all males around. Still, her playfulness hinges on recontainment, so that the appropriation may still signal an unconscious entrapment in male stereotypes (and expectations) of young women. At times, Issy is very much a stereotype of girl-child eroticism. In answer to tenth riddle in FW I, vi—"What bitter's love but yurning, what' sour lovemutch but a bref burning till shee that drawes dothe smoake retourne?" (FW 143.29–30)—we get a babbling river of Issy girl-talk, piping sweetly for her Pipette: "Are you enjoying, this same little me, my life, my love? Why do you like my whisping? Is it not divinely deluscious? . . . But don't! You want to be slap well slapped for that. Your delighted lips, love, be careful! Mind my duvetyne dress above all! It's golded silvy, the newest sextones with princess effect" (FW 147.35–148.8). If the listener likes her "whisping"—a wistful lisping—it is a diminutive lure that draws him (or her) in. And then to have her only teasingly resist, giving the "I say no to say yes" message while she protests the importance of preserving her carefully purchased dress, implies a sexual politics that allows agency to women and girls only as it launches no final refusal on the man's pursuant agency. This is a problematic locus from which to have radical *écriture* spring. However, Issy's "say-no, say-yes" flirtation opens up the ambiguity between what desire wishes to say and what society dictates one must. Poised upon one of the most dreadful clichés (which has been cited as justification for rape), still it flowers into the radical *acceptance* (as opposed to interpretive violence) implied within the fluidity of language that Issy enables. Words (and women) speak in two directions at once. This duplicity—a negative stereotype of untrustworthy women and words—enables a countergesture of allowance and flow. Her split speaking echoes not only verbal parapraxes but also the slide between unconscious desires and the struggle for self-conscious (perhaps societally ordered) control. So control of the feminine is now internalized as a struggle in Wakean women. Issy's youth mixes innocence with savvy agency in a way that calls into question the radical distinction between youthful innocent and willful woman. She controls—and doesn't. Speaks—and slips. So that language (and clichés) are grasped and then exploded in a coupled gesture.

It seems important to acknowledge the perseverance of *some* form of gender cliché, even amidst the *Wake*'s radical *écriture*. Indeed, Joyce's final text draws on social stereotypes just as they might float through the unconscious in a dream. But there are also the individuated aspects of dreams, the quirky revisions and "perversions" of such containments. What is culturally absorbed thus mixes or clashes with more personal expression. This tension does not necessarily progress in *Finnegans Wake*; rather, it is constantly recycling in a variety of scenarios.

Cyclical roles are not deterministic containments in the *Wake*, however, and one of the chief strategies for evading stereotypic containments is for women (and men) to dissipate their identities and fan out into a rainbow of possible identities. This occurs in terms of gender and sexuality, which I discuss in the following chapter, and it also is a means of evading the more violent forms of national identity, which I explore in the chapter beyond. The slippage of identity in the *Wake* is one way of avoiding aggressive displacements and reducing their impact. Although stereotypes pepper the aggressive discourses of the *Wake*, dissipation and self-splintering is poised directly against such negative gestural politics.

The *Wake* most persistently parodies control of the other through the roving force of *gossip*. Society, as an abstract and fluctuating force, issues judgments and speculates on extremes, trying to limit and contain the more fluid realities. Both Earwicker and Anna Livia are the foci of scandal, he for his voyeuristic pleasure in watching little girls and women urinate, dance, and otherwise perform for him unknowingly, she for her own realization of sexuality (and supposed facilitation of his). In the first book of the *Wake* (I, iv), Earwicker's fall—either as drunk off a ladder or humiliated from public and political life—is reconfigured repeatedly through gossip. At one point he is discovered by "Fama," the personification of rumor, and resurrects as a figure spied on board the S.S. Finlandia. He is found "under an islamitic newhame in his seventh generation, a physical body Cornelius Macgrath's (badoldkarakter, commonorrong canbung) in Asia Major" (FW 98.7–10). In his seventh regeneration he is resurrected as "Cornelius Macgrath," a giant Irishman[45] and a "bad old character." Unfortunately, he is discovered to have "bepiastered the buikdanseuses from the opulence of his omnibox" (FW 98.12–13) pestering dancers (or throwing piasters at them) from his theater box. And so "Wires hummed." Macgrath, as a great Irish figure, is, with "regrettitude," pushed out of office and resigns even from life, being "recalled and scrapheaped by the Maker" (FW 98.15–17). This is one of many repeated scenarios in which Earwicker is celebrated, deprecated, and dismissed through gossip. Earwicker most often defends himself by refusing fixation of his identity. He is a *"pan*triarch" (FW 74.11), wild and Dionysian in his lack of control and also splintered into a panorama of identities that belie the violence of identification. Later, in *Finnegans Wake* I, viii, the washerwomen will likewise scandalize themselves over Anna Livia's sexual provocations. After disapproving the "dirt" in Earwicker's shirt and "mak[ing] his private linen public" (FW 196.16), they turn to Livia, who is "nearly as badher as him herself" (FW 198.9). She is accused of pimping for her husband, going out and seeking loose women and "throwing all the neiss little whores in the world at him!" (FW 200.29–30). Moreover, they speculate, "she must have been a gadabout in her day, so she must, more than most" (FW 202.4–5). Her fluid nature is condemned by the "stones" of women, whose voices solidify rumor into "fact." In this way Joyce critically reviles the social tendency to externalize moralisms and to fix facts, so that, historically, Parnell's political career ends from a mishandled scandal, and fictionally Joyce's own characters must forever die, mutate, and split in the face of judgments based more on rumor than fact. Fluidity is thus not exclusively gendered as feminine in the *Wake*, and evasion of control of society becomes generally more important, a broader map of the crucial focus Joyce had on releasing women from masculine control. Joyce seems most interested, in the *Wake*, in moving beyond social stereotyping, less than establishing a particularly liberating *sexual* politics. The sexual politics of the text, then, circulate more readily around social censure than gender issues. Women's figures, like men's, mutate and fan out into an alphabet or rainbow of various selves and portions, evading the more controlling voices of the *Wake*. The gradual opening of women's voices within Joyce's works serves as the vehicle for such a change, making gender implicitly, if not explicitly, central to thematics of liberation.

When Shaun announces to the rainbow girls that "the word is my Wife, to expanse and expound, to vend and to velnerate," he echoes an earlier claim of Stephen's, with regard to Shakespeare and Ann Hathaway in the "Scylla and Charybdis" episode. Stephen there argues that the artistic desire to control words runs parallel to the necessity of controlling women's sexual appetites. I see Joyce's own practice—his control of words and female characters—as a progressive struggle against this controlling compulsion, with his parody operating predominantly as a form of disengaging the mastering grasp implicit in such a formulation. As Joyce practices letting women speak their desires, his language becomes less severely tied to some single, authorized intention or meaning. Instead, his words are let play in parts of *Ulysses* and more fully in *Finnegans Wake*, giving over to a pleasurable exhibition of desire in language. Not coincidentally, women in the *Wake* more freely voice non-meaningful or non-reproductive desires, and Anna Livia Plurabelle serves as a model both for sexually desiring woman and for the author, penning letters and speaking a steady babble of desire and affection.

These associative linkages multiply across the text, leaving the word, in its mis-spells and -speaks, as the only anchor to the range of references. The body of the word then *procreates* meaning, taking a radically affirming association between woman, body, and words that moves beyond the parodied resistances of *Portrait* and *Ulysses*. At one point in *Finnegans Wake*, Issy apologizes for a brief distraction, explaining that she "was listening to every treasuried word I said fell from my dear mot's tongue" (FW 146.26–28), the combination of "mother" with "mot" (word) implies the creative, interpretative possibilities of language. A word may give rise to legions of interpretations so that, like desire, meaning flows outward. This model, as it operates in *Finnegans Wake*, functions as a continuous transgression of the control of the word, never turning back toward a single interpretative or intentional construct.

Joyce moves away from a simple (and silencing) objectification of woman in favor of a complex attempt to ventriloquize female desire, a move that paradoxically releases women from male control *within* Joyce's novels, even as it remains within the "pornosophical" control of Joyce's male imaginary and, at times, constrained by culturally learned modes of heterosexual desire. Indeed, the recreation of woman as a mirror to male desires strongly suggests a narcissistic construction of heterosexuality implicit both in Joyce's culture (and still our own). However, this position is necessarily complicated by a critical reading of Joyce's use of doubling and associative counterpoint in his representation of homosexuality in *Finnegans Wake*. There, narcissism is a model for textuality, a confirmation of the implication of autobiography and realism as mimetic projects. By deconstructing narcissism in his representations of gay and lesbian clichés, Joyce rearranges the trajectory of desires as they operate in the consciously deployed play on the unconscious in *Finnegans Wake*.

In the Original Sinse: The Gay Cliché and Verbal Transgression in Finnegans Wake

From his earliest writings, James Joyce associated transgressive sexuality with language. Words beyond control, words that exceed interpretation—in *Dubliners*, such indistinct language is associated with sexual ambiguity and "perverse" behavior.[1] The man with bottle green eyes in "An Encounter" takes transgressive pleasure in the circling of his own words, while his fantasies of whipping boys and girls create discomfort in the young boy who listens. Although this pedophile is not exclusively interested in young boys, the uneasiness the narrator feels defines his reaction through homophobic fear, as the boy becomes anxious to evade the older man's desire.[2] The stereotype that views the pederast *as* homosexual is thus caught up, in this story, with words that mesmerize their own speaker, who appears to be caught in a kind of verbal narcissism or autoerotic speech. In "The Sisters," sexual ambiguity is similarly aligned with uninterpretable speech, as an elder priest's "failing" is elusively discussed within the hearing of a young boy he tutored. Troubled by allusions that constantly fade into gaps, the boy subsequently dreams, in his sleep, of the "heavy grey face of the paralytic" following him and "murmuring" to him (D 11). The uninterpretable is linked to the paralytic and paralysis, negatively cast as frozen and infertile, although the locus of this infertility arguably lies more with Dublin society and its suppression than with the sexual desires themselves. In this manner, gay stereotypes that Joyce incorporates into his writing function as points from which to instigate the very dissolution of both social and verbal clichés. Language ceases to be predictable when sexuality is no longer normative. Desires consequently inform the unconscious in Joyce's work, inducing changes in the way language functions.

I will here be examining the parallel disruption, in *Finnegans Wake*, of reductive social assessments of homosexuality and prescriptive notions of how language operates. Stereotypes of sexuality are invoked by Joyce at points where verbal clichés begin to be displaced by parapraxes and misrecognitions. Joyce invokes and parodies two familiar stereotypes of homosexuality: the notion that "same-sex" desire arises from narcissism and that it might also be a source of paranoia. Both these denigrative analyses of sexuality were put forward in Freud's work in the early 1900s, and they appear to have been derived from broader cultural biases of the time.[3] If Joyce refrains from valorizing such stereotypes, he continually uses their effects thematically. His textual gestures are in many ways split between a playful inward narcissism and a radically aggressive paranoid insistence. The effects of sexual stereotyping exceed the plot and characterological development, disrupting the language and mimetic framing of Joyce's fiction. I aim to here clarify the ways in which one might read these effects as a "perverse" form of textuality that hinges upon the parodic representation of the splinter between homosexual desire and resistance. In the late 1970s, Colin MacCabe noticed the link between sexual and textual perversity in Joyce's writing, and work on the connection between theses phenomena has been taken up more recently by Jean-Michel Rabaté, who argues that the slippage into non-meaning in *Dubliners* functions as the opposite of orthodoxy and opens a certain "perversity" of non-meaning.[4] Critics however have shied away from focusing fuller attention on Joyce's use of stereotypes, emphasizing the transgressive aspects of Joyce's work more readily than the invocation of reductive clichés of homosexuality. However, denigrative stereotypes of gay sexuality have recently been critiqued by Jonathan Dollimore, Michael Warner, and others.[5] With these revisionary readings in mind, I will be examining Joyce's recurrent use of clichés of homosexuality in the *Wake*, arguing that his deployment and subsequent disruption of these stereotypes are intertwined with his changing form of textuality.

What is narcissistic art? Does it refuse to speak beyond its own hearing, murmuring to itself without regard for social reaction, resisting every interpretive foray or "curative" critical exercise set to draw it back into the normative circle? Perhaps the narcissist's (in)distinction, the wavering line between internal and external forms of communication, troubles the interpretive process, so that, with its challenge to binaristic forms of evaluation, narcissism becomes the supreme scapegoat of all forms of representation. In 1910, Freud aligned narcissism with homosexuality, arguing that its emphasis on sameness signals a self-enclosing circle of desire, unhealthy in its implications.[6] Such denigrations of same-sex love implicate the tendency toward non-reproductive pleasure in a mythos of egotism (Narcissus) that circulated in Joyce's various contexts even before his encounter with Freud's theories in his work on

Leonardo da Vinci (1910).[7] In Joyce's writing, narcissistic forms of representation are repeatedly associated with homosexuality, both in the pleasurable engagement with sensate aspects of language and the "perverse" transgression of mimesis, itself a form of mirroring. Women's desires especially are cast in terms of narcissistic self-enrapture, whether on a homo- or heterosexual model. In contrast, whenever male homosexual desire is represented in Joyce's work, it circulates around a model of paranoia—yet another Freudian cliché—so that it slips through only in parapraxes that erupt as two men endeavor to repress any slide into homosexual desire. Freud not only identified homosexuality as the cause of paranoid anxiety, but he also linked that illness to narcissism, based on its self-enclosed view of the world as a reflection of its own self.[8] As Joyce distinguishes his approaches to male homosexuality and lesbian desire, he casts them on a continuum of two extremes. Lesbian language moves beyond simple narcissism in the *Wake*, opening onto a more "fertile" notion of the unforeclosable nature of word-play and meaning, while the murmurings of gay desire are met by a violently doubled and repeatedly resplit mode of representation that threatens to break down Joyce's more radical parody and shift his work to a defensive/aggressive form of textuality from which stereotypes repeatedly emerge. I will here be suggesting that a dialectic between the extremes of seduction and aggression—narcissistic pleasures and paranoid defenses—ultimately defines the parodic critique of stereotyping that undergirds the textual flow of *Finnegans Wake* more generally, placing the perverse language of sexually transgressive practices at the center of Joyce's avant-garde experiment with words.

Before pursuing two localized readings of lesbian and gay clichés in "The Mime of Nick, Mick and the Maggies" and "The Tale of Burrus and Caseous," I would like to briefly sketch the framework of my application of the terms "narcissism" and "paranoia" to concepts of textuality in *Finnegans Wake*. Woman-as-narcissist is initially represented as a heterosexual construct in Joyce, where women are guilty of being either oblivious to social realities or to male desires. Joyce thus renders Gerty MacDowell as a sadly pathetic narcissist, engaged in denial of the bleakness of her romantic and marital outlook, whereas, in Molly Bloom's monologue, he turns narcissism toward a savvy awareness of the female body, which can develop into autoeroticism or even lesbian desire. In *Finnegans Wake*, female narcissism slides between an autoerotic focus and an older woman's desire for a younger woman, in whom she sees a former self. As this narcissism translates into language, women's words are often the softly erotic babble that renders little word-sense and much sensation. Male homosexual desire, in contrast, is met by homosexual panic and paranoid defense in Joyce's work, and the language that circulates around these scenarios is often pressed, by Shaun and his associates in their moralistic stances, toward aggressive attempts to rigidify and control language. Both the repressed potential for homosexual desire and the parapraxes that reveal it are agents of betrayal for the Shauns of *Finnegans Wake*. And betrayal is, as Lacan notes, one of the key anxieties motivating the paranoiac.[9]

In simplest terms, paranoia designates a psychological delusion, a persecution complex in which a subject perceives behind the visible a web of maleficent meanings. On Freud's analysis, the paranoiac is unable to accept the interplay between the ego and superegoistic functions, so that he or she externalizes fault and/or evaluative agency, displacing this sense of an internal split onto some other—a persecutor who is located radically outside the self.[10] Psychoanalyst François Roustang suggests that

> the paranoiac is someone who, paradoxically, is threatened with losing his own limits. That is why he needs to provoke the other into becoming his persecutor. The other will thus protect him from the threat of dissipating like a liquid; he will set a border which the paranoiac must constantly confront in order to reestablish the certainty of his existence in a circumscribed physical or psychic space.[11]

If paranoia is linked to a variety of manifestations, such as erotomania, delusions of grandeur, and persecution scenarios, I will be focusing on the paranoiac's compulsion to control language, texts, and any variety of forms in which meaning can occur. *Finnegans Wake* employs a structural use of paranoia, so that rigidly paranoid attempts to reduce language are loosened by their opposite—narcissistic language that fails altogether to return any rationally defined, containable, and communicable meaning. As Joyce integrates the *gay clichés* of lesbian-narcissism and gay-paranoia in his writing, he shifts the gestural politics away from the very structures of cliché and containment, elaborating a textualizing web that plays between transgressive pleasures and interpretive allowance.

I begin with Joyce's ventriloquism of lesbian desire, since it links up with received discussions of the jouissance of *Finnegans Wake* that Joyce's representations of gay desire/anxiety complicate.[12] It furthermore enacts the gestural link between body and language developed in Joyce's representation of women. Joyce's use of lesbian eroticism arguably represents the form of homosexual desire Joyce could appropriate with the least threat to his own heterosexual identity. If lesbian sex disavows the heterosexual call to propagation and traditional, familial hierarchies of power, it can be used for erotic titillation within the heterosexual, male imaginary. After silencing women's voices repeatedly in *Portrait*, Joyce begins to experiment with the ventriloquization of female desires in *Ulysses*. Freeing women from the function of symbol, he works to inhabit their thoughts and represents their minds as shifting and as fluid as many of the men's in *Ulysses*. And yet as he does this, Joyce appropriates the cultural stereotype of woman as narcissistic object. In the previous chapter, I discussed the ways in which female narcissism—in Gerty MacDowell's character and more radically in Molly Bloom's—is cast through the male gaze and so never wholly "narcissistic" nor fully self-enclosed. This destabilized cliché of female narcissism influences the introduction of sensate and playful language in *Ulysses*, and this process is most pronounced in the places where lesbian eroticism emerges.

By the end of *Ulysses*, Joyce's pressure on the narcissistic model of female desire transforms into the potential advent of lesbian eroticism. If in contrast to Gerty, Molly Bloom knows that when she looks in the mirror, it "never gives you the expression" (U 18.414), Molly in fact uses a mirroring model of self-observation in her sexual fantasy. That is, Molly repeatedly covets a man's ability to be aroused by a woman's body, to the extent that her thoughts threaten to convert the male position into her own. She thinks of how her own body can "excite myself sometimes its well for men all the amount of pleasure they get off a womans body" (U 18.1379–80). At one moment, this envy of male arousal becomes an explicit thought of Molly's: "God," she thinks, "I wouldnt mind being a man and get up on a lovely woman" (U 18.1146–47). Here, Molly voices something close to lesbian desire, but it is contained by the social code of heterosexuality: she would have to *be* a man to have this experience. Molly's ability to identify with male sexual desire may be "safe" heterosexual fantasy, which gives her pleasure in her own body even as an understanding of her desire is formulated through the dominant male culture's understanding of it. On the other hand, her fantastic identification with the male gaze may suggest a shift of position, so that she, as (fe)male identified, could "get up on a lovely woman." As Molly plays with cross-gender identification, she threatens to destabilize traditional gender alignments of subject-object (male-female) relations. When she thinks to herself, "God I wouldnt mind being a man and get up on a lovely woman" (U 18.1146–47), is this narcissism—the egotism of her own successful self-objectification? Or is it a moment of lesbian desire?[13]

I suggest that in employing an ambiguity about Molly's preferences, Joyce is pushing on the tensions within narcissistic construction. In *Group Psychology and the Analysis of the Ego*, Freud distinguishes between the heterosexual form of desire, which treats the other as object, and homosexual desire, which instead identifies *with* the object's sexual desires. This distinction, however, assumes already a radical separation between forms of desire.[14] As Michael Warner observes, Freud assumes a gender-alignment with object/subject positions, so that in order to choose an other, the male must choose woman. As Warner comments, however, "no matter how much he [man] wants to think of the Other as woman, it remains true that men are others to him as well, just as women are fellow beings. When another man, this 'other who is also the same,' becomes the object of desire, has the male subject failed to distinguish self and other?"[15] Freud says yes, but Warner finds the strands to unravel this willful distinction between homo- and heterosexual love. Not only does Freud fail to anchor his privileging of male identification in the Oedipal scenario, but he also bases his distinctions on an (arbitrarily claimed) exclusiveness of identification and attachment.[16] Moreover, Lacan's subsequent definition of love presses on Freud's attempt to mark out such distinctions. Love of any kind is constructed on "one's own ego that one loves in love, one's own ego made real on the imaginary level." As Warner notes, "[Lacan] definitively removed any possibility of making narcissism a basis for a normative hierarchy between hetero- and homosexuality. Homosexuality may indeed be a way of loving one's own ego, but so is heterosexual romance."[17]

Jean-Michel Rabaté has observed Joyce's repeated obfuscation of the gender of voices and characters in the *Wake*.[18] As the stereotype of woman-as-narcissist is centrally deployed, its extension into a stereotype of lesbian desire likewise implicitly destabilizes the opposition between hetero- and homosexual love, for Joyce's layering of voices and images enacts a parody of such distinctions. As women's voices allude to the possibility of lesbian seduction, so too do these words engage in the *jouissance* that plays upon aural and tactile sensations in language. ALP's and Issy's babble of words may disrupt normative approaches to interpretation, eschewing the categorical and definitive hierarchies of reference. Yet their associative words also threaten to remain a clichéd version of narcissistic language, turning forever back on itself.

Issy, who is most often engaged in seductive babble, is transformed into Izod in "The Mime of the Mick, Nick and the Maggies," where she is described as "a bewitching blonde who dimples delightfully and is approached in loveliness only by her grateful sister reflection in a mirror" (FW 220.7–9). Issy, Izod's prefiguration in the *Wake*, is notoriously schizophrenic, marking a contrast to the externalized, paranoid split between the male twins, Shem and Shaun. The mirror that is externalized in their relationship is embedded within Issy's own mind. She talks to herself, constantly glancing at the mirror, the social image she has internalized. Whenever Issy's words extend outward, however, her audience appears to be directed toward either men or women or both. Initially, one notes that she enjoys tantalizing males, although she occasionally rebels. One of her most Wakean modes of resistance is to slide into non-meaning, into pleasurable sounds that are not necessarily directed toward men. Her language fades playfully into the indistinct as she lisps out her "vowelthreaded syllabelles," for example, "Have you evew thought, wepowtew, that sheew gweatness was his twadgedy?" (FW 61.6–7). This childish lisping plays on the erotic evocation of indirect sound. Issy seems to achieve seduction only in and through the stereotypes that construct her as a childish nymphet. It is as if Joyce needs the recognition value of stark types to give force to the subsequent movement away from such containment in Issy's very words. Indeed, the women in the *Wake* speak an associative flow that is crucial to Joyce's shift from "controlling" words in that last text, so that both the control and its escape are alternately modeled.

Issy is, however, no simple nymphet. She often demonstrates a direct interest in her own sexual appeal and a cynical awareness of social codes—the necessity of attracting a male suitor. Her footnotes to the school lessons, in book II, chapter ii of the *Wake*, give glimpses of a playful boast of sexual awareness. "My six is no secret, sir," she laughs (FW 273n7). And when the teacher describes "fickers who are returnally reprodictive of themselves," she footnotes, "I enjoy as good as anyone" (FW 298.17–18 and f.1). Both in terms of reproduction and reprodiction, Issy is prepared. She picks up on saucy allusions and is sassily scandalized by the lesson's reference to something that is "as plane as a poke stiff." "The impudence of that in girl's things!" she snaps (FW 296.29–30 and 296n5). And much as Issy's sexuality appears to be defined toward men, she has no illusions about marriage. "One must sell it to some one, the sacred name of love," she thinks (FW 268n1). If she is pubescent, like Nuvoletta or Gerty, Issy seems more aware of her body as a tool of attraction and is far from abashedly modest, and thus the social parameters that direct her toward heterosexual relations are at points acknowledged with a somewhat cynical wink.

In the school lesson, Issy brags to a suitor that she has learned the language of love from her schoolmistress. As Issy taunts her love, whom she calls "smooth of my slate," to "eat my words for it as sure as there's a key in my kiss," she reveals that she has already learned the relation between words and desire, and she uses her banter as a form of sublimated exchange, likening the "verbe de vie and verve to vie." Complaining of her "intended, Jr, who I'm throne away on," she suggests that her "impending marriage" will be a subjection to the intention of another, even as it will be her social elevation. Most important, however, we learn that prior to her "fall," she has enjoyed some form of education, linguistic and perhaps also sexual, under to tutelage of an older woman. Teasing the object of her seduction, Issy brags about this experience: "I learned all the runes of the gamest game ever from my old nourse Asa. A most adventuring trot is her and she vicking well knowed them all heartswise and fourwords" (FW 279n1). She knows the ruins of marriage, told by her old nurse Asa, as she also knows all the secrets ("run," in Old Norse) of it.[19] The adventuresome "trot" (or whore) may very well, or *ficking* well, know all the arsewise and forward ways. Her name furthermore suggests that the nurse is associative in her very nature: "As a. . . ." As Issy claims, at least, she now knows "the ruelles of the rut," whether they be directed toward homo- or heterosexuality. Rue-elles may signal a path (Fr: *rue* = street) or grief to come, or it may cast aspersions on the nature of her sexual experiences—as a street-walker perhaps. The word "ruelle" is, however, French slang for "vagina," and so might again refer to lesbian desire. And "rut" may of course signal sexual experience as readily as it points to social stagnation.

Joyce seems to have acquired his notion of lesbian sexuality from the Victorian social codes, which allowed that a schoolgirl might engage briefly in "romantic friendships," so as to learn the ways of relating to some other (necessarily male) companion to whom she would be wed when she reached maturity.[20] In "The Mime," however, Joyce inscribes various sexual ambivalences that potentially destabilize this model. There, Joyce's occasional allusions to lesbianism are more pronounced, and he parodies Freudian "cyclological" (FW 220.30–31) interpretations of childhood sexuality by interlacing his depiction of the child's game Angels and Devils (or colors) with sexually loaded parapraxes. This is where Joyce truly plays on the "Studium of Sexophonologistic Schizophrenesis" (FW 123.18–19). Whereas elsewhere in *Finnegans Wake* references to lesbianism seem rare or can only be traced through the play upon ambiguous pronoun references, here allusions are relatively direct. Lesbian eroticism and other forms of sexual transgression are both named and variously alluded to, as the children of Chapelizod play their "twilight games."[21]

The play begins as the Floras ("Girl Scouts from St. Bride's Finishing Establishment") flirt with the boys, Glugg and Chuff. Or rather, Izod flirts with them. The text moves between descriptions of a group of girls and a single one:

> Aminxt that nombre of evelings, but how pierceful in their sojestive-
> ness were those first girly stirs, with zitterings of flight released and
> twinglings of twitchbells in rondel after, with waverings that made
> shimmershake rather naightily all the duskcended airs and shylit bea-

conings from shehind hims back. Sammy, call on. Mirrylamb, she was
shuffering all the diseasinesses of the unherd of. Mary Louisan
Shousapinas! If Arck could no more salve his agnols from the wiles of
willy wooly woolf! If all the airish signics of her dipandump helpabit
from an Father Hogam till the Mutther Masons could not that Glugg
to catch her by the calour of her brideness! Not Rose, Sevilla nor Cit-
ronelle; not Esmeralde, Pervinca nor Indra; not Viola even nor all of
them four themes over. But, the monthage stick in the melmelode jawr,
I am (twintomine) all thees thing. (FW 222.32–223.9)

Minxlike and batlike, these so-jestive girls circle around (in rondel) in
the descending dusk, beckoning each other behind (or "shehind")
Glugg's back. At the moment of desire ("Sammy, call on!") and also of
delayed verbal gratification (a pause: semicolon), Izod consolidates into
a "she" who suffers from either dizziness or diseases. She seems to want
Ark—Archangel Mick or the rainbow girls (Arc)—to save her (his
"agnols," or lambs) from the wolf. Yet for all the help of the alphabet,
Glugg cannot name the right color and so win the sexual chase. In fact,
the objection seems to be that Izod is not any particular shade of herself,
but "all these things" at once. She is a self-enacted pantomime and a
narcissistic self, caught up in the phrase "twintomine." In "The Mime,"
Issy splinters into the "rainbow girls," all associative aspects of herself
and also, at times, playmates. Glugg is aroused and endeavors to catch
her, but here he fails to name her as only one thing. Izod's complexly
(non)consolidated identity plays a chief role in the transference from
narcissism to sexual desire. Her multiple identification with aspects of
herself can turn outward, so that she desires another woman with whom
she is identified, simultaneously. In Freud's work on homosexuality, no
such confusion between identity and desire can occur. In "The Mime,"
however, female eroticism explicitly depends on the breakdown of such
dichotomies. This is not to say that Joyce radically theorizes some new
form of homosexuality. If these textual implications carry the *Wake*
toward this deconstruction of self/other oppositions in women's relations, the moments where lesbianism seems to be most thematically
described in the text return it to a highly contained version of that form
of desire.

As the children's play progresses and Izod's desires for male seduction are thwarted, one of the voices nonetheless foretells the inevitability of her marriage:

she'll meet anew fiancy, tryst and trow. Mammy was, Mimmy is,
Minuscoline's to be. In the Dee dips a dame and the dame desires a
demselle but the demselle dresses dolly and the dolly does a dulcy-
damble. The same renew. For though she's unmerried she'll after truss
up and help that hussyband how to hop. (FW 226.14–19)

The voice predicts a heterosexual attachment, so that Izod may have children—the dolly Issy desires. First, however, there is a chain of desire between women, where each older woman, in desiring to *be* her younger self, also actively desires another, younger woman with whom she can identify. Here we have the cliché of narcissism that Joyce takes up, with desire hinging upon a likeness to one's own self. Yet the "Dame" who "desires a demselle" (damsel or demoiselle) must be thwarted if propagation is to be carried through.[22] The closing parapraxes, however, suggest that she might teach hopping to a band of hussies, rather than to a "hussyband." Joyce traces the heterosexual taboos on lesbianism, while also covertly pointing to their potential for instability.

Joyce takes these clichés of lesbianism as self-absorbed interest in a former self (or, from the girl's point of view, as prepubescent sexuality being instructed), and he transforms the very process of verbal association upon which stereotyping can be based. That is, narcissism as cliché of the woman may be linked to lesbianism in the *Wake*, but the very construction of cliché is unraveled again by the language lesbians speak. For stereotypes are immaterial, abstracted from context and conditions, so that the body (and bodily acts) deploy a kind of specificity that displaces categoricals and clichés. Moreover, as lesbian "assaucyetiams" fuel the associative pleasure of Joyce's own words, his textuality derives inspiration from Proust's similar association of lesbian erotics and language.

Verbal association is explicitly linked to lesbian association in Marcel Proust's *Remembrance of Things Past*,[23] a subtext to Joyce's "The Mime of Mick, Nick and the Maggies." Proust published *À l'ombre des jeunes filles en fleurs* (*In a Budding Grove*) in 1919 and won the Prix Goncourt that year. The Joyces moved from Zurich to Paris during 1920 and were surely caught up in news of its success. Describing a visit to the beach at Balbec, Proust's narrator recalls his intrigue upon seeing a beautiful group of young women traversing the beach. One day, as he waits before the Grand Hotel, he sees "at the far end of the esplanade, along which they projected a striking patch of colour, I saw five or six young girls." This group he variously describes as "a flock of gulls" with "birdish minds," as "a luminous comet," and as "young flowers" of various kinds.[24] With their spectrum of colors they make up "a single warm shadow" that attracts him singularly.[25] Proust's rapture at their beauty emerges from his sense of an interplay between his ability to partially distinguish their separate identities and then see them again as a fusion of attributes:

> Although each was of a type absolutely different from the others, they all had beauty; but to tell the truth I had seen them for so short a time, and without venturing to look hard at them, that I had not yet indi-

vidualised any of them . . . and when (according to the order in which the group met the eye, marvellous because the most different aspects were juxtaposed, because all the colour scales were combined in it, but confused as a piece of music in which I was unable to isolate and identify at the moment of their passage the successive phrases, no sooner distinguished than forgotten) I saw a pallid oval, black eyes, green eyes, emerge, I did not know if these were the same that had already charmed me a moment ago, I could not relate them to any one girl whom I had set apart from the rest and identified.[26]

The young women are identified as types that both differ and mingle in their impression. Likened to a rainbow or a series of musical phrases, the girls are remarkable to Proust at this moment just prior to individuation, in that his own inability to distinguish them "permeated the group with a sort of shimmering harmony, the continuous transmutation of a fluid, collective and mobile beauty."[27] Later, he likens the project of distinguishing them to "those too rapid readings in which, on the basis of a single syllable and without waiting to identify the rest, we replace the word that is in the text by a wholly different word with which our memory supplies us."[28] This combination of the various attributes of beauty—its range of types—excites Proust most for its interassociative possibilities. These possibilities can give rise to competitive anxieties, however. Earlier, Proust's narrator had been reflecting on how love is not real in the sense of being necessarily attached to its object, but rather hangs on an arbitrary chain of associations, where the next love must in some respect resemble the former and desire only floats until it can fasten itself to the next.[29] In Proust's depiction of obsessive love, in fact, the fastening is fierce, and with obsession arises jealous suspicions that Albertine—the one the narrator eventually singles out in the group—is mixing herself up in a lesbian affair with another member of the group, Andrée.

If Joyce occasionally plays upon scenarios of the obsessive control of women, here his use of Proust opens onto a different trajectory, pursuing lesbian eroticism as his emphasis. This (dis)identity in women works as a collection of various types and attributes, as the Floras of Joyce's "Mime" make repeated appearances in various rainbowlike transformations throughout the *Wake*. The lovely seaside girls of Proust's narrative are playfully translated, but in a manner that retains the same emphasis on their oddly non-individuated, nonconsolidated status:

And these ways wend they. And those ways went they. Winnie, Olive and Beatrice, Nelly and Ida, Amy and Rue. Here they come back, all the gay pack, for they are the florals, from foncey and pansey to papavere's blush, foresake-me-nought, while there's leaf there's hope, with primtim's ruse and marrymay's blossom, all the flowers of the ancelles' garden. (FW 227.13–18)

98   GESTURAL POLITICS

Here Joyce spells *rainbow* backwards with the initials of the girls'
names, and the "gay pack" is likened not only to flowers but to various
attracting gestures, such as "flouncey" flirtation, or pandering to "true-
papa's" blush, pleading with one's lover not to "foresake," the hopeful
flower, springtime's ruse, the promise of marriage. All are flowers of a
handmaid's (ancille) or whore's (ancelle) garden.[30] Joyce has already
spelled "Raynbow" forward in an earlier passage, where the girls are
likened to music ("cadenzando") and colors:

> Say them all but tell them apart, cadenzando coloratura! R is Rubretta
> and A is Arancia, Y is for Yilla and N for greeneriN. B is Boyblue with
> odalisque O while W waters the fleurettes of novembrance. Though
> they're all but merely a schoolgirl yet these way went they. I' th' view
> o' th'avignue dancing goes entrancing roundly. Miss Oodles of Anems
> before the Luvium doeslike. So. And then again doeslike. So. And miss
> Endles of Eons efter Dies of Eirae doeslike. So. And then again does-
> like. So. The many wiles of Winsure. (FW 226.30–227.2)

Anna Livia Plurabelle is also here, associating her myriad identities with
the rainbow of female attributes. Or is it also that she, by identifying
with the schoolgirls, "does like" them, both in that she does things as
they do, but also in that she is fond of them. The problem here is that
one cannot distinguish between associations and "assaucyetiams" that
include sexually transgressive desires. Narcissism thus calls into question the distinction between self and other, and within Joyce's "narcissistic" language here, homo- and heterosexual forms of desire are over-
lapped, pressing on attempts to radically distinguish the two.

Moreover, within lesbian "narcissistic" pleasures, a non-competitive
element liquifies the binaries that create agonistic energy within Joyce's
prose. As Issy, Nuvoletta, and ALP occasionally slip into narcissistic
modes, their associative play allows non-competitive relations between
women, so that in contrast to paranoiacs, they refuse to draw boundaries
while they likewise evade the controlling gesture toward language. This
elision of competition between women in Joyce's model of lesbian desire
marks the difference between agonistic and accretive forms of meaning in
The Wake. Anna Livia Plurabelle, for example, negotiates the relations
between her desire for her daughter, her sympathetic identification with
her, and her awareness of the competition between herself and the young
woman in the eyes of her husband, Earwicker. In her closing soliloquy,
Anna Livia thinks of the way in which her husband—"wick dear," she
calls him (FW 625.17)—may be turning his sexual desires toward a
younger woman, one who is often, in the book, their daughter Issy:

> But you're changing, acoolsha, you're changing from me, I can feel. Or
> is it me is? I'm getting mixed. Brightening up and tightening down.

Yes, you're changing, sonhusband, and you're turning, I can feel you,
for a daughterwife from the hills again. Imlamaya. And she is coming.
Swimming in my hindmoist. Diveltaking on me tail. Just a whisk brisk
sly spry spink spank sprint of a thing theresomere, saultering. Saltarella
come to her own. I pity your oldself I was used to. Now a younger's
there. Try not to part! Be happy, dear ones! May I be wrong! For she'll
be sweet for you as I was sweet when I came down out of me mother.
My great blue bedroom, the air so quiet, scarce a cloud. In peace and
silence. I could have stayed up there for always only. It's something
fails us. First we feel. Then we fall. And let her rain now if she likes.
(FW 626.35–627.12)

"Acoolsha" is a term of endearment, which could be directed any-
where.[31] "Or is it me is?" she asks. Although it seems clear, from the
more extended context, that Anna Livia is addressing her husband, suddenly identities become blurred. She might be herself changing, and she
might be changing into Is, or Issy.[32] As in a dream, the references overlap and spread; Earwicker is also a "sonhusband." From a momentary
inability to distinguish between herself and the object of her affections,
ALP reasserts that the "son/husband" is now turning toward a younger
woman, an "Imlamaya," or perfect illusion.[33] Rather than fight her
usurper, Livia can accede her position to the younger woman who might
take her place in Earwicker's affections and desires. This because, in her
thoughts, Anna Livia accepts an identification with the younger woman
as a glimpse of her former self, when she too was a young virgin, her
innocence or her "blue bedroom" like a womb. Instead of competing,
erecting distinctions and boundaries, here a woman lays more emphasis
on her bond with the daughter. The fall she seems to mourn, both in her
own past and in her daughter's future, is the loss of the heavens and of
the girlish idealization of love. In Joyce's construction of female identifications, narcissism, even in its altered form, eliminates the aggression
implicit upon realizing the alienation or difference encoded within identification. Narcissism becomes the ability to simply embrace a contiguity, a similitude that links the distinct subjects. Rather than splitting off
against her daughter in a competitive gesture, Anna Livia accepts the difference and tunes her affection to an identification with her former self.
When she says, of her potential rival, "let her rain now if she likes," of
course she is allowing the younger rival to reign, but she is also aware
that the younger one will "rain" or cry and fall from the clouds, and in
this she recalls the earlier story in *Finnegans Wake* of the suicide of Nuvoletta, or "little cloud."

This non-competitive form of association presses parodic (dis)iden-
tification toward a more benign form. Likewise, the pleasure of such
associations opens up the potential for autoeroticism as it grades into

lesbian desire, emphasizing not so much an eroticization of sameness as Freud would argue, but more sympathetic connections and—at times—the abandonment to pleasure. Anna Livia Plurabelle, as Joyce's most prominent figure of writing woman, relates to her words as to her sexuality, in an indulgent form of pleasure that troubles the distinction between autoeroticism and lesbian sex. Tales of her earlier days tell of the worst offense she has offered society:

> first of all, worst of all, the wiggly livvly, she sideslipped out by a gap in the Devil's glen while Sally her nurse was sound asleep in a sloot and, feefee fiefie, fell over a spillway before she found her stride and lay and wriggled in all the stagnant black pools of rainy under a fallow coo and she laughed innocefree with her limbs aloft and a whole drove of maiden hawthorns blushing and looking askance upon her. (FW 204.14–20)

Young Livia falls over a spillway and lies laughing and "innocefree"—free from marriage—wriggling with her limbs aloft in such a foolishly pleasurable way that it makes the maiden hawthorns blush. More scandalous yet, she somehow has landed in the stagnant black pools under a fallow coo—of pleasure perhaps (or beneath a cow, one gathers). Not only is this pleasure not channeled through any apparent male desire, but for Livia it seems to be most threatening in its completely self-directed enjoyment. This kind of sexual or linguistic free play, along the sensate pleasures of language, leaves "askance" the voices of social restrictions. In *Three Essays on Sexuality* (1905), Freud argues that the abandonment of the reproductive function is the common feature of all perversions. He claims that society identifies sexual activity as perverse if it entails giving up the aim of reproduction and pursues pleasure as an aim in itself.[34] As Brown has argued, Joyce was interested in a range of non-reproductive sex, finding even the advertising for birth control titillating.[35] In *Finnegans Wake*, perverse language is more productive than a reduction to univocal meaning, if by "productive" one can understand the proliferation of meanings that resist any crystallization into a single intention or reference.

The musical and physical aspects of Livia's writing is crucially thematized, as well as presented in Joyce's radical style. In erotic touching, she plays music upon her body, a much bawdier extreme of the rhythmic music Stephen Daedalus beats upon his arms in *Stephen Hero*. Mature Livia takes pleasure in music that sounds like another reference to lesbian pleasures:

> For coxyt sake and is that what she is? Botlettle I thought she'd act that loa. Didn't you spot her in her windaug, wubbling up on an osiery chair, with a meusic before her all cunniform letters, pretending to rib-

ble a reedy derg on a fiddle she bogans without a band on? Sure she
can't fiddan a dee, with bow or abandon! Sure, she can't! Tista suck.
Well, I never now heard the like of that! (FW 198.22–28)

Before all her "cunniform" or cunnus-form letters or progeny, she plays
an erotic me-music, the pose of the muse who draws them away from
definitive meanings as she plays upon her own pleasure. What is she
doing, but playing a fiddle, or riddling with the (rain)bow of younger
women? "Tista suck," she may well be. And if she plays with "abandon," we also hear echoes of Willingdon's urge to "get the band up,"
with regards to sexual activity, in book I. Music and sexual play both
enfold and rupture the meaning-sense of language here. Autoeroticism
and narcissism are indistinguishable, again playing on the cliché that
sameness supposedly constructs homosexual desire. And yet Joyce's language—as with Anna Livia's desire—does not collapse into a single
sameness or a homogeneous mass of non-meaning. Meaning is alternately dispersed and extended by the cross-referentiality that resists
attempts to separate autoeroticism from homosexuality and from heterosexual desires.

In contrast to Joyce's permissiveness toward lesbian desire, potentially erotic relations between men are constantly subjected to separation, which is reasserted at such a level of intensity that violence often
erupts. Repeatedly, suggestions of male-male association meet immediate resistance, particularly where a mirror effect occurs. Twins and doubles react to a double threat, that which might belie individual unique-
ness (so that sameness poses a threat of erasure or obfuscation of a
distinctive identity) and that which might also suggest an erotic association, a narcissistic desire for the self mapped over the other.

Narcissism, as a compelling sameness, is a nightmare between men
in the *Wake*, and aggressive gestures throw up radical distinctions whenever such a possibility threatens. This is similar, and I am venturing historically related, to a phenomenon Eve Sedgwick has observed in
Romantic novels, which she terms the "paranoid Gothic," where "a
male hero is in a close, usually murderous relation to another male figure, in some respects his 'double,' to whom he seems to be mentally
transparent."[36] In this scenario, homosexual panic transforms into a dif-
ferentiating aggression, much as in *Finnegans Wake*, although Joyce
plays less upon the problem of mental transparency between twins.
Sedgwick rightly points out that critics need not read these moments as
psychological clarifications of some gay consciousness (much as Freud
seems to), but rather more fruitfully and historically should understand
paranoia and homosexual panic as problems arising from "the entire
spectrum of male homosocial organization" as it insists on heterosexuality and stakes itself in a polarization against homosexual relations.[37]

Two forms of aggression in the *Wake* most consistently allow male-male relations to maintain a repression of homosexual transfigurations: competition for female attention and war upon the father. This continues a trajectory from *Ulysses*, where, as Jennifer Levine has argued, the line between hetero- and homoerotic pleasure blurs when men form homosocial bonds around the images of women.[38] In the *Wake*, homosocial tensions are even more closely linked to eroticism that troubles the line between hetero- and homosexual desires. In "The Mime," for example, while Chuff and Glugg compete for Issy's attentions, verbal innuendos mark the return of a repressed sense of homosexual possibility. If Chuff is yet another version of huffy Shaun, his name also invokes *chuff chums*, a term for homosexuals.[39] While the innuendoes accompanying Chuff and Glugg's competitions for the rainbow girls in "The Mime" suggest a homoerotic repression, this suggestion becomes humorously more pronounced through an excess of parapractic slips of the tongue in Shaun's telling of the tale of Burrus and Caseous in *Finnegans Wake* I, iv. These two figures, who are parodies of Brutus and Cassius, alternately sing the praises of one "sweet Margareen" and then make war upon the father, temporarily bonding before their displaced desires return to resplinter them again.

As characterological constructs of Shaun and Shem—created within Shaun's defense against his double and brother—Burrus and Caseous show signs of homosexual panic, being repeatedly troubled by sexual innuendoes that Shaun seeks to suppress. The characters' overwrought doubling forms a manifest link between narcissism and strict interpretations of the mimetic project, so that the scenario functions as a model of aggressive and overreaching parody, in contrast to Joyce's own parodic gestures in the passage. Moreover, Joyce's association of agonism with homophobic anxiety functions as a nodal pressure point for the language of the *Wake*, where attempts to control "perverse" or transgressive language are undermined by the repeated parapraxes of Burrus' pronouncements in favor of traditional channels for sexuality—marriage and institutionally structured propagation (i.e., the family). As heterosexual desire is given a name, homosexual references parodically undermine the implicit gesture of repression, and the line between hetero- and homoerotics is called into question, riveting the more general problem of distinctions and interpretation in the *Wake*. Faced with indistinction, the paranoiac steps up adamant claims of difference, reflecting on an inner failure to accept and comprehend the split within himself. On Lacan's analysis, paranoia therein becomes a representational problem:

> At the basis of paranoia itself, which nevertheless seems to us to be animated by belief, there reigns the phenomenon of the *Unglauben*. This is not the *not believing in it*, but the absence of one of the terms of belief, of the term in which is designated the division of the subject. If,

indeed, there is no belief that is full and entire, it is because there is no belief that does not presuppose in its basis that the ultimate dimension that it has to reveal is strictly correlative with the moment when its meaning is about to fade away.[40]

Repeatedly in his works Lacan identifies a basic ambivalence within the subject, a split between that which is conscious and that which exceeds the subject's control and knowledge—the element of alienation within the self. Here, this split circulates around the tension between belief and uncertainty. Unable to accept the inevitability of some failing within belief, "the moment when its meaning is about to fade away," the paranoiac angrily reacts to destabilized language and representation. The pun, the split word, easing toward the arbitrariness of sound play, would therefore provoke in the paranoiac the greatest distraction.

The split within desire is also, according to Freud, what so troubles the paranoiac. In the essay on Leonardo da Vinci, which Joyce owned, Freud argues that if a subject does not make a homosexual object choice he always either "still adheres to it in his unconscious or else protects himself against it by vigorous counter-attitudes."[41] As Sedgwick argues, however, this is more a symptom of the historical construction of sexuality that an abstract form of desire. In a homosocial culture that insists on male heterosexuality, any betrayal of desire might inspire a cycling escalation of phobia and insistence. In Shaun's stories and lectures, homosexual panic as a form of homophobia is confronted repeatedly by the parapraxes that suggest the ever-present possibility of homosexual desire. And the crucial tension that I am pressing here is that of whether the paranoiac is typed as homosexual or homophobic. For Freud, he is implicitly both, as the paranoiac's neurosis arises predominantly from *repression* of homosexual desire.[42] That is, some primary ambivalence, a split within the self that all subjects experience, antagonizes the paranoiac. For Freud (at times) this ambivalence is necessarily the undecipherable splinter of desire that shifts between hetero- and homosexual foci. For Shaun, this splinter functions as a form of internal betrayal, as he struggles to control his inner consciousness. The "betrayal" within language that Joyce so often marks is itself encoded within the division between twins, who function both as distinct characters and, at other times, as one mind divided against itself.

Burrus and Caseous appear after the last of the riddles of *Finnegans Wake* I, iv broaches the problem of "byhold"ing at once the split or twain parts of the mind:

> if a human being duly fatigued by his dayety in the sooty . . . could . . . byhold at ones what is main and why tis twain . . . *what* would that fargazer seem to seemself to seem seeming of, dimm it all?

Answer: A collideorscape! (FW 143.4 . . . 28, my ellipses)

In question (and answer) number nine of *Finnegans Wake* I, vi, HCE appears gazing into the mirror of his "seemself," seeing the "twain" parts he struggles to "byhold at ones," giving, not a smooth composite portrait of contrary selves combined, but a "collideorscape"—the colliding image of his psychological landscape.[43] As Clive Hart suggests, HCE is "seeing in the mirror of the kaleidoscope an inversion of his ego and/or id" while he narcissistically, also, gazes at himself.[44] In the passage that addresses Burrus and Caseous, Shaun is, as John Gordon notes, attempting to refute the allegation that he and Shem are mirror selves, twins and doubles.[45] Narcissism, as a scenario of troubled mimesis founded on the act of scapegoating, is therefore also put to question.[46] This problematic form of representation draws to it a tangle of related desires: the desire for individuation, the desire for a woman, and the urge to destroy the father. The articulation of each of these desires is punctuated with reversals punning on homosexual desire. It is perhaps no coincidence that Shaun chooses to employ an allegory of desire cast in metaphors of eating.

With the tale of Burrus and Caseous (and their love for Margareen), Joyce comically overlaps the story of Brutus and Cassius's conspiracy against Julius Caesar with culinary metaphors, punning Brutus into "Burrus" and Cassius into "Caseous," bringing out a story of butter (French *beurre*) and cheese (*caseous*: cheesy). Shaun, in his struggle to distinguish himself (as "pure" butter) from Shem (as gaseous, vile, and derivative) invokes, albeit messily, the law of the excluded middle, such that binaries must be distinct and free from any third space or hybridity:

> I cannot now have or nothave a piece of cheeps in your pocket at the same time and with the same manners as you can now nothalf or half the cheek apiece I've in mind unless Burrus and Caseous have not or not have seemaultaneously sysentangled themselves, selldear to soldthere, once in the dairy days of buy and buy. (FW 161.9–14)

The piece of "cheeps"—as cheap cheese in the pocket—has to persist by the law of the excluded middle, so that one cannot both have and not have it, just as one must either "half" it or leave it whole. Contrarily, however, Joyce fools this notion with its very language: he changes *and* to *or*, so that one cannot both have it *or* not have it. The binary is not so securely split; it is, rather, a choice that Shaun lacks. And as Shaun attempts to deny any contiguity between himself and Shem, he is also endeavoring to excise the bit of Shem he finds in himself. But if Burrus, like Shaun, moralistically interrupts all potential falls into "low" and cheesy exchanges (with a kind of constant "but!"),[47] the two coconspirators Burrus and Caseous still have a hard time, being "seemaultaneously sysentangled themselves." The first level—the speaker's predominant meaning, prior to his parapraxes—is the thought that Burrus and Cassius might (or must) simultaneously disentangle themselves from one another. Nevertheless, they only "seem" to be simultaneous, or twinlike, just as they fail to disentangle identities, turning rather to integrate (Greek: *sys* = together)[48] themselves. The language doubles irreconcilably here, as do Burrus and Caseous. As Shaun fails to disentangle Shem's image from his own, references to a dreaded intimacy with Shem's (mirrorlike, male) body erupt on a latent level of reference. "Cheek" hits a first register with cheese, but it is also a crude term for buttocks, slipping into sexual innuendo.[49] To make matters worse, *cheese* is crude slang for the residue that clings under the foreskin: smegma.[50] If Caseous also echoes *gaseous* at moments, then Joyce is riddling the scenario with puns on the bodily grotesque, and Burrus, as "Butter," accrues the rather obvious (Butt) locus of one of Joyce's many physical preoccupations.

The revulsion is too much for Shaun, the doubling too terrible. He argues that if they are not wholly distinct, Burrus and Caseous operate much as an original and its parody might:

> Burrus, let us like to imagine, is a genuine prime, the real choice, full of natural greace, the mildest of milkstoffs yet unbeaten as a risicide and, of course, obsoletely unadulterous whereat Caseous is obversely the revise of him and in fact not an ideal choose by any meals. (FW 161.15–19)

Shaun may be feeling vulnerable in the rear—he even slips and refers to himself as "grease" (possibly Greek) and "milkstoffing," echoing *milksop*. Moreover, the metaphor of eating cannot but help Shaun's anxiety, and a paranoid struggle to both patrol his boundaries and distinguish his identity ensues. Is it surprising then that as Caseous is associated with gaseous Shem, the ever-perfect Shaun is, like Burrus, so inflexibly moral as to be near "risicide," or killed with self-parody (Latin: *risus* = laugh)[51]?

The tension between twinned factions functions much like the troubled line between representation and its original. Shaun's attack on Shem echoes Plato's denigration of art as a mere copy of external likenesses that degrades the original, substituting a beautiful shell that lacks *eidos*, essence, idea, or—in language—original intention. With Shem and Shaun, the question may be which is the stable portrait and which the slide into denigrative parody. Here, Caseous is much like a parody of Burrus, cheese being a reworked revision of butter, never as "prime" or pure as his brother or partner, Burrus. As Shaun struggles to label Burrus "pure" and Caseous as secondary, verbal denotations and connotations intertwine, so that the reader must ask which is the primary meaning of Shaun's words, and wonder if homosexual innuendo might not supplant the more innocent or pure design.

And on an ever-more-thematic level, the scenario is shot through with this struggle to supplant (by betraying) an original authority—the calling into question of any authorization. Burrus's "risicide" also refers to the regicide for which Brutus and Cassius were cast into hell and, in Dante's *Inferno*, condemned to be chewed in Satan's mouth. "It is why," Glasheen notes, "they appear as decently chewable foods—butter and cheese, Burrus and Caseous."[52] The murder of Caesar here transforms into a second form of binary aggression, where twins or coconspirators in the *Wake* often recombine in order to face off against the father.[53] Caesar here is "sisar," and he is cast as a main role in the family salad, made up of "Murphybuds" (potatoes) and "hot young Capels and Lettucia" (FW 161.29). "Pfarrer Salamoss" is attacked by Burrus and Caseous, who are rebelling against his authority. Within the family salad then, "there's many a split pretext bowl and jowl" (FW 161.31–32); so that what was perhaps once lying "cheek by jowl" in the womb or simpler terms of friendship and supposed unity is inevitably split and even warring. Thus, in "sisars" salad hierarchy prepares to fall.

Joyce works a clever triple pun here on "Brutus," drawing in references to as many as three different figures who struggled with scenarios involving betrayal and conspiracy. The most consistent referent would be Marcus Junius Brutus (also known as Quintus Caepio Brutus) who lived 85–42 B.C., near Philippi, Macedonia. Brutus had been pardoned by Caesar after joining Pompey in a rebellion against him earlier, but in 44 B.C. he joined ranks with Gaius Cassius Longinus's plot to oust Caesar, finding his dictatorship too stringent and hoping to shift the republic toward democracy.[54] Tyrants are, in the Burrus and Caseous passage, said to be "unbeurrable" (FW 162.2), and one wonders if they are sweet or foul ("brutherscutch or puir tyron," FW 163.8–9). If Brutus seems to have felt Caesar too "unbeurrable," still he operates as a betrayer, too, given Caesar's prior pardon. In a possible secondary pun, Caesar was intimately betrayed by Decimus Junius Brutus Albinus, who had been a protege of his before joining the conspiracy for his assassination.[55] It seems most likely, however, that Joyce is invoking still another Brutus, Lucius Junius Brutus, of the late sixth century B.C. This Brutus as the supposed founder of Rome, having ousted the Etruscan king Lucius Tarquinius Superbus. He suffered the same fate as "sisar" in the tale, as records claim that he condemned his own sons to death when they joined in a conspiracy to restore the Tarquins.[56] Finally, Burrus and Caseous are also, in part, Ireland, as "sell high, buy low" (FW 161.13 "selldear to soldthere") alludes to Parnell's famous remark, "when you sell, get my price."[57]

Anxiety about betrayal most often circulates around the construction of paranoia in Joyce. For Shaun, this splintering of positive and negative identities (good leader and tyrant) functions as a form of internal betrayal, as he shifts back to his concern for control over his inner consciousness. Although here, after one last blow at Caseous, he appears to resignedly gesture toward acceptance of contraries:

> Thus we cannot escape our likes and mislikes, exiles or ambusheers, beggar and neighbour and—this is where the dimeshow advertisers advance the temporal relief plea—let us be tolerant of antipathies. *Nex quovis burro num fit mercaseus?* I am not hereby giving my final endorsement to the learned ignorants of the Cusanus philosophism. (FW 163.12–17)

McHugh notes the overlap of the last passage and the Latin phrase, "ex quovis butyrum num fit merus caseus": "from any butter there is not made pure cheese." *Nex*, however, means murder (Latin), suggesting that violence against the one (tyrannical Burrus? is he?) will not set the cheesy one right. Shaun, however, resists any suggestion that he "give an unconditional sinequam to the heroicised furibouts of the Nolanus theory" (FW 163.23–24), and indeed he is here struggling against Bruno of Nolan's theory that contraries combine. Joyce once summed Bruno's work in a letter as "a kind of dualism—every power in nature must evolve an opposite in order to realise itself and opposition brings reunion etc. etc."[58] If Shaun here lumps Bruno (the Nolan) with Nicholas of Cusa, Joyce also arguably thought of Bruno and Nicholas of Cusa together as two adherents to the "coincidence of contraries" position, since Cusa's work on the coincidence of contraries in God is believed to have influenced Bruno.[59] Shaun, however, humorously qualifies his concession to Cusa, saying that he hopes to eventually prove that "both products of our social stomach . . . are mutuearly polarised the incompatabilily of any delusional acting as ambivalent to the fixation of his pivotism" (FW 163.34–164.3). Even as Joyce introduces the question of how one should interpret the "coincidence of contraries" theory—as full combination or complex heterogeneity—Shaun oscillates between interpretive extremes. It is no use pretending an ambivalence about the fixation of Shaun's binary; he must radically distinguish himself from Shem. And this adamant denial of split reference and ambiguity gives rise to increasingly violent verbal gestures that create stereotypes, denigrative parodies, and instigate a variety of wars. It is no coincidence that Shem's turn to violent verbal expression is accompanied by a denial of bodily desires, alphabetic slips, and pleasurable puns.

For Shaun, contraries do *not* combine; rather, they create a competitive ambivalence that must be controlled. This is accomplished not by associative acceptance, as in the case of Anna Livia, but by rigidifying hierarchical structures and aggressively denigrating Shem and elevating Shaun himself. As Lacan notes, in instances of doubling, aggression is almost inevitable: "The subject's desire can only be confirmed in this relation through a competition, through an absolute rivalry with the other, in view of the object toward which it is directed. And each time we get close, in a given subject, to this primitive alienation, the most radical aggression arises—the desire for the disappearance of the other in so far as he supports the subject's desire."[60]

As soon as Shaun resolves his problem of contraries, temporarily accepting the combination but theoretically resisting, he has to introduce the next level of restorative heterosexual "fixation": "Positing, as above, too males pooles, the one the pictor of the other and the omber the *Skotia* of the one, and looking wantingly around our undistributed middle between males we feel we must waistfully woent a female to focus" (FW 164.4–7). As he attempts to posit two male poles or opposites who mirror one another (like Narcissus to his pool), Shaun requires a female "to focus" what I am supposing is their (hetero-defined) identities. To oblige them, "the cowrymaid M.," otherwise known as "Margareen," appears. Music overhead plays "*I cream for thee, Sweet Margareen . . . O Margareena! O Margareena! Still in the bowl is left a lump of gold!*" (FW 164.18–20). She is, of course, fake butter, so a tricky substitute for Burrus. She will be later called "Margery," slang for an effeminate in the early twentieth century.[61] Moreover, there is some question as to Margareen's true sex. As a parenthetical aside assures us:

> (I am closely watching Master Pules, as I have regions to suspect from my post that her "little man" is a secondary schoolteacher under the boards of education, a voted disciple of Infantulus who is being utilised thus publicly by the *seducente infanta* to conceal her own more mascular personality by flaunting frivolish finery over men's inside clothes, for the femininny of that totamulier will always lack the musculink of a verumvirum. My solotions for the proper parturience of matres and the education of micturious mites must stand over from the moment till I tackle this tickler hussy for occupying my uttentions.) (FW 166.20–29)

If *Finnegans Wake* often works to blur sexual dichotomies and to frustrate attempts to demarcate male and female identities, the reader is here left with an uncanny uncertainty as to whether the object of voiced sexual desire is male or female. "Master Pooles" may be referred to those two who are "mutuearly polarised," the poles of Shem and Shaun in one here. And as McHugh suggests, it might also be one of Joyce's jabs at Wyndham Lewis, who mocked Joyce as "James Pulman" ("Pulley") in *Childermas*.[62] But "pooles" and "pules" also puns on "poule"—the

French for hen, suggesting the emersion of the brother's identities in ALP's own. Contrarily, the figure who is apparently masculine is suddenly "her," if prior reference functions, and I gather that "she" is the object of Burrus's and Caseous's attentions. They are a "little man"—a young boy she has seduced—who is used by her to hide her "more mascular" personality. She *or he* wears "frivolous finery" over men's underclothes. This casts aspersions on Margery's sex—is "she" really a woman? Are they/the "little man" really men? As the voice (perhaps Issy's) asserts, "the femininny of that totamulier will always lack the musculink of a verumvirum." This translates roughly into "the femininity of a complete woman (Latin: tota mulier) will always lack the masculinity of a real man (Latin: verus vir)."[63] My guess is that this is a suggestion that Margareena's femininity reeks of "mascular" airs, being too virile, in effect, not to be male. Still, the referent is uncertain and may undermine the masculinity of the twins, as a "masculink." What is clear, however, is that Margareen (Margery) fails to help Burrus and Caseous ward off homosexual panic, and the emotion transforms into competitive aggression.

The turning of Burrus and Caseous to attack and deprecate Margareen is, in a partial sense, a replay of the "risicide" of sisar, given the pun on "sister" in that name. Here, Margareen may in fact be "The Very Picture of a Needless Woman" (FW 165.15–16), if her presence is necessary more as mediation of desire. Sedgwick points out that "'to cuckold' is by definition a sexual act, performed on a man, by another man" and she argues that its central position in a piece of literature "emphasizes heterosexual love chiefly as a strategy of homosocial desire."[64] Where women are sometimes celebrated with apparent appreciation, misogyny is still a component, and here it quickly breaks out. Margareen is promptly stereotyped as a whore, "whose types may be met with in any public garden" (FW 166.5–6), and her fickleness provides the core of triangulation: "Margareena she's very fond of Burrus but, alick and alack! she velly fond of chee" (FW 166.30–31). Her split affection instigates yet another conflict between the coconspirators, who now turn on one another in a competitive gesture. When the two fight over her, Shaun eventually reclaims his word (and wife-*as*-word) as "sacred" and unchanging. Shaun's voice ends the episode with a lecture on the necessity of controlling one's words and women: "My unchanging Word is sacred. The word is my Wife, to expose and expound, to vend and to velnerate, and may the curlews crown our nuptias! Till Breath us depart! Wamen. Beware would you change with my years" (FW 167.28–31). Shaun's concluding lecture—to the rainbow girls—asserts the necessity of consolidating authorial position over the word *and* women. The tension between women's associative unravelings of "productive" forms of meaning, and the subsequent disruption of the interpretive attempt to control and possess language, is thus answered, in Joyce's parody, by a paranoiac insistence on absolute control. But such radical gestures break with the more rhythmic and sensate body of words (and the body in possessive focus), thereby losing the thing for which they grasp.

As the troubled tension surrounding the (non)differentiation between homo- and heteroerotics is repeatedly refigured in Joyce's writing, so too does his experiment with parody pull more radically against the paranoiac's attempt to delineate boundaries. I am suggesting that in *Finnegans Wake* narcissistic models of a psychologically inflected mimesis work in radical contradistinction to a paranoid mode of textuality, where single meanings are insisted upon, desires denied, and identities fixed. The paranoiac resists any social attempts at objectification, much as in *Finnegans Wake* HCE resists society's move to assess, judge, and assign a representation to him. As the paranoiac anxiously endeavors to evade social judgment (and the pain of his own superego), he himself becomes aggressively certain of his own assessments. Recall Roustang's characterization of the paranoiac as one who needs a persecutor to secure his own boundaries. If establishing the certainty of one's own existence is the primary goal of paranoia, the paranoiac's most likely opponent would be that which lies opposite of certainty—the possibility of chance and arbitrary occurrence. Just as paranoiacs cannot accept subjective transience, they cannot likewise mime the necessary shrug that pays tribute to chance. Anything that evades logic or reason would therefore threaten the paranoiac, even as, paradoxically, he/she requires this threat to establish his/her identity.

Paranoia may therefore be understood not only as a mental illness caught up in issues of control and defense, but also as a form of textuality that repeatedly and compulsively stresses the intentional and interpretive control of each word and belief issued forth. As the medium through which the paranoiac initially engages his/her supposed nemesis, language would haunt the paranoiac, being as it is a tool that so often evades control. Working to press language toward its more logical or rational potential, the paranoiac turns away from a word's playful and coincidental effects as they arise from the supposedly faulty body of language, its misspells, seductions, and crossed references. The paranoiac will likewise try to fix representation as a stable, objective form, losing the lyrical rhythms Joyce so richly works in. As literary interpretation and forms of analysis slide away from more flexible gestures of mediation, they run the risk of falling into paranoid extremes.

The undecidability that haunts the paranoiac therefore transmutes into a distrust of representation. Lacan's analysis of the splinter within belief translates into a problem of interpretability, such that the paranoiac insists upon the certitude of his interpretation (as paranoids classically do) in a gesture that marks the denial of arbitrariness, pure sensate pleasure, and non-meaning. In this manner, paranoia also functions as the structural opposite to a key term in Joyce's aesthetic practice—parody. Both words take their initial stem, *para-*, from the Greek for contiguity (alongside another), while paranoia's second root, *nous* (mind), specifies that one is in a sense beside oneself mentally, not fully centered nor clear of boundaries. The subject is in effect doubled or blurred. Parody, on the other hand, indicates a critical contiguity of one text (or subtext) to another, such that identities are overlapping without full distinction nor collapsible into sameness. Moreover, in Joyce it marks the presence of a rhythmic process of (dis)identification and gestural embodiment.

Joyce's radical experiment with language and forms of historical narration in *Finnegans Wake* might then be implicated in the struggle against paranoid control of his medium. Indeed, representations of homophobic patrol of physical and psychic boundaries function as a critical hinge in his move away from univocal forms of narration and into the textual *jouissance* that circulates around Anna Livia's and Issy's words and has been so famously described by Kristeva, Cixous, and others. The loosening of control, however, threatens to dissolve an identifiable position for the other, potentially resulting in a narcissistic form of communication that never extends beyond a benign, self-fulfilling interpretation. The narcissistic text cannot be opened through interpretation, just as the paranoid form resists any reading but the author's own (which can never be surrendered to the reader for judgment). Narcissism and paranoia thus define the extremes of Joyce's gestural politics, and the *Wake* moves between invoking stereotypes and pressing toward verbal transgression.

In III, iii, when asked by the four judges whether "any orangepeelers or greengoaters appear periodically up your sylvan family tree" (FW 522.16–17),[65] HCE responds "Buggered if I know!" While on the surface the judges seem merely to be asking if there are any Protestant constabularies (orange-peelers)[66] or naive fools (since "green" has meant naive since the eighteenth century, and to "Play the goat" is to be a fool), they may also be wanting to know if there were any lesbians, "orange" being slang for female pudend from the Restoration period, or if there are not also Irishmen interested in "goaters" or posteriors. HCE responds with his own double language:

—It all depends on how much family silver you want for a nass-and-pair. Hah!
—What do you mean, sir, behind your hah! You don't hah to do thah, you know, snapograph.
—Nothing, sir. Only a bone moving into place. Blotogaff. Hahah!
—Whahat?
—Are you to have all the pleasure quizzing on me? I didn't say it aloud, sir. I have something inside of me talking to myself. (FW 522.18–26)

The *blot* was low slang for the anus, by the 1930s, and HCE teases the tribunal by pimpingly pressing for how much "family silver" they will offer for a nice pair ("nass-and-pair"), before shifting to references to the "bone" (penis) and ass. But more troubling still to the tribunal is the difficulty HCE has in telling any direct truth. Engaged in a narcissistic form of self-directed talk, HCE refuses to make the judges the sole reason for his words. His own pleasure counts at least as much. This self-directed pleasure is rewarded then with the usual stereotypes in return:

—You're a nice third degree witness, faith! But this is no laughing matter. Do you think we are tonedeafs in our noses to boot? Can you not distinguish the sense, prain, for the sound, bray? You have homosexual catheis of empathy between narcissism of the expert and steatopygic invertedness. Get yourself psychoanolised! (FW 522.27–32)

The one who cannot keep "the sense" and "the sound" separate must be guilty of homosexuality, that which murmurs at the margins and in the parapraxes. HCE is said to be guilty of stereotypical invertedness, or rather "steatopygic," which is defined as "abnormal protuberance of buttocks." What would be hidden comes to view, and what the judges wish rather to comprehend ("What do you mean, sir, behind your hah!") fails to arrive.

Textual perversity is here sketched out as a kind of self-enclosed pleasure, the game of the narcissist. Homosexuality is taken as a way in which one lacks distinctions and turns language narcissistically in on itself. By weaving *gay clichés* into the *Wake*, Joyce is thus addressing the potential critique of narcissistic art, which uses the mirror only to reproduce the self, and which can never speak beyond the economy of its own pleasure. What is troubling about narcissism, in the strictest sense, is that, as a form of self-love turned inward, it avoids the social relations, is more imaginary than reality-based in its affections, feeding its own desires without need of external input. Narcissistic art would be fantasy, escapism, utopia, in that it would seek its ego ideal by mapping it over the other, never truly seeing or encountering the other. Homosexuality/heterosexuality has been therefore construed along the axis of imaginary/real, an axis crucially problematized by *Finnegans Wake*. The text plays out Joyce's own sometimes private pleasure; but language itself, wrought as it is with unconscious desires and swerves, pursues its own sensate association. *Finnegans Wake* in that sense allows language to rise off the canvas in the intensity of its own effects. If one were "to communicake with original sinse" (FW 239.1–2), one would perhaps reclaim some original intent or purer form of language. But the terms are already adulterated, and to press for such "original *sin*se" commits the sin of performing an aggressive separation from and exclusion of the sensate, disruptive elements of language that make up its medium. And it would be also to exclude laughter, that which shakes the boundaries between self/other, will/desire, meaning/pleasure, and a range of separations. If "this kissing wold's full of killing fellows" (FW 248.24–25), Joyce parodies such a bond, adding both humor and pleasant non-sense in an oscillation between aggressive gestures that threaten to crystallize patterns into stereotypes (and words into clichés) and the movement toward release of competitive boundaries, so that he may, in that sense, "entwine our arts with laughters low!" (FW 259.7–8).

CHAPTER 5

In the Wake of the Nation: Joyce's Response to Irish Nationalism

In 1909, during a brief sojourn in Dublin, James Joyce wrote to Nora, back in Trieste, his impressions of the hotel where she had once worked: "The place," he says, "is very Irish. I have lived so long abroad and in so many countries that I can feel at once the voice of Ireland in anything. The disorder of the table was Irish, the wonder in the faces also, the curious-looking eyes of the woman herself and her waitress. A strange land this is to me though I was born in it and bear one of its old names."[1] On that same visit to Dublin, however, Joyce also writes to Nora,

> I felt proud to think that my son . . . will always be a foreigner in Ireland, a man speaking another language and bred in a different tradition.
> I loathe Ireland and the Irish. They themselves stare at me in the street though I was born among them. Perhaps they read my hatred of them in my eyes. I see nothing on every side of me but the image of the adulterous priest and his servants and of sly deceitful women.[2]

Joyce moves between two extreme views of Irishness, both of which hinge on different understandings of strangeness and are repeatedly implicated in the act of stereotyping. On the one hand, the Irish are imaginative and even magical, identified by a certain voice and look of "wonder." They are, in a sense, both "curious-looking" and curious. And then again, they are strange and "foreign," threateningly given to betrayal both in instances of sexual relations and in terms of politics. And indeed, as Seamus Deane has suggested, foreignness may very well lie at the heart of the Irish relation to language, so that Joyce's dual consciousness defines both his relation to Ireland and his resistance to racism and stereotype.[3] Yet Joyce's feelings toward Ireland were never exactly nationalistic in nature. He alternately loved and loathed his homeland, praising it at times and then, as in a letter to Stanislaus, condemning it as an "ignorant and famine-stricken and treacherous country" (*Letters*, 2:288). Read through the eyes of Joyce, the Irish are alternately too distant and too familiar, too morally rigid and too dissolute. He cannot hold them at a distance without stereotyping them, nor can he be subsumed comfortably into their national identity. Irishness thus becomes a notion defined in and through contraries for Joyce, and in that sense his own writing is definitively "Irish," weaving as it does the alternating idealism and betrayal of a stream of notions that eventually create a new view of cultural, national, and group identity. I will be pursuing here Joyce's treatment of Irish nationalism, first as a topic of changing emotional affect; then as structural disruption of perception in the "Cyclops" episode of *Ulysses*; and finally as it influences the polysemous language and voices of *Finnegans Wake*. Without an image of the nation to unequivocally embrace, Joyce's struggle to represent Irishness necessitated a more general revision of representational processes in his writing, so that parody became central to Irishness, as "hyber irish" splinters into several hybrid identities. In *Finnegans Wake*, this link between Joyce's early impression of nationalism and his parody culminates in a revision of "hyber Irish" language in order to evade paranoid nationalistic extremes. Joyce there struggles to remake Irishness in a revisionary understanding of betrayal, not in terms of antiloyalty but as a transgression of limits and a mockery of societal (and readerly) expectations.

In a sense, Joyce began his career as an ardent voice of disillusioned Irish nationalism. In the summer of 1891, at nine years of age, his first experiments with poetry and prose culminated in a poem entitled "Et Tu, Healy."[4] This piece eulogized Charles Stewart Parnell, who had died that year after public scandal over his long-standing affair with Katharine O'Shea brought on his political ruin.[5] As historical narratives now suggest, Parnell had led Ireland to the brink of Home Rule in the 1870s and '80s, and many Irishmen—including Joyce's father—had been shocked and angered by his dismissal from Irish politics. While no copy of "Et Tu, Healy" remains, Joyce's brother Stanislaus remembers it as "a diatribe against the supposed traitor, Tim Healy, who had ratted at the bidding of the Catholic bishops and become a virulent enemy of Parnell."[6] If this was one of Joyce's first artistic efforts, it was also his first publication: John Joyce had it printed and circulated to all of his friends that year.[7] Although juvenalia arguably counts for little in the balance of Joyce's extensive mature work, the poem reflects a formative moment in Joyce's attitude toward Irish politics, given that he persistently writes Parnell's fall and loss into all of his works, even as his treatment of it shifts from diatribe to humorous recapitulation.[8] *Finnegans Wake*, as Joyce's last work, is still peppered with figures who stutter Parnell's stutter, deny accusations of sexual infamy, and fall victim to conspiracies in Phoenix Park.[9] Stanislaus interprets the significance of Parnell for his brother strictly as a lesson in social hypocrisy and betrayal, but, as I will be arguing, Joyce's early impression of Irish politics guided his treatment of Irish nationalism toward textual gestures that radically oscillate between sentimental memory and defensive distantiation.[10] Parnell's specter left no simple mark; rather, it constituted the beginning of a parodic quandary, to which objects of desire and admiration were subsequently subjected. In Joyce's work, all configurations of belief, commitment, and sentiment are thereafter split. And although many modernists rebelled against the sentimental specifically in its relation to the *domestic* sphere, Joyce most ardently resists that term in its link to nationalist nostalgia, which in his work is both fetishistically denied and insistently replayed.[11] National sentiment may be less a full denial of parodic fracturing, although it insistently invokes the impossible desire to retrieve unified identity, a fantasy of original and pure Irishness in some pre-post-colonial unity that never, for Ireland, existed.[12]

Joyce's revision of Irish history and communal identity presents an alternative view of nationalism and cultural identity, notions that have been placed under increasing scrutiny by contemporary critics.[13] Joyce initiates a complex critique of nationalist extremes and builds, out of that critique, a new concept of interaction between culture and subjects that calls into question the nature of group identity and ideological subscription. Groups become constitutively porous and unstable, and yet their galvanizing force creates new representations that continually recycle and renew identities forged by the associative link between subjectivity and communal identity. And this revision of group identity is integrally related to Joyce's conception of the literary project. Colin MacCabe, for example, finds that "rather than engaging in the direct espousal of political positions, Joyce's work poses new questions about the relation between reader and text," such that Joyce eschews any gesture toward a metadiscourse or any imaginary position of unitary subjects.[14] Thus he makes the reader aware of his/her own construction within contradictory discourses, creating the "conscience" or consciousness of an audience he could not locate, for a form of political awareness that did not yet exist.[15]

There has been a major impetus to reclaim Joyce as Irish in his politics, but too often such endeavors have turned only a blind eye to the implications of Joyce's parody. In 1980, Dominic Manganiello published a book-length study of Joyce's politics, in which he worked to counter previous treatments of Joyce as an apolitical writer, arguing that Joyce was strongly invested in Irish politics while critical of its extremes.[16] What has followed, in recent years, is a long overdue movement to reclaim Joyce as Irish, political, and engaged with the issue of his national identity throughout his career. Critics have focused attention on Joyce's use of Irish myth (Tymoczko), his manipulation of language (Deane), and his criticism of racism and imperialism (Cheng).[17] These studies are for the most part cautious in their claims, aware of Joyce's ambivalent eye as it was directed toward Ireland. Some have, however, gone to extremes, so that Emer Nolan attempts to reclaim from the margins of Joyce's works a sympathy for Irish nationalist separatism and even, at moments, for violent forms of rebellion.[18] While I take exception to Nolan's work, my intervention here is not to roll back the long-overdue scrutiny of Joyce's relations to Ireland, but to focus specific attention on the ways in which Joyce incorporates and changes the effects of his ambivalence toward Ireland and Irish nationalism. For it would be too tempting to forget his complex parody of Irish nationalism in the face of the recent recovery of Joyce's Irishness, even given Joyce's tendency to disrupt categories and play out elaborate mutations of received ideas. Joyce's politics are not readily defined by the ideas that are most familiar in our understanding of national sentiments and political positions. Rather, he initiates a complex critique of nationalist extremes and builds, out of that critique, a new concept of interaction between culture and individual subjects that calls into question the nature of group identity and ideological subscription. This critical reconsideration culminates in *Finnegans Wake*, where Joyce infuses betrayal into the typological constructs that enable stereotyping, thereby diffusing the borders of both reified national identity and his own stereotypes of Irishness.

Joyce's political critique of nationalistic adherence is constructed through his literary writing, where the stakes of his own artistic identity are caught up in his relation to future audiences and past contexts. Politics here are specifically tied to the cultural implications of Joyce's literary work, a link that for Joyce was always especially troubling. His split response to Ireland was in fact complicated by the drive for a nationalist art, which was initiated in 1842 by Thomas Davis's Young Ireland movement. Backed by their paper, *The Nation*, the movement called for independence not only in political action but in thought, arguing that the Irish needed to develop a sense of cultural nationalism that would be distinctly their own. Although disbanded a few years later, the Young Ireland movement had a lasting impact on the ways in which Irish literature has been valued.[19] Joyce is sensitive to Ireland's struggle toward independence but leery of "a narrow and hysterical nationality" that arises from Thomas Davis's call for the arts to fuel patriotism (CW 82).[20] According to Ellmann, Joyce sought admission to the Irish Revival's inner circle in 1902, a group less inclined to radical nationalism. However, after initial gestures of interest and support were extended (and, in some cases, retracted), Joyce and the Revivalists grew disenchanted with one another. To the end of his life, Joyce held a sliver of disdain for the movement, refusing to be identified with it and rejecting Yeats's later invitation to join the Academy of Irish Letters.[21] Mary Reynolds has noted, however, that while Joyce may have taken distance from the Revival out of ill-ease with a naive sentimentalization of the rural Irish, he also worked to exceed Yeats and Synge in his ability to represent West Ireland's allure in "The Dead."[22] It is within this double gesture of adherence and resistance that his Irish politics resides.

This tension within politics becomes explicit in moments of interpretive doubling, which Joyce initiates in *Dubliners*. There, he begins to sort out the tensions of his resistance to literary nationalism and his attachment to the figure of Parnell. The results are several stories that hold open split possibilities, denying any attempt to clarify a final decision. In "Ivy Day in the Committee Room," he paints a bleak view of Irish political canvassing in 1904, where the atmosphere of uncertain alliances and lukewarm politics maintains. The story concludes upon a fine irony, a moment of aesthetic approval that may affirm or undermine Joe Hynes's praise of Parnell. Hynes creates a precarious tie between the various canvassers in the room, as he recites his poem, "The Death of Parnell." The piece functions less as an aesthetic object, however, than as a central memory that pulls on the common, if thin, thread of emotion in the room, invoking a joint memory of hopes surrounding his political endeavors. It is met by "a silence and then a burst of clapping" (D 135). When applause die down, Mr. Henchy turns to Crofton, a Conservative member who has been most reserved about Parnell, and asks, "What do you think of that. . . . Isn't that fine? What?" to which the text laconically returns: "Mr. Crofton said that it was a very fine piece of writing." Joyce dangles the ambiguity of whether Crofton has *assented* to the sentiment apparently stirred in others, or whether he has merely praised the poem's aesthetic merit and distanced himself from the ideological content. Joyce further troubles this tension between aesthetics and nationalism in "The Dead," where Gabriel Conroy attempts to resolve two parallel resentments: his refusal of cultural nationalism— ignited by Miss Ivors—and his envy of the strong, idealist passions brewed by Michael Furey and images of Western Ireland associated with Gretta and her past. In Gretta's memories, Furey is cast much like an Irish martyr, his death a gesture that refuses compromise. At the story's end, as Gabriel watches the snow falling "general all over Ireland," he allows that "he had never felt like that himself toward any woman"— so unequivocally in love that he would rather die than part from his lover. At this moment, Gabriel partially identifies with—but also remains distinct from—Furey's form of sentimental extremism. He admits he cannot fully identify with his purity of conviction. So when he reflects on the snow "all over Ireland," this is not a benign dissolution of tensions—some general embrace of all humanity. Rather, he realizes that he can only attain resolution by allowing—rather than suppressing—the presence of complex adherences and partial (dis)identification.[23]

In *A Portrait of the Artist as a Young Man*, Joyce continues this development of Parnellism and resistance to intolerant literary nationalists, but he pitches both positions at starker extremes. In contrast to Gabriel's generous acceptance of the divide within his own emotions, Stephen's final epiphany shows that he will accept nothing, resist all, and appropriate Parnell's martyrdom in his self-proclaimed exile.[24] Joyce therefore initiates his move into self-parody by structuring a terrain of hostile extremes that are never resolved but must be constantly re-integrated through his parodic style, so as to keep contradictions intact. As a child, Stephen's first context is constituted through binaristic perspectives, set between the terms of warm and cold, mother and father, and the two brushes of maroon and green that signify Irish politics for Dante. Stephen's world accelerates between these polar oppositions as he grows older, witnessing the family fight over Parnell, which he later replays in disputes with his mother over religion. Stark moralisms structure Stephen's world so that when he takes over the narrative—most directly when it transforms into diary entries by the novel's end—he must struggle with the urge to harshly judge Cranly, E.C., and himself.

The parodic structure that informs *Portrait* tends toward the ironic. As I mentioned earlier, both the trajectories of the ironic and the satiric are part of Joyce's parodic impulse, since parody slides between an undecidable split root that points both to the ironic, self-questioning mode. When parody is more ironic, it plays on the split intentions and ambiguous sympathies of its own author, whereas satiric parody launches itself more clearly as an intervention in the social arena. The progressive self-parody that begins even in *Stephen Hero* is more than subjective self-alienation; it becomes a textual gesture that presses on the limits of representation, demonstrating the ways in which narratives are complex echoes of the subject's struggle toward critical self-consciousness. This is reflected as well in Joyce's approach to the novel. As David Lloyd has observed, Joyce not only resists the novel's pronounced assimilative project—that of creating a narrative in which the individual and various "sociolects" are drawn into a unifying cultural representation—but his "novel" is moreover distinct from the dissident Irish novel, which applied a "translational aesthetic." Instead, Joyce's fictionalizing process insists upon recurrent heterogeneity in its very formal and textualizing structures.[25] This emerges as Joyce shifts from ironic to satiric modes of parody. While Joyce's early works play out the subject's impossible struggle toward self-determination, in *Ulysses* and *Finnegans*

Wake he transforms this struggle progressively into a comical dialogue between social and representational fixities and the dissonances that enable subjective and societal change.

Halfway through *Ulysses* the "Scylla and Charybdis" episode ends with Stephen Dedalus' failed appeal to literary Dublin, and Joyce's narrative experiments change and accelerate, shifting toward more elusive, fractured collections of perspectives that are themselves often at extremes.[26] In his study of Joyce's notes and revisions of *Ulysses*, Michael Groden singles out "Cyclops" as one of the most radical stages in Joyce's move away from interior monologue and toward narratives that pursue a greater relativity of perspective.[27] The episode sets up a polar opposition repeatedly mocked in *Finnegans Wake*; it concerns itself with Irish nationalist discourses launched either in the aggressive grousing of publicans or the high-toned celebration of Irishness. In this manner, the episode provides an astute study of how racialism leads to racism, not only through the obvious excesses of the Citizen's angry, negating discourse but also in the celebratory stereotyping of the mock-heroic passages, which serve as an inverted mirror to the Citizen's "low" version of racialism. Moreover, the two cycloptian narrations operate as an oppositional construction of the political and literary aspects of ardent nationalism, forcing a revision of Joyce's textual process so that "politics" becomes more deeply encoded as a mocking repetition of aggressive gestures and polarity itself.

The episode begins as Joe Hynes—the author of "The Death of Parnell" in "Ivy Day in the Committee Room"—crosses the purview of the nameless narrator, a debt collector who has just been pursing one Michael Geraghty for money owed Moses Herzog—"the little jewy" as the narrator calls him (U 12.30). Hynes and the narrator head off to Barney Kiernan's pub, as Hynes wishes to speak to the Citizen. As various commentators have noted, the "Citizen" is a famous local nationalist so ardently identified with his passion that he no longer has a proper name.[28] He is pure type. In this episode, Joyce exercises an understandably harsh critique of radical nationalism, using the debt collector's narrative to emphasize its relation to violence and antisemitism.[29] Readers have invoked this episode repeatedly to point to Joyce's own dislike of racism and his critical distance from nationalism.[30] Many have, however, responded to the Citizen's chauvinism by implicitly celebrating Bloom's own self-celebration at the episode's close. While Bloom is perhaps the only sympathetic character in the realistic narrative, his angry appropriation of martyrdom functions as a continuance of the binaristic purification that Joyce is here critiquing. I would like to press on the specific nature of Irish nationalism's construction in this episode, as Joyce's own narrative polarities may tempt one to replay the symptoms of cultural paranoia that can haunt radical nationalism.

In "Cyclops," we discover a storyteller who initially seems quite accessible, one who drinks, spits, and thinks within the Dublin context. The nameless narrator's perspective soon emerges as a threat, however, as antisemitism combines with the generally negative cycloptian views of others and the degradation of a benign Leopold Bloom. Readers are probably inclined, within their reading of the I-narrative, to swing radically away from the narrator's perspective and latch onto Bloom as the anchor, the pivot point, the one admirable character in the scene. I am arguing, however, that Joyce is both trying to shake us from this habit and, moreover, to present not just the negative extreme of racism but to set it up as a mirror of high celebratory racialism. As Enda Duffy notes, Frank Budgen's initial interpretation of the episode set the terms for our current reading, so that "critics invariably characterize 'Cyclops' as a set-piece in which Joyce, with the heartfelt agreement of his readers, sends up chauvinistic and ignorant Irish nationalism. . . . Many critics, however, with Bloomlike nervousness, retreat from Poldy's own cliches. . . . They thereby implicitly dismiss the elaborate and hilarious interpolations as merely a surfeit of satire."[31] The double parody of nationalism in this episode presents, on the one hand, a denigrative report that participates in a foolishly extreme Irish nationalism, while on the other hand inflated parodies raise the so-called ordinary language of the Citizen and thoughts of Bloom to dramatic heights, ironically exposing the frequent inconsistencies and failures of such celebratory typification. Readers who identify with Bloom in this episode therefore not only overlook the parodies, but they miss the broader critique of celebratory stereotyping in literature. And the I-narrator, traditionally referred to as the "realistic" voice in this episode, is in many ways as unreliable as the accompanying mock-heroic passages. Both the structure of the narration and the action of the episode deny access to any pivot-point or grounding. Even Bloom, so immune to conflict and self-reification through most of the day, here gives in to the polarization that breeds violence—although he physically suffers no more than the threat of a biscuit tin.

Such radical reification and overstatement of one's identity can signal an unusual instability embedded within one's consciousness. Analyzing this state in paranoiacs, François Roustang has noticed that they insist ardently on their individuality and construct a conspiratorial world to help them reify their imaginary, psychic boundaries.[32] In actuality, however, the very crisis that gives rise to the paranoiac's disease is an inability to accept the split within themselves and the porousness of their own identity. I introduced the analogy of paranoia and textuality in the previous chapter, as it relates to Joyce's appropriations of lesbian and gay language. Within my analysis of stereotyping, it is that gesture most given to aggression and ever more violent reductions of the Other. Here, the very problem of betrayal, which defines the anxiety of the homophobic aggressor, grades into the more general question for Joyce of the Irish betrayer. This turns into paranoia, on Jacques Lacan's analysis, in that the paranoiac's chief struggle is with the oscillation between belief and disbelief, which he cannot accept within his own consciousness.[33] The inability to fully control one's own identity and thoughts is what most persecutes the paranoiac; the slide of the conscious into the unconscious echoes the disintegration of willed intention into arbitrary and coincidental action, linking it implicitly to the problem of interpreting (sometimes capricious) parody. Moreover, as Freud has noted, the split the paranoiac must—and cannot—manage represents the interplay between ego and superegoistic functions, the relationship between self and self-evaluation.[34] Paranoiacs may be postulating a defensive stance, but they are often aggressive, and, according to Lacan, their harsher gestures definitively arise from a discomfort with self-separation and judgment. For fear of being judged, the paranoiac engages in brutally negative assessments of others. A paranoid form of textuality might reveal a gap or rift, as it more insistently (but unconsciously) separates transgressions from judgmental remarks. Joyce self-critically maps such a textuality in the "Cyclops" episode. I am not, however, arguing that the Citizen or the I-narrator are paranoid in a clinical sense, much less that Leopold Bloom is. Lacan's discussions of paranoia are not formulated exclusively in terms of clinical application but, as he insists, bear directly upon the more general problem of our culture's attempts to navigate the distortion that is invariably a part of perspectival relativity. Paranoia arises from the inability to come to terms with the fact that we are all constructed subjects without any fixed, core being and that our assessments of the world are inextricably caught up in subjective experience. As such, this is the general problem of modern and postmodern subjects. It is this very porousness of identity and the unreliability of narration against which the paranoiac reacts. Clinical paranoia is then only an extreme response to the absence of objective historical grounding and essentialized identity, problems that modernists like Joyce, Woolf, and Eliot repeatedly addressed in the 1920s and 1930s. Paranoia shares with radical nationalism the problems of self-isolation, agonistic anticipation, and eventual and probable chauvinism. The structure of nationalism need not be paranoid, but as it approaches more closely to purification and insistence on some originary self, it can become indistinguishable from that disease.

The nameless narrator, interestingly enough, begins the episode with complaints about trouble with his "eye"s. He commences his tale by complaining that his *eye* ("I") has been nearly shoved out by the brush of a passing sweep:

> I was just passing the time of day with old Troy of the D.M.P. at the corner of Arbour hill there and be damned but a bloody sweep came along and he near drove his gear into my eye. (U 12.1–3)

Naturally, this alludes to Homer's Cyclops, who receives his final insult from Odysseus in the form of a lance in the eye. Defending against this possible destruction of perspective is fairly traumatic, and the narrator persists, in his encounter with Hynes, in attempting to dramatize and magnify upon the seriousness of the event. Even when the narrator moves on to his tale about the "foxy thief" who Moses Herzog has hired him to track, his need for affirmation of the self emerges homonymically, as he repeatedly reports, "Ay, says I" to Joe's inquiries: another way of saying "yes" in Irish idiom, perhaps also relevant to Joyce's decision to end the book with several "yes"s from another character.[35] Affirmation can extend ties, can create stability, and can—certainly—give a sense of ending, but here with the nameless narrator it is more a signal or warning. The struggle to achieve self-affirmation happens not only as a repetition of "Ay"s, but also through the process of constructing a narrative, and it may be a subtle hint that the more assertive the narrator is the less stable the narrative will be—despite its familiar, seemingly realistic form. The colonial stereotype, according to Homi Bhabha, is complex and contradictory in its mode of representation, "as anxious as it is assertive." Any attempts to purify or "normalize" these tensional differences will employ a system of representation that is "structurally similar to Realism."[36] Indeed, this seemingly more realistic narration establishes its identity through suppression of differences that leads to an equal and opposite emergence of force against the selected target of aggression.

It should not be surprising then that a paranoid construction of identity emerges in Joyce's parody of Irish nationalism, given Ireland's struggle with a hybrid identity and a colonized consciousness. Beginning with Henry II's declaration of England's sovereignty over Ireland in 1171, Irish culture faced English suppression for over seven hundred years of Anglo-Norman occupation. Moreover, the dual Irish/English legal system and the Statutes of Kilkenny (1366) denigrated Irish customs, language, and literature. Irish/English intermarriage was forbidden, as was any Protestant appropriation of Irish culture, dress, and language. Cultural integration inevitably occurred, but always under the threat of government prosecution. When James I and later Cromwell instigated campaigns to "plant" Protestant colonies in Catholic Ireland, ever more stringent laws were enacted to protected a wealthy Protestant class faced by restive Roman Catholics. From 1672–1701, Catholics were deprived of the right to inherit land, excluded from public life and many of the professions, stripped of their arms, and even limited to owning horses of a lesser value. In 1728, they lost the right to vote.[37] Poverty and near erasure of their language and culture led them to rebel and eventually, in the 1800s, to initiate the movement to retrieve Irish culture. Joyce was not insensitive to the pain of this agonistic background, but he seems more keenly intrigued by the effects of the dual system. And while he could admire nationalist politicians like Arthur Griffith, he particularly disliked the racism that so often accompanied their movements. Joyce praised Griffith's ideas, his speech on advocating commercial boycotts and nationalistic education, and in a letter to Stanislaus, he claims that

> [i]n my opinion Griffith's speech at the meeting of the National Council justifies the existence of his paper [*Sinn Féin*]. . . . [S]o far as my knowledge of Irish affairs goes, he was the first person in Ireland to revive the separatist idea on modern lines nine years ago. He wants the creation of an Irish consular service abroad, and an Irish bank at home. What I don't understand is that while apparently he does the talking and the thinking two or three fatheads like Martyn and Sweetman don't begin either of the schemes.[38]

Joyce admired Griffith's bravado, eventually making his acquaintance on his last visit to Dublin in 1912. Much as Joyce is drawn to Griffith, however, he is repelled by the racism such ardent nationalism brings. "What I object to most of all in his paper," Joyce wrote, "is that it is educating the people of Ireland on the old pap of racial hatred."[39] In "Cyclops," Joyce demonstrates the ways in which a decolonization of the mind, when too extreme, can swing out against other marginalized groups, most particularly the Jews. Joyce is, as Cheng notes, critically aware of the ways in which the Irish internalize the hierarchy of oppressor/oppressed and displace it onto others.[40] In this episode, he not only ridicules the Citizen and Irish nationalist extremists who engage in chauvinism; he also mocks the radical re-appropriation of reified and supposedly pure identities.

Joyce's attention to this gesture of extremism is embedded in the very structure of the "Cyclops" chapter, which plays between two mirrors of positive and negative exaggeration. While the I-narrator's descriptions disparage and reduce the scene into stereotypes and clichés, the mock-heroic interpolations lift characters to archetypal heights. "Giganticism," as it has been called, gives us an initial celebration of the Citizen's own self-supposed stature:[41]

> The figure seated on a large boulder at the foot of a round tower was that of a broadshouldered deepchested stronglimbed frankeyed redhaired freelyfreckled shaggybearded widemouthed largenosed longheaded deepvoiced barekneed brawnyhanded hairylegged ruddyfaced sinewyarmed hero. (U 12.151–55)

Using a familiar stylistic tick of Joyce's "initial style"[42]—the double adjective merged into a single word—this passage both turns upon Joyce's own style, expanding the list of adjectives to the point of ridicule, while it also parodies the high celebrious tone it employs. The "nether extremities" of this "hero" are "encased" in "buskins dyed in lichen purple" and girdled with "a row of seastones" engraved with images of Irish heroes. The list of these heroes spans over half a page of text, cuing one in to the impossibility of such a number of "seastones" and also, within it, listing such figures as "Patrick W. Shakespeare," humorously mocking the tendency to claim that *all* great figures must, by definition of their greatness, be Irish. According to the I-narrator, in contrast, the Citizen is sitting in Barney Kiernan's pub, "having a great confab with himself and that bloody mangy mongrel Garryowen, and he waiting for what the sky would drop in the way of drink" (U 12.119–21). It is important to recognize that this is not a realist narrative any more than the mock-heroic interpolations, as both passages hold their cycloptian views at the extreme of disparagement and celebration, respectively.

Joyce's representation of the process of stereotyping here is nonrealistic in the immediate sense, for the mirror it presents is heavily distorted. On the other hand, the textual presentation of stereotypes fits with Joyce's integration of naturalism and forms of expression that might be screened out of an idealized perspective. Just as readers of the "Nausicaa" episode might laugh at Joyce's deflationary tactics—as when Leopold Bloom enjoys the voyeuristic excitement of Gerty MacDowell's panties but then faces the fleeting grief of unsticking his flesh some moments later: "the foreskin is not back. Better detach. Ow!" (U 13.979–81)—so they are faced with Stephen Dedalus chanting an antisemitic rhyme to Bloom in "Ithaca." Groden notes that Joyce had originally planned to have Stephen enter the pub in "Cyclops" as well, but removed him from the chapter later, perhaps fearing his association with Stephen would seem to implicate him in antisemitism.[43] As Stephen and Bloom are walking toward Bloom's house later in the evening, he recites the rhyme about the little Jewess who kills Harry Hughes. Bryan Cheyette has suggested that Stephen functions as "racial opposite" to Bloom's Jewishness. He not only *is* Catholic and lacking in many aspects of identification with Bloom, but he appears at times to participate in the Dublin penchant for antisemitism. Although he resists Deasy's slurs against Jews in "Nestor," he later indulges in this rhyme and other shows of potential racism.[44] In this manner, the grotesqueries of stereotyping and characters' resistances and capitulations to these views are integrated into the exchanges of *Ulysses*. Characters of closer sympathetic proximity are hardly celebrated; it is only in this manner that Joyce conveys a *realistic* Dublin, well beyond more traditional narrative forms.

Joyce's trajectory toward absolute contraries, as it culminates in "Cyclops," leads to a crisis in his artistic conception of "Irishness" of community and of a nation. Not only on a narrative level, but within the action of the I-narrative, the tension between purification and heterogeneity seems to compel the publicans' actions. The Citizen launches an argument in support of the Gaelic league's drive to teach "the shoneens" their "own language." The Gaelic league worked not only to reinstate an Irish language, but it also encouraged writers and scholars to revive an interest in the "original" literature of Ireland, to instill a sense of culture and redefine Irish national character.[45] Joyce undercuts this when Garryowen, the Citizen's mongrel wolfhound, composes his own verse; "spoken somewhat slowly and indistinctly in a tone suggestive of suppressed rancour" he recites a poem in request of water (U 12.738–39). The Irish wolfhound himself stands as a contradiction of purification. The national dog of Ireland, the wolfhound was in fact a mongrel bred of many breeds in an attempt to recreate the lost pedigree, and Garryowen is later mock-heroically called "the famous old Irish red setter wolfdog" (U 12.714–15) on account of his many combinations. This parody of purification extends both to literary practice and also to historical writing. Joyce's high-flying parodies have a range of sources; he appropriates poetry and ballads, but also directs a mocking eye toward newspapers and the histories they eventually feed. At one point, the Citizen ridicules a skit from the *United Irishman*, about a Zulu chief's visit to England: "A delegation of the chief cotton magnates of Manchester was presented yesterday to His Majesty of Alaki of Abeakuta by Gold Stick in Waiting, Lord Walkup of Walkup on Eggs, to tender to His Majesty the heartfelt thanks of British traders for the facilities afforded them in his dominions" (U 12.1514–17). The absurdity enjoyed by the publicans is an inverted mirror to their own aggressions, and their image likewise, laughing at such mockery, presses us to consider the regress of ridicule, for we too occupy the Citizen's own position as we read overblown news accounts and mock-heroic interpolations.

When Bloom ascends to the heavens then, it would be hard to find more than amusement, although the tendency to polarize against the Citizen may well produce an elative identificatory sensation. Bloom exits in high biblical mode:

When, lo, there came about them all a great brightness and they beheld the chariot wherein He stood ascend to heaven. And they beheld Him in the chariot, clothed upon the glory of the brightness, having raiments as of the sun, fair as the moon and terrible that for awe they durst not look upon Him. And there came a voice out of heaven, calling: *Elijah! Elijah!* And He answered with a main cry: *Abba! Adonai!* And they beheld Him even Him, ben Bloom Elijah, amid clouds of angels ascend to the glory of the brightness at an angle of fourtyfive degrees over Donohoe's in Little Green like a shot off a shovel. (U 12.1910–18)

Bloom is lauded in much the same language that introduced the Citizen at the scene's opening. Here, Bloom has avoided the extreme of agonism in its negative form: he does not fight back but flees the hostilities in the bar. Still, he has engaged in Joyce's more favored form of aggression by using words. Near the episode's end, Bloom gives in and falls into a fury ironically like the Citizen's own. "Three cheers for Israel!" he shouts as he leaves the pub, issuing the delayed toast, albeit without a beer in hand. He then calls back "Mendelssohn was a jew and Karl Marx and Mercadante and Spinoza," proposing yet another list of heroes who are not what they seem. As Wolfgang Hildesheimer has noted, Mercadante was not ever known to have been Jewish, and, as has been most often noted, Bloom himself is not technically Jewish.[46] After Stephen has recited his antisemitic rhyme in "Ithaca," Bloom thinks, "he thought that he thought that he was a jew whereas he knew that he knew that he knew that he was not" (U 17.530–31). The reader learns that Bloom has been baptized three times, once as a Protestant, once "under a pump" as part of a hostile prank, and once by the Catholic Church in Rothgar, most likely in preparation to marrying Molly (U 17.542–47). Finally, Bloom's mother, as she appears in "Circe," is Irish Catholic, and her name in "Ithaca" (Higgins) seems to confirm this. In that Bloom is something of a hybrid of religious and national identifications, his desire to celebrate the very stereotype used throughout the hour to denigrate him is more a defensive appropriation than a positive act of redefinition. Bloom's Jewishness can be turned inside out, however, so that the broad category of "Jew" *does* apply to Bloom as a social category Dublin attaches to him, even if it does not apply to him technically. This plants the seeds of destruction within the prejudicial category and, if it does not destroy the category, it shows that the category of "Jew" was always, in fact, a collection of hybrid identifications and occasional contradictions when applied to a particular case. And so the I-narrator in "Cyclops" will ask, "Is he a jew or a gentile or a holy Roman or a swaddler or what the hell is he?" (U 12.1631–32).

Bloom's salience in *Ulysses* arises from his general resistance to this gesture of self-reification. A scrutiny of the various ways of forming an identity and an interest in the nature of association underpin Joyce's work here, so that an initial critique of polarized identities might give rise to some other notion of subject formation. According to Philippe Lacoue-Labarthe's analysis of the subject's constitution, identity need not be locked into gestures of aggression against the Other, nor determined through a stark opposition between those who are like us and those who are different. Rather, subjectivity can be formed through an oscillating process of multiple and changing identifications with a variety of sometimes contrary types.[47] Responding to René Girard's argument that society founds itself always and inevitably upon the violence of exclusion, in the act of scapegoating some arbitrarily chosen other, Lacoue-Labarthe suggests that the subject can instead *desist*, can refuse to fully identify, thereby avoiding the violence of such an Oedipal scenario that locks into more vehement forms of identification. Rather, the subject can productively vacillate between multiple figures: "its only chance of 'grasping itself' lies in introducing itself and oscillating *between* figure and figure." (175). This vacillation serves as a kind of filiation that avoids stabilization, schematization, and its rivalrous aggressivity, and instead follows movement (*Typography*, 101–38, 165–76, and passim). One might therefore move away from a polarized sense of nationalism by emphasizing the importance of the mode—or *gestural* inflection—of representation in this move. Social identities, which are shaped by a variety of cultural representations, need not focus on purification and exclusion, and narratives might well practice a more associative pattern of historical integration. In this societal difference, representational differences emerge: the distinction between denigrative parody and its more blithely humorful benevolence. These different textual gestures may be distinguished only by subtle degrees of difference, but those degrees determine the difference between innovative representations and stereotypes or clichés of character.

In "Cyclops," the publicans wonder "why can't a jew love his country like the next fellow?" (U 12.1628–29). The notion of one man identifying with multiple histories—say, the history of Ireland and also the tribes of Israel—seems beyond their grasp. Bloom on the contrary tries to forge an identity between Jewish persecution and Irish martyrdom, one that might lend equal status to both histories and tie them together. Bloom is not the first to associate Ireland and Israel in *Ulysses*. In "Aeolus" one of the newspaper men, J. J. Molloy, recites from memory a speech given by John F. Taylor, which compares Ireland's struggle with England to the troubles of the Jews under Egypt at the time of Moses. Taylor imagines the Egyptian high-priest's words to Moses as an exact parallel: "Why will you jews not accept our culture, our religion and our language?" (U 7.825). In *Finnegans Wake*, Joyce employs this tactic of overlaying histories to extend interest in Irish (and other) emancipation. He does not, however, collapse association into full sameness, and I therefore read the *Wake* as a response to Leopold Bloom's failed attempts to define a nation.

This failure occurs at the episode's climax, when Bloom is faced by the Citizen as he shouts a toast in which Bloom does not join: "Sinn Fein! says the citizen. Sinn fein amhain! The friends we love are by our side and the foes we hate before us" (U 12.523–24). The battle cry of Fenianism translates as "Ourselves! Ourselves alone!" so that the boundaries of nationalism are pulled forever tighter. "Before" the Citizen stands, of course, Leopold Bloom, who will not have a drink, nor buy a round, nor advocate Irish sports, and who unwittingly insults the memory of Irish martyrs (to the Citizen's mind) when he calls for the end of the death penalty. If the Citizen's definition of nationalism is a negative cliché inbred with violence, Bloom's alternative definition, provided through the reductive lens of the I-narration, hardly supplies an option, swinging as it does simply to an opposite position:

—But do you know what a nation means? says John Wyse.
—Yes, says Bloom.
—What is it? says John Wyse
—A nation? says Bloom. A nation is the same people living in the same place.
—By God, then, says Ned, laughing, if that's so I'm a nation for I'm living in the same place for the past five years.
So of course everyone had the laugh at Bloom and says he, trying to muck out of it:
—Or also living in different places.
—That covers my case, says Joe.
—What is your nation if I may ask? says the citizen.
—Ireland, says Bloom. I was born here. Ireland.
The citizen said nothing only cleared the spit out of his gullet and, gob, he spat a Red bank oyster out of him right in the corner. (U 12.1419–33)

Bloom naively emphasizes sameness, probably in contradistinction to the hostile emphasis on differences that has just nearly spat in his face. Ned and Joe mock Bloom's gesture, in that it gives a comic image of nations as individuals. This definition of the nation in terms of an individual was not unfamiliar, however, in Joyce's time. In fact, as he attempts to construct a modern or *post*modern history of Ireland,[48] Joyce turns back to nineteenth-century notions of history to pick up on Thomas Carlyle's directive to write history as the story of the world's great men. Carlyle argues that

Universal History, the history of what man has accomplished in this world, is at bottom the History of the Great Men who have worked here. They were the leaders of men, these great ones; the modellers, patterns, and in a wide sense creators, of whatsoever the general mass of men contrived to do or to attain; all things that we see standing accomplished in the world are properly the outer material result, the practical realisation and embodiment, of Thoughts that dwelt in the Great Men sent into the world: the soul of the whole world's history, it may justly be considered, were the history of these.[49]

Taking up Carlyle's initiative, Victorian essayists Leslie Stephen and John Morely edited the *Directory of National Biography* and the Men of Letters series, respectively, publishing profiles of the country's "great men."[50] Stephen's daughter, Virginia Woolf, parodically reappropriated this version of history, inscribing women into the center of her essays in the *Common Readers* and changing Orlando, as a figure for English political and literary history, into a woman, as well. Joyce, for his part, parodies Carlyle's historical concept much as he parodically treats Homer's *Odyssey*. Just as Leopold Bloom ironically matches Homer's heroic Odysseus, so Earwicker-Finnegan-Et al. in *Finnegans Wake* is one "great man" mapped over Ireland's geography in various ways, containing hoards within his leviathan figure. Or rather perhaps *not* containing them, as Earwicker's identity slips forward with each new punnical and historical association, so that the iconic figure fissures into a mutable community of associative identities that refuses to be permanently fixed.

In *Finnegans Wake*, Joyce's critique of giganticism transforms into a critique of Leviathans, of the notion that a nation as one great identity can contain the multiple identities of all its constituents. The boundaries of flesh and psyche are decomposed and made porous by their "burial" in *Finnegans Wake*. At the invited request of Harriet Shaw Weaver, Joyce maps a giant beneath Phoenix Park. His presence is signalled at the *Wake*'s very opening:

The great fall of the offwall entailed at such short notice the pftjschute of Finnegan, erse solid man, that the humptyhillhead of humself prumptly sends an unquiring one well to the west in quest of his tumptytumtoes: and their upturnpikepointandplace is at the knock out in the park where oranges have been laid to rust upon the green since devlinsfirst loved livvy. (FW 3.18–24)

The giant corpse lies beneath Phoenix Park and then, alternately, under all of Dublin, just as America and Europe are mapped over Ireland at different levels of the book. This is because "Dyoublong" is also "Echoland" (FW 13.4–5), and so the body decays while, in some part, it also maintains across elaborate associations. Humphrey Chimpden Earwicker is most often associated with the body—as is Finnegan and later, as we will see, Yawn. Earwicker's "character" is an associative extension most like to a Leviathan. Yet even if he is "as globeful as a gasometer of lithium" (FW 131.35–36), "Here Comes Everybody" is not exactly a generic everyman who can absorb all differences in some odd, assimilative melting pot. Rather, associative similarities may bind his "multiplemes" without erasing the differences that force up the splintering of the narrative throughout the book. As John Bishop has demonstrated, the giant that Joyce buries under Phoenix Park (and, on more elaboration, buries beneath, in, and through *Finnegans Wake*) emerges only as the "comedy nominator to the loaferst terms" (FW283.7–8) whose nightlife generates "comic denominations."[51] No single name or trace can confine him, and the very body that should be buried shifts and transforms meaning:

> "This is the body," stripped of pronominal definiteness and caught at the transubstantiative moment in which "word is made flesh," and primarily only flesh. It enables HCE to mean nothing, in other words, in much the same way that the body "means" nothing. Whether or not one buys a reading this definitive is finally not crucial because its purport is everywhere evident anyway. Sleep is absolutely transubstantiative in force: turning the whole world into the body of the sleeper, it incarnates everything.[52]

In its obstinant refusal of meaning—to mean *nothing*—the body functions as a meaningful limit to the *conceptual* grasping that occurs in linguistic interpretation. It is dumb materiality, the flesh or word alone, and as such marks the limits of immortality and reason both. And as a body *politic*, this "body" knows no essential fixity but catches its identity in a fluctuating, associative web. It defines an antidefinitional mode of meaning that works by associative possibilities rather than deterministic categories, essences, and containments.

History, as the narrative of national identity that is echoed on the level of individual trauma, finds its central crisis and so a temporary clarity (of sorts) in book III, chapter iii of *Finnegans Wake*. There, a figure called Yawn has lain down "on the mead of the hillock" (FW 474.1–2), with "one half of him in Conn's half but the whole of him nevertheless in Owenmore's five quarters" (FW 475.6–7). In one sense, Yawn lays stretched over Ireland, a hill the four senators Gregory, Lyons, Tarpey, and MacDougal must climb to inspect. In another sense, he echoes a picture of Earwicker passed out on the floor of his pub at closing (FW 474.4). One motif of this chapter is the historian's assessment of Ireland, scripted over a tribunal's psychoanalytic judgment of

Yawn, as he is associated with Shaun, Shem, HCE, Issy, and ALP. It is a satire of social judgment that hinges on the corrupt construction of a national identity, as the Four seem to be endeavoring, at moments, to conjure the image of Ireland, Patrick, and the *Wake*'s parodic representative, H.C.E. Hugh Staples reads III/iii as the projection of a conflicted Irish history wrought through Yawn, who may resemble a sleeping Shaun, Jaun, or transform into HCE and ALP variously, but which, as Staples reminds us, "is not a character in the sense that he has unique human attributes, but a symbolic entity in whom the family conflicts have become projected into the conflict of Irish history."[53] This portion of *Finnegans Wake* then suggests a reading of Joyce's reconfiguration of Irish history and Ireland as the babbling of various communities of speakers who dwell both within the consciousness of some one figure while also melting into the surrounding social landscape. Aggressive attempts to constrain and purify an Irish national identity are persistently ridiculed in the comic failure of such endeavors by the four representatives of Ireland's "gossipocracy" (FW476.4), who here try to call forth and cross-examine HCE as he is associated with the Irish heroes Patrick and Finnegan. To do this they must identify the father with the son, HCE with Shaun, Jaun, or Yawn, for they are endeavoring to pass judgment on Ireland and, in that act, to call it forth and reify the Irish national identity. They peer at Yawn:

> More than their good share of their five senses ensorcelled you would say themselves were, fuming censor, the way they could not rightly tell their heels from their stools as they cooched down a mamalujo by his cubical crib. (FW 476.29–32).

Visiting the babe of Ireland (Jesus, Yawn, etc.), the Four are a mamalujo—*Matthew*, *Mark*, *Luke*, and *John*, and also, according to McHugh, mamalucco (in Italian)—simpletons, given to simple-minded wonder.[54] Joyce is poking fun both at government tribunals and scholarly assessments.[55] Their attempts to "read" Yawn stem from a need to see themselves, a vision so obscured that they can not tell "their heels from their stools." The narrator has earlier described their motives as "For he was ever their quarrel [fight, but also quarry], the way they would see themselves" (FW 475.19–20). Joyce is emphasizing the way in which the compulsion to judge the Other reflects the subject's need to consolidate his or her own identity. The subject purifies his sense of who he is by aggressively externalizing the traces of any negative and contradictory thoughts onto the Other, and so the identity of the Other is often contingent upon our own need to exculpate ourselves.[56] Joyce's parody answers such a gesture with its emphasis on the undecidability as to where self and other (or prior text and new) differentiate. It is the possibility of affinity that often provokes the most aggressive quarrels in the *Wake*, and this operates as a recurrent response in the text to the ambivalence parody writes into gestures of (dis)identification, even to the point of diffusing the function of linguistic reference. As verbal meaning slips away from paranoid gestures and out toward associative possibilities, identity becomes less a list of attributes and more a way of connecting to (and releasing) various alterities.

In III/iii, as the Four are estimating their identity by cross-examining Yawn as to his nature, past, and in search of some dirt on the pater, HCE, the "map of the souls' groupography rose in relief within their quarterings" (FW 476.33–34). Their vision—a hallucinatory hope for the outcome of their interview with Yawn—is a map of Ireland as a group of souls set together in a geography that binds the four corners of Ireland. But more important, they would study that relation as a "groupography," what might be a study of the connections between groups both within and across particular geographic locations. Ready to map the workings of Irish community, they are run aground as they spread their "nets"—"fine attractable nets, their nansen nets" (FW 477.20), for they encounter a problem with Yawn's language:

> There is this maggers. I am told by our interpreter, Hanner Esellus, that there are fully six hundred and six ragwords in your malherbal Magis landeguage in which wald wand rimes alpman and there is resin in all roots for monarch but yav hace not one pronouncable teerm that blows in all the vallus of tartallaght to signify majestate, even provisionally . . . (FW 478.7–13).

Of all Yawn's "ragwords" he has not one word for "magistate," the great state of Ireland. The speaker calls Yawn's language a "landeguage," a language of or created from the land, one gathers. Like the quarters of Ireland, Yawn's language remains split—as does his identity. He will later be accused of plagiarism when the Four recognize traces of Shem in his work. Here, when they demand of Yawn, "Whure yo!" (who are you and also where are you), Yawn responds that he is "Trinathan partnick dieudonnay," invoking communication of the Trinity (FW 478.26), which Joyce sets up in the "Scylla and Charybdis" episode of *Ulysses* as a model for association that resists both reduction and separation. "Trinathan" designates both a triple-portioned nathan, Jonathan Swift (earlier nathandjoe), and also a tripart nation that exists only in nicks and parts but that is nevertheless "god given" or *dieu donné*. Yawn's response also teasingly refers to Patrick, saint of Ireland, who the Four seek to call forth. As they cross-examine Yawn, they ask if he is "in your fatherick"—or pater of Ireland, Patrick. Yawn answers "The same. Three persons," identifying with HCE so that the association reaps greater meaning. Interestingly enough, however, as Yawn responds that he is a "Trinathan," he then turns to ask for the object of his own desire. "Have you seen her?" he asks, "Typette, my tactile O!" (FW 478.26–27). In terms of base plot, he might be calling out for an incarnation of Issy. More likely still, he could be Swift asking for his Pipette, the term of endearment for his Stella. Most obviously, however, Yawn is longing for a letter, a little bit of type, a "tactile O." Letters in *Finnegans Wake* associate loosely with meaning, so that one ceases to erase their particularity in favor of the "whole" meaning of a word, and they often move away from conceptual meaning toward sensate meanings, which only signify on the level of visual, aural, or here tactile sensation. Joyce interrupts this natural process of suppressing misspellings in favor of meaning, and Yawn implicitly links that process of interruption to a resistance of reified personal and national identity. That is, as he accedes to his identity with the Pater, his desire for something else, his "typette," turns him away from the gesture of consolidation and toward flirtatious Issy or a letter that has no meaning but is, one gathers, pleasantly tactile. The body once again emerges as disruptive of meaning, but not without (here a pleasant) significance.

Such slippage within language can be linked to the resistance to normative forms of community. For, as Giorgio Agamben has argued, in his analysis of "the coming community," we should set aside terms like "identity" and work instead to understand the processes that collect under the rubric of community. Agamben, moreover, stresses the relevance of *language* as it taps into the nature of communication *as being* (in both Heidegger's and Aquinas' senses). Language and being are not fixed forms but modes of rising forth; they are not essences but processes of exposing oneself or meaning to all potentialities.[57] Agamben understands the difficulties of postmodern society in terms of the movement between singularity and universal categories, and he finds that singularity always *exceeds* the category that enables its movement toward identity. Focusing on the Latin term "quodlibet" (translated "such that it is"), he argues that the particular finds itself "such that it is" through the general category, while also discovering itself "such that it is *not*," when taken in light of that category. Thus the excess or marginalized difference comes to light in that relation, rather than simply waning in the face of its social subscription. I am suggesting likewise that critics must focus their analysis on the contemporary dilemma of *language* in order to turn toward a crucial rethinking of politics. For words have become the spectacle that organizes social being, through advertising and media proliferation, and should not be understood as separate tools or finite things, but as meaning in the process of becoming. As with words, so with subjects in the community. A subject is as s/he is only in her attachment to—and definition through—society, never to be fully subsumed or erased as a particular.[58] In *Finnegans Wake*, Joyce seems to be less interested in exceeding the boundaries of the State than in forging a more fluid form of national identity or "groupography," wrought through a uniquely porous language made of the body of letters that continually disintegrate and reform. And as language in the *Wake* mutates, so inextricably does the collective community shift and change its boundaries and definition. The words thus move beyond what the plot scenarios so insistently replay: the drama of the individual oppressed by the community—or the portrait of a nation making war on some imaginary, marginalized enemy from within the culture.

In *Finnegans Wake*, when Yawn finally does endeavor to consolidate his various selves, it is not surprising that this moment occurs in anger, as he is answering accusations that his language is not his own. The Four suspect plagiarism or at least admixed authorship: "The gist is the gist of Shaun but the hand is the hand of Sameas. Shan-Shim-Schung. There is a strong suspicion on counterfeit Kevin" (FW 483.3–5). Yawn rises indignant, asking why they betray him, why "you will celebrand my dirthdags (birthday and death day) quoniam, concealed a concealer, I am twosides uppish, a mockbelief insulant, ending none meer hyber irish" (FW 484.13–15), accusing them of being split and part non-Irish while he himself rises up as Irishness incarnate (by his own terms). He recalls saving them from the "Hekkites"(Hittites and hectates: witches),[59] recalling how he taught them the "WXYZ and PQRS of legatine process" and brought them "from the loups of Lazary" (laps of luxury, but recalling resurrection of Lazarus) "and you have remembered my lapsus langways" (FW 484.25). He is aggrieved that they recall only his slips of the tongue, or "collapsus" of back promises. He erupts in two long words, combined translations of "I" and then indignantly invokes his high parentage and peerage and past education. This is the gesture of control and potential violence that Joyce now replays as a response to his own early sense of the centrality of betrayal in Irish politics.

In *Finnegans Wake*, then, Joyce finally succeeds in rupturing the paranoid opposition between self and community. He achieves this by diffusing language and narrative beyond the binary and by overwhelming the text with humor. As Roustang has suggested, the paranoiac can begin to disrupt the megalomania and radical patrol of boundaries around the self with the help of humor, particularly when that humor is directed toward the self. Joyce's own suggestive identifications with Parnell inspire sentimental protection of his image, but in *Finnegans Wake* the scenes of betrayal quickly turn from pathos to pratfall, shifting from high-toned rhetoric to small-minded gossip and comically childish spats.

In this manner, Joyce provokes the laugh that shakes the boundaries that crystallize the form of paranoid nationalism he parodies in the "Cyclops" episode of *Ulysses*. This split relation to Irish nationalism transforms into a fluctuating integration of opposites in a form of "spoken" community in *Finnegans Wake*. Humor and missed intentions form this community and "betrayal" becomes a constructive category that allows miscommunication to bind and unbind without leading to aggressive forms of identification and judgment.

Yawn eventually admits that he cannot reify his identity and that he suffers from an anxiety about slipping forward into a different self in some future: "I felt feeling a half Scotch and pottage like roung my middle ageing like Bewley in the baste," he complains, "so that I indicate out to myself and I swear my gots how that I'm not meself at all, no jolly fear, when I realise bimiselves how becomingly I to be going to become" (FW 487.15–19). He repeatedly admits of a run away from fixity, as he contemplates his various selves. He may reify in anger and defensiveness later, when HCE's voice rises through his own, but the national discourse of Ireland is then marked—as was Parnell's—by a persistent stutter. As Yawn collects himself into the voice of the father, HCE (FW 532–34) stutters incessantly, disseminating his identity and implicitly also Ireland's. The Four try to bring him into focus with the help of radio waves (Zin . . . zin . . . Zinzin, FW 500.29, 31, 34) so that eventually he rises in true Parnell form. He defends against accusations of sexual transgressions—not adultery, however, so much as child molestation: "On my verawife I never was nor can afford to be guilty of crim crig con of malfeasance trespass against parson with the person of a youthful gigirl frifrif friend" (FW 532.18–20). HCE boasts his dignity, invoking both his genealogy and his immaculate English: "I am bubub brought up under a camel act of dynasties long out of print, the first of Shitric Shilkanbeard (or is it Owllaugh MacAuscullpth the Thord?), but, in pontofacts massimust, I am known throughout the world wherever my good Allenglisches Angleslachen is spoken" (FW 532.7–11). His Anglo-Saxen (Angelsachse) is laughably (lachen) full—*all* full—of glitches (Allenglisches). Much earlier in the *Wake*, in chapter I/i, Earwicker stutters the fissure within the nation, as he brags of his "nonation wide hotel and creamery establishments which for the honours of our mewmew mutual daughters, credit me, I am woo-woo willing to take my stand, sir . . . there is not one tittle of truth, allow me to tell you, in that purest of fibfib fabrications" (FW 36.22–24, 33–34). Error, lie, and fabrications—the general distortions of realistic images and fall into parody and hearsay—these gestures disrupt the singularity of nations and individual identities. If, as Benedict Anderson has argued, "communities are to be distinguished, not by their falsity/genuineness, but by the style in which they are imagined," Joyce's imagining of Ireland is radically different from the polarized perspectives of "Cyclops."[60] Here, Earwicker's stutters seem to reveal the truth he seeks to hide, so that his assertions often flow through contradictions, and the Ireland that emerges from his figure is a nation of contrary beliefs and assertions, with a history that oscillates between highs and lows but that may also splinter beyond polarities in the future. It would still be a future of dissonance, but one less defined by insistent and aggressive forms of representation.

Irish "betrayal" thus turns into a humorous play on words that betrays initial meanings for multiple others. Eschewing a fixed and idealized vision of Ireland, Joyce loosely reweaves Irish discourse, so that even in the recourso, when the Irish identity should return to itself, it does so only as a series of particulars that Joyce insistently lists (FW 614.27–615.10). Joyce does not then abandon the nation but reconfigures it as a community of dissonant voices, contraries that reify and soften, marked by a rhythm of various forms of becoming. In terms of Jürgen Habermas's recent emphasis on normative categories of identity that inform a subject's legal status, my work here might suggest an analogy between the "norm" and the "noun" or the way in which words can redefine subjects in relation to communal interpretation.[61] Rather than identifying and developing one mutual horizon of communal meanings, one might think in terms of the multiple strands of meaning that can define a word differently. So a "coming community" might share one denominator (or name), but it might not hold the same meaning. This is just to suggest that interpretations of Joyce's own reworking of the postcolonial construct might well inform current discussions of multicultural communities, where no normative value system can prevail, but some means of discussing and mediating conflicts between values needs to be established. While Joyce does not exactly celebrate his new community—it might well be considered his "nightmare of history"—he offers a version of the nation, community, and history that allows diversity to maintain and complex associative identities to supplant reification and aggression. In this sense, Joyce recreates Ireland in his work as a "nonation," the notion of a nation torn between its own historical erasure and its identification *as* that which has been erased, a community constituted through the rift within its self-conception (or notion). As Muta poses the problem to Juva, toward the end of *Finnegans Wake*:

> MUTA. So that when we shall have acquired unification we shall pass on to diversity and when we shall have passed on to diversity

we shall have acquired the instinct of combat and when we shall have acquired the instinct of combat we shall pass back to the spirit of appeasement?

JUVA. By the light of the bright reason which daysends to us from the high. (FW 610.23–29)

CHAPTER 6

Rhythmic Identification and Cosmopolitan Consciousness in Finnegans Wake

toute âme est un nœud rythmique ["every soul is a rhythmic knot"]
—Mallarmé, *Oeuvres complètes*

Whence followeup with endspeaking nots for yestures
—FW 267.8–9

In *Finnegans Wake*, Joyce represents consciousness as a web of relational rhythms, oscillating tensions that alternately knot into aggressions
("nots") and loosen into associative "yestures" that nod assent. If, as
Mallarmé thought, every soul is a rhythmic knot, in Joyce this is charted
by gestures that shift between paranoid negation and narcissistic affection; such gestures will be defined not by some movement of arms or
limbs, but as a way of relating to context, self, and others. As parodic
constellations of pregiven possibilities, they will be captured along a
swerve of thought, a characteristic way of negotiating similarities and
differences, of bridging situatedness and translocations (as well as
trans*locutions*). Such alternate entanglements and disassociations occur
not only within the subject but range across the spectrum of voices in
Finnegans Wake. Some of these voices turn in upon themselves while
others confront societal interdiction. Some respond to the threat of associative displacement with aggression, struggling to control the self, the
other, and—most important for Joyce—the word. "Characteristic" gestures thus emerge as patterns etched in the unconscious, deeper than
memory, yet always shifting and accreting across the layering flux of
identifications.

For Joyce, one of the most pervasively difficult aspects of Dublin in
his youth seems to have been negotiating the moralist strictures imposed
by religious, educational, and nationalist ideologies. The "knot" of
Joyce's soul was in that sense tightened by the "notshalls" of his environment. Throughout this book, I have been suggesting that Joyce's

writing progressively works loose the bonds of this constraint, so that the textual gestures of his fictions reflect an oscillating play of resistance to and humorous allowance for societal dictates. As his work records the fluctuation between conscious and unconscious directives, desire is ever more radically delivered up as sexual, aggressive, affectionate, and otherwise—so that it develops a disruptive agency in the face of moralistic constraints. Joyce effects this disruption by fusing words with the body, both in the embodiment of verbal physicality in alphabetic bits and in the playful parapraxes that point toward human bodily functions and transgressive acts.

In this chapter I will be examining the ways in which Joyce's use of gestural language and parodically (dis)identified character creates a history that is both worldly and local, and a sense of character that is both generally recognizable while locally particularized. Politically, if Joyce has been identified as a cosmopolitan modernist, *Finnegans Wake* redefines that term as a consciousness that develops, moving between transnational and local instances and moderating general categories with the specificities that disrupt them. Authoritarian modes of reading Joyce are therefore misleading, I will suggest, in their favor of mastery as a supposedly central drive in his most unmasterable text, *Finnegans Wake*; the old insistences on reading Vico's imperialist history and Jung's politically questionable model of archetype as Joyce's own signal instead the desperate scramble for critical certainties. Across the oscillation between general typological constructs and disruptive parapraxes and word play, Joyce's cosmopolitan model works toward repeated boundary crossings, tethering perspective to its local context while also pushing it out toward difference in a manner that works to eschew biases and aggressions. In specific scenarios, narcissism and paranoia are at play, but in terms of the *Wake*'s oddly worldwide and simultaneously hibernian references, a mediation of the general assessment and individuated perspective is persistently performed.

Why cosmopolitanism? It was the term attached to Joyce several decades ago, indicating his disaffection for nationalist passions to some literary critics, but also signifying an elitist disdain for real politics to others. As the term has been previously understood, it described an *attitude* of the transnationally mobile upperclass who, under the influence of Stoicism, claimed universal citizenship as a license to either withdraw from local politics or to claim intellectual mastery of world political problems.[1] Recently the term has been reclaimed and reconfigured by thinkers like Homi Bhabha, James Clifford, and Bruce Robbins.[2] Bhabha and Clifford particularly are invested in formulating a cosmopolitan notion of hybridity, dwelling in cultural identities that are always admixed and contingent in their identifications. In Pheng

Cheah's analysis, this allows them to describe "the symbolic and fluid nature of human identity and existence, as opposed to the givenness or organicity of the natural and nonhuman."[3] It also allows a new model of subversion, for Bhabha, one that can work the rifts between the natural/cultural, reality and its representation, political necessity and freedom from constraint.[4] For Robbins, however, it is most useful as a way of recasting the situated intellectual's conscientious investment in world politics, whereby the cosmopolitan experiences "a density of overlapping allegiances rather than the abstract emptiness of nonallegiance."[5] Such a concerned thinker will not assume the easy arrogance of universalism, but neither will s/he surrender empathetic social agency that may cross national and subject-identified borders. In contrast to universalism, humanism, and internationalism, contemporary cosmopolitanism, for Robbins, holds on to the *value* of difference while never overlooking the complex negotiations between his/her situatedness and this desire to understand other cultures.[6]

I am suggesting that Joyce is neither this formerly accepted (and then disdained) version of elite cosmopolitanism linked to imperialist gestures,[7] nor is he a member of the politically conscientious set that now recovers the term. Indeed, in her "Thoughts about James Joyce" jotted down for Richard Ellmann, Nancy Cunard recalls an abrupt phone call from Joyce in 1937, after having sent him a questionnaire assessing sentiment on the Spanish Civil War and Fascism. She picked up the phone to hear him blurt out his outraged at all this concern about politics: "A ten-minute monologue follows. He will not answer it because it is 'politics.' Now, politics are getting into everything—mentions a meeting of PEN, which has a charter stating that politics shall never be discussed at its meetings."[8] As I have suggested, Joyce was not apolitical, but his "politics" dwell less in explicit position-holding than in gestures, curiosities, and textual dissections. They are manifest in textual gestures that weave conscious awareness with unconscious drives, producing a map of social interactions, saturated with analysis and comic commentary on the impact of aggressive gestures and the amelioration seduction and connective associations bring. In the context of vocal exchanges and verbal extensions, the *Wake* thus portrays a politics of its own. Moreover, in its textual gestures, it evades the imperialism once links to cosmopolitanism. Here, instead, cosmopolitan consciousness is engaged in a perspectival mapping, which simultaneously remarks Joyce's situated subjectivity, formed by Dublin and Europe, as well as his extended curiosity for the differences and analogies with other cultures' histories and languages.

The world's history is inscribed palimpsestuously on the tablet of Joyce's localized interest in Ireland. This is not a counter-imperialist gesture in which Ireland, by way of reversal, contains all the world within its archetypal history. Rather, Joyce's final work conveys the perspectival mapping that accompanies any attempt to assess the world beyond one's self-known and constitutive context. Instead of invoking universalism, Joyce conveys a cacophonic perspective roped to particular drives, intensities, and—from his experience—a subject-position created by Irish culture, language, and lore. In all this, Joyce is acting as cosmopolitans do: to reach beyond the claims of religion, class, and nation. Yet this reach never erases the particularity of Joyce's own culturally constituted perspective.

The Earwicker family and broad characters of the *Wake* function likewise not as traditional archetypes, which maintain a narrative of inherited cultural similitudes, that function only as necessary reference points around which a myriad of historical, fictionalized agents can be fleetingly comprehended. My intention here is to roll back claims for universalization and archetypal "truths" in *Finnegans Wake*, which might be tainted by the very imperialistic gestures Joyce so ardently denied. Ultimately, *Finnegans Wake* becomes a text of prerational or "after" thoughts, dwelling on materiality and semiotic scraps, and in this flotsam of thought Joyce engages the problem of how to narrate a history that, like its gesturally inflected medium, language, refuses to be contained by logical boundaries and linear plots.

In his seminar on history and myth, Lacan warned that "history is the greatest phantasm." Behind historical claims of fact and reality, myth always lurks, pulling in both the historian and the dreamer. For Lacan, *Finnegans Wake* is one of the most troubling examples of myth's overpowering draw:

> The proof is that Joyce, after having carefully borne witness to the symptom of Dublin, whose soul only comes to life from his own, does not fail, most extraordinarily, to fall into the myth of Vico that supports *Finnegans Wake*. The only thing that saves him is that even so *Finnegans Wake* itself is presented as a dream, and, moreover, one that indicates that Vico is a dream as well; and finally, that the babuskas of Madame Blavatsky, the Mahanvantara is all that follows, the idea of a rhythm. . . . One never retrieves, or if one does, it's called turning in circles. One finds.[9]

Lacan's suspicion of the Imaginary, which suppresses the Real, is vented in his amazement at Joyce's shift from the realism of *Dubliners* to the fantastic mythic circling and displacements of *Finnegans Wake*. The only thing that "saves him [Joyce]" is that Vico is merely a dream in the *Wake*. In the river of such an unconscious, one only makes discoveries by pursuing the rhythm that moves between retrieval and relapse, creating the circularity of *Finnegans Wake*. History is not a teleology, nor even a chain of facts; it moves between ripples of conscious claims and unconscious distortions of the real. And this dream—this history—is never entirely subjective nor focused upon one character's dreams; neither is it universally rational and clear, as an ideal history: "There is no better proof than Joyce," Lacan adds, "that the collective unconscious is a symptom, because one can not say that *Finnegans Wake*, in one's imagination, does not participate in this symptom . . . it is the symptom, the symptom that there is no way to analyze."[10] This symptomatic invocation of a collective unconscious is not a universalizing reach, or "truth," in Joyce's work; yet neither is it a full evasion of communal thought, marked by a dive into the fantasies of one fractured mind. It represents a flow of rhythmic associative reaches that model for us a particular form of cosmopolitanism, one that accesses global differences while retaining a situatedness in Dublin and in Irish history. On another plane, it dips from conscious thought to unconscious desires, which then return to redefine truth, belief, and cognition. These processes are echoed across the text in the (de)formations of character, where retrieval and loss repeat the rhythmic (dis)identities that turn the text of a few figures into a world cacophony.

GESTURAL LANGUAGE AND VICOVIAN HISTORY: JOYCE'S EXPROPRIATIONS

When Joyce expropriated Vico's historiography, he was invoking an eighteenth-century, Italian philosopher of humanism in order to ground the antihumanist, postmodern project we now call *Finnegans Wake*. The only thing humanist about *Finnegans Wake* is that it has a name, a thin square boundary that contains the radically dissolute and disruptive scraps of stories, tales, characters, and "alphabites" within it (FW 263n1). So why was Joyce so compelled by Vico's work, as to make it a central structuring force in his own reconfiguration of history? In a letter to Harriet Shaw Weaver, Joyce cautioned that, "I would not pay overmuch attention to these theories [Vico, Bruno, et al.], beyond using them for all they are worth, but they have gradually forced themselves on me through circumstances of my own life. I wonder where Vico got his fear of thunderstorms."[11] Joyce seems to have been fascinated by Vico's image of the first great men, giants frightened into caves by thunder across the sky. Himself afraid of thunder, Joyce's delight in contiguous fancy might just as well have inspired his interest. But Vico's giants and social theories in many ways justify imperialist politics; in fact, the author explicitly claims that his science of history is "a philosophy of authority," which examines the power nations. Thomas Hofheinz has suggested that "Vico's approving vision of the rise of Christian empires through 'righteous and blameless wars' . . . might have pinched a raw Irish nerve in Joyce."[12] Indeed, the valorization of hierarchy and nationalist aggression appears to stand in contradiction to both Joyce's personal views and his textual "perversity" as it disrupts normative systems. Vico exhibits a tendency toward historical determinism, believing that "the human mind is naturally impelled to take delight in uniformity" and arguing that history operates along a scheme of necessity, that "it had, has, and will have to be."[13] It seems odd that Joyce, who was so pleased by chance disruptions and coincidence, came to employ a philosopher with such a stratifying system.

If Joyce's works indicate a strong suspicion of colonizing gestures, he also never fully *erases* hierarchy or imperialism for a fanciful view of the future. He is too wedded to a skeptical form of realism. Instead, he forces a complex dialogue between chance and predetermination, between imperialism and its impending downfall, between broad humanistic categories and the particularities that elude their grasp. In this manner, the *Wake* constantly challenges the tendency to read for a single position, directing attention to the gestural movement between positions. French theory and its appreciation of the particularity and the humor in Joyce's word-play has in many senses given us the *Wake* as a text that can and does resist Vico's system of authority. I am suggesting in tandem with this work that the *Wake* not only critiques but also *uses* the systems of containment as points around which to negatively tether interpretive possibilities. For if, as I have argued in chapter 4, some of the pleasure of this text lies in its narcissistic self-direction, it requires also that outward form of communication and sliver of meaning to be what it is: a literary text in some ways engaging its readers. *Finnegans Wake* is not some coy figuration, turning its meaningful glance away like a parody of the object of desire; it is a text that constantly reaches out with jokes and allusions to provoke an interpretative dilemma and response. Interpretation is the crucial question of the *Wake*, the question of how one reads this book or, for that matter, *anything* now that such a text has been written.

John Bishop has proposed one of the most compelling explanations as to why Joyce was drawn to Vico. Vico has been treated as a humanist historiographer, but he was initially neglected on account of the general scandal over his picture of early man as a pre-enlightened being:

> The foresightfully radical snap of thought that made Vico unread and misunderstood in his own day—the same decades of the eighteenth century in which Pope wrote his *Essay on Man*—was his supposition

that our political forebears [Bishop is punning on "Our Family Furbear" in *Finnegans Wake*], men in a state of nature, were not enlightened rationalists who could agree on social contracts and protective alliances, but semi-bestial clods who had barely thrown off their fur, speechless giants who rutted, bore furry children, and left them to wallow in their own excrement while they themselves roamed off to sate their appetites.[14]

Vico's controversial innovation was to include the prerational within a narrative of history, a possibility Joyce weighed as well in a context increasingly informed by Freud, where the child's "prerational" mind had become an important origin for his or her own "history." Bishop suggests that Joyce moderated the Freudian emphasis on the family romance with a broader sense of history as reaching back beyond our fathers, so that we remember what we could never have known, perhaps a gesture of the unconscious passed on through generations that can no longer name or narrate the effects that have constituted them. Joyce therefore takes up, on his own terms, the problem of how to narrate preconscious or "nighttime" history, rediscovering narrative only in the disruption of linearity and its supposed telos.

PARODIC HISTORY AND THE TEMPORAL PUN

Noting the "hiccupping parabolics," Bernard Benstock explains that "rather than a continuous narrative, the *Wake* consists of packets of linked, blended, and interrupted narratives, and a mélange of voices performing narrative services independent of a central intention. Not only does the *Wake* contain multitudes, but these multitudes interact and interconnect at junctures determined by accidental and coincidental factors, the net result of which is an almost seamless garment only marginally affected by chapter separations."[15] Indeed, the flow of these various voices, with associative echoes of other voices within each, can hardly be called "narrative" in any strict sense. But stories are certainly told and retold, and meanings are in effect given even as they fade away through parapraxes and redirected allusions. In this manner, meaning is attained only at the juncture of its dissolution in the *Wake*, playing out the struggle between conscious narrativizing and the drift of desire, play, and materiality in the unconscious and in language. The construction of history that arises from such a textualizing process is therefore necessarily split between traditional forms of narrative and punnical references, which repeatedly disrupt initial interpretations.

History in the *Wake* is not synchronic in the simple use of the term, for the past and future—like predestination and revision—function in a dialectical tension, just as all the world, while not being wholly defined by Dublin, is reconfigured through its locale. Indeed, the book commences with a construction of interpretation that points to such a use of history:

> Sir Tristram, violer d'amores, fr'over the short sea, had passencore rearrived from North Armorica on this side the scraggy isthmus of Europe Minor to wielderfight his penisolate war: nor had topsawyer's rocks by the stream Oconee exaggerated themselse to Laurens County's gorgios while they went doublin their mumper all the time: nor avoice from afire bellowsed mishe mishe to tauftauf thuartpeatrick: not yet, though venissoon after, had a kidscad butttended a bland old issac: not yet, though all's fair in vanessy, were sosie sethers wroth with twone nathandjoe. (FW 3.4–12)

From the *Wake*'s very opening, a double mapping occurs, constituted twice in both historical and geographic doublings. North America, suggested indirectly in "North Armorica" and "Lauren's County" (in Georgia), is invoked, yet this emerges through punnical slips off of references to the settlement of Howth's Head, a "scraggy isthmus" near Dublin.[16] Moreover, temporally, the reader is asked to remember what has not yet (passencore) occurred. So, for instance, the first half of this opening sentence is the string of words that ends the *Wake*: "A way a lone a last a loved a long the . . ." (FW 628.15–16). This process of reading through memory is not a reaching back but a springing forward to the book's end. This contrachronological move is marked further by the next paragraph, which proceeds to list events that have not yet occurred.[17] This reverse chronological imperative—the command to know the future so as to negotiate the present—takes the reader through a constant "vicus of recirculation."

History operates here much like a pun. Sir Tristram can be historically traced to "Howth Castle and Environs," since a Sir Amory Tristram was the first earl of Howth.[18] The narrative, however, leaves behind Dublin history and focuses on "Sir Tristram," interrupter (violer) of lovers. This is then an association, derived from the similarity of Tristram's name to that of the legendary Tristan (of *Tristan and Iseult*), who finds himself wooing the woman he has been sent to escort back to her betrothed, Sir Mark. The referent is an odd composite of character possibilities.[19] In this manner throughout the *Wake*, small, seemingly insignificant details, like the sound and look of names, forge the link between identities. Rosa Marie Bosinelli has suggested that Joyce may have been drawn to Vico's use of bodily metaphor in his work: "Fleshy, carnal, corporeal words abound in the passage that is Vichian both in terms of the language used and in the open allusion to the 'cyclewheeling history,' where 'the slow fires of consciousness' characterize 'a dividual chaos, perilous, potent, common to allflesh, human only, mortal' (186.4–5)."[20] As Vico's own language reveals the resistant underside of his authoritarian philosophy, Joyce appropriates such language only to expand its force in his own work. The homonymic influence recurs continuously, due to the *Wake*'s submersion in the unconscious. This dissolute language may also reflect a sympathetic interest in Vico's argument that all history is reflected in the development of language.

The split within the pun carries over to a split within character, making Joyce's work also the history of the psychoanalytic process—simultaneously marking history with the fluidity of conscious and unconscious compulsions. After Vico's work, modern histories moved gradually away from a focus on the deeds and influences of "great men," examining more progressively the societal influences and fluctuations in common human behavior.[21] Joyce maps out externally—as wars and scandals—that which occurs also internally as a form of self-accusation. Choosing not merely to record such skirmishes, Joyce constructs his history as a collection of street gossip, humorously embracing the unstable discourse as a determining factor in the development of historical narratives.[22] The trauma of the *Wake* is in many ways the attempt to manage relations between individual subjects and accumulated gossip. By the time Joyce had begun writing the *Wake*, he was himself the center of much rumor and speculation. In a letter to Harriet Shaw Weaver, he comments on "a nice collection . . . of legends about me" and lists several absurd ones with apparent amusement.[23] Just as Joyce's shifting syntax destabilizes narrative in the *Wake*, so his rerouting of history through scenes of public gossip and scandal undermines the possibility of establishing (or identifying) "facts." His appropriation of this cycle of endless retrials functions not like the move toward some final verdict; instead, it critically (and comically) mimics the tedious yet seemingly necessary structure of social formation. The details of gossip derive in part from real events, but these are always configured through the clichés of memory, broad stereotypes and familiar tales of good and evil that subjugate reality to the demands of myth. If gossip tenders the "truth" of the moment, stereotype is always its constitutive law. Subsequently, in the face of such absolutes, identity dissipates. In *Finnegans Wake*, where character is recreated and dispersed through social exchange and, on a more individuated level, through psychoanalytic oscillations, the text's characterology is necessarily fluid and changeable. Thus Joyce parodically deconstructs identity as he "mirrors" the obscure and countrafactual origins of history and the cycling aggressions woven into its narrations.

If characterization and history are constituted by gossip in the *Wake*, gossip is, after all, nothing nastier than fiction, and as such it cre-

ates (and decreates) characters with easy authority. Although understanding historical detail is crucial to any reading of the *Wake*, the process by which the text assembles these details could hardly be said to
work within the bounds of normative historical methods. Joyce's history
is split between two operations: moralism (its catalytic impulses) and
desire, that which overflows borders and dissipates control. While historical narratives traditionally engage questions of causality and issue
claims as to how an event comes about, Joyce is drawn toward coinci-
dences, such as homonymy or a meeting of opposites, so that he often
teases the reader's expectation to find causally determined explanations.
He weaves a loose composite of gossip around figures who intersect by
virtue of similar roles, fates, or actions—actions like the falling:
Finnegan's fall from the scaffold, Halvard Solness' fall from the steeple,
man's fall from grace, Parnell's fall from power, and a nearly infinite
number of other falls, large and small, are written into the *Wake*. In the
second chapter of book I, HCE seems to stand in as an archetype for
them all, but his actions are particularized in ways that distinguish him
from any of the historical and mythological characters he resembles as
he is "subjected to the horrors of the premier terror of Errorland"
(FW 62.24–25).

I would like to briefly revisit HCE's characterology, familiar though
he is to *Wake* scholars. My point of interest is the associative nature of
his construct, which allows Joyce broad-ranging social and historical
commentary. He is the figure of cosmopolitan consciousness in that he
maintains a thin thread of local reference while being extended toward
a series of differentiated figures. He is "transhibernian" (FW 55.20), in
that he is extended toward (and his actions understood by) these other
legends even as he is located in Ireland. HCE's "fall" begins when he is
met in Phoenix Park by "Gasping Gill," known later simply as "the
cad" (FW 36.35). He bids HCE good day and asks the time. Later, the
cad tells his wife that HCE falters suspiciously, and this gets elaborated
on and passed to a Mr. Browne (FW 38.26) and then is passed along
again. In the manner of gossip, it soon takes on the proportions both of
a major political crime and a scandalous sexual transgression. Moreover, the nature of dreaming allows rumor to expand along the veins of
guilt-anxiety in the unconscious, just as Leopold Bloom's worries in
"Circe" give fruit to long scenes of protestation and defense. Joyce suggested, in 1936, that "there are, so to say, no individual people in the
[*Wake*]—it is as in a dream, the style gliding and unreal as is the way in
dreams."[24] Indeed, HCE is not an umbrella figure or grand Leviathan,
but the silky thread of possible—but never fully probable—connections.
As HCE's indictments progress, stories told about one martyr are confused and collapsed into another's tale by virtue of foggy memory and

associative assimilation. HCE is fleetingly identified with—and in some part becomes—a variety of mistried men and scapegoats, such as Christ (FW 58), Parnell (FW 87), Cromwell (FW 45), and Thomas à Beckett (FW 77). He is likened to those who have failed, on some level, in terms of sexual transgressions: Swift, Shakespeare (FW 58), and Parnell; and he is also like those who fall, such as Humpty Dumpty (FW 45). He is occasionally transmuted into a visionary, like Confucius (FW 36) or a great man, like the giant who lies under Phoenix Park (FW 36). And he has his biographical associations as well. Joyce himself is on trial, in a sense, as the "King, having murdered all the English he knew," is exiled by the jury, which shouts "Shun the Punman!" (FW 93.1–2, 13).[25]

HCE nonetheless always differs parodically from such historical influences, and this very difference disrupts any simple notion of him as a categorical container of other men. He is, for example, associated with Parnell by virtue of the similarities in rumors about his and the Irish Leader's alleged crimes. Parnell was accused of ordering by letter the murders of Lord Frederick Cavendish and Thomas Burke in Phoenix Park; however, the government's key witness, Patrick Delaney, had been released from life imprisonment on the condition that he be willing to testify against Parnell. HCE is actually accused in court by a "poor delaney" who "reported the occurance in the best way he could" (FW 84.8, 12).[26] Yet incidents differ, so that HCE is said to have engaged in hand-to-hand combat with an assailant in the park—an elaborated version of his verbal accostal by the cad. He is not accused of directing the murders of statesmen, although as likened to Joyce, he has "murdered all the English he knew." At the eventual conclusion of the tale of HCE's assault, the listeners mishear a bit, and ask "Herwho?" and this slip leads to speculation about his alleged Don Juanism. Although exonerated in the case of the Phoenix Park murders, Parnell was destroyed politically by scandal surrounding his long-term relations with Katherine O'Shea, the wife of Captain O'Shea.[27] Again, however, HCE's transgression is different and seems to be constituted by "having behaved with ongentilmensky immodus opposite a pair of dainty maidservants" (FW 34.18–19). There is indication of "partial exposure" while drunk, either to urinate or for the pleasure of flashing them a view of his personal parts. Later, the jury asks if "the prince in principel should not expose his person?" (FW 89.6). In other modes of sexual transgression, he has, like Shakespeare, been seduced by a woman. Only for HCE, these are multiple Liliths in the form of the rainbow girls or Issy (incest). If "It was the first woman, they said, souped him" (FW 58.28–29), his are most often not older (as for Shakespeare, in Stephen Dedalus's biocritical presentation) but younger. He is likened to "dear old grumpapar" who is "gone on the razzledar" on a young star. But he also has his "gel number two" who he's "fair mashed on" (drunk or in love) (FW 65.12, 23, 25). This culminates in a comedy of gossip, apparently at the bar(room):

> it's as simple as A.B.C., the two mixers, we mean, with their cherry-bum chappy (for he is simply shamming dippy) if they all were afloat in a dreamlifeboat, hugging two by two in his zoo-doo-you-doo, a tofftoff for thee, missymissy for me and howcameyou-e'enso for Farber, in his tippy, upindown dippy, tiptoptippy canoodle, can you? Finny. (FW 65.27–33)

And indeed it is both "Finny" and funny. At times Joyce will break the scene of gossip so we glimpse that it is no real history but tall tales of amusement already told in a dream. "Ack, ack, ack" laugh and cough the audience (FW 65.34). Here, identity is less the focus of aggressive fixation than the font of amusement.

HCE's identification with Parnell spreads over most of the *Wake*, but it is never a consistent or monologic narrative. It is more scattering into dashes along the text, and so functions much as gossip does. For every single similarity HCE bears to a historical or mythological figure, he boasts twenty differences. These variations are most all comical differences, so that readers cannot seriously contend that Joyce gives us a mimetic presentation of Parnell; rather, he parodies his trial and the Catholic moralism that destroyed his career, mocking his attackers but also trivializing the crisis by minimalizing HCE's crime. Thus "the book of Doublends Jined"[28] will proliferate "till Daleth, mahomahouma, who oped it closeth there of the. Dor" (FW 20.15–18). A world cycle ("Mahamavantara" in Sanskrit) runs from cover to cover of the book, or door ("Daleth" is "Delta" respelled in Latin) to Dor (sleep, French).[29] Between deepest sleep and wakefulness, which (almost) closes the door to the unconscious, Wakean cycles move by dream logic.[30] Shifting between associative flow and nodal conflict, Joyce retells the tale of all falls. Before society can pull down a figure—make it fall—it must first fix that figure's identity. That is, before something can be judged it must first be held stable and be analyzed statically. And so Wakean characters are constantly slipping away from inquiries that seek to pin them down. Joyce's cyclical history of gossip is then an evasion of rumor as well.

ARCHETYPOLOGIES AND THE
POLITICS OF PREDETERMINATION

Lacan once commented that stereotypes never speak, but are always spoken.[31] The 1950s in Joyce criticism were in many ways proof of this assertion. Stereotypes of women, most particularly, were bandied about in discussions of *Ulysses*, while *Finnegans Wake* slowly found its way to accessibility through its recasting in Jungian terms.[32] In his 1929 essay on *Work in Progress*, Samuel Beckett warned *Finnegans Wake*'s future critics that "the danger is in the neatness of identifications." Arguing that the *Wake*'s integration of philosophical abstraction and empirical event could not be pressed into tidy composites, Beckett disparaged those who might try to "wring the neck of a certain system in order to stuff it into a contemporary pigeon-hole. . . . Literary criticism," he concluded, "is not book-keeping."[33] Despite this warning, the first book-length interpretation of the *Wake* employed a rigid model of archetypology to organize the massive detail of the text. Joseph Campbell and Henry Robinson's *Skeleton Key to "Finnegans Wake"* characterized the *Wake* as a "prodigious, multifaceted monomyth" with five main characters all functioning as stable, categorical structures to which elements of history repetitiously adhered.[34] Suppressing Joyce's ironization of the "hierarchitectitiptitoploftical" (FW 5.01), this application of Jungian archetypes to character was provisionally accepted by critics, for it extended early symbolist readings of *Ulysses* and made Joyce's most difficult work accessible. While Campbell and Robinson were hardly simplistic in their formulation of archetypal character, their understanding of the process of repetition was one-sided, tilted heavily toward an integrated awareness of the possibility of *repeated identities* (as sameness) rather than toward the dissonance and variance that repetition allows. Without an understanding of such dissonance, they concluded that characters were repeated in non-shifting cycles that returned toward, more than they wandered from, points of origin. Their book, *A Skeleton Key to Finnegans Wake* (1944), has since been broadly criticized,[35] although most all Joyce critics realize the immense debt owed it. And indeed, the influence of their archetypology remains strong in contemporary readings of the *Wake*.[36] In general, the emphasis on a return to identities, rather than a more precise mapping out of Joyce's associative tangents, has left a persistent thread in receptions of the *Wake*.

Scholars may be most familiar with Jung's notion of archetypes, yet the concept of archetypal system derives conceptually from Plato's *eidos*, and was first used by Philo Judaes (20 BCE – 50 CE) to describe the *Imago Dei* in man, the image of God that operates as man's determining possibility.[37] Joyce became familiar with archetypal systems through his reading of classical thinkers such as Plato, whose *eidos* was that of forms that reside in the mind of God, and St. Augustine, who argues that God's *ideae principales* determine the world. Jung argues that St. Augustine's system of *ideae principales* is an archetypal model *contained within* God's understanding. For St. Augustine, God not only kept the *ideae principales* in his mind, but God's Word (the verbum) was a perfect, objective whole to which man's language could only fragmentarily aspire.[38] It seems odd that critics would then apply archetypal reading to a text so bent on replaying the "babel" of language that contrasts to God's "Word." Discussing Joyce's use of the portmanteau word in *Finnegans Wake*, Derek Attridge warns that, "there is no escape from its insistence that meaning is an *effect* of language, not a presence within or behind it, and that the effect is unstable and uncontrollable."[39]

Yet in some part the continued attachment to categorical constructs of identity has been accepted as one of the inevitabilities of reading the *Wake*. This seems to arise in part from a broad critical reliance on early summaries of Giambattista Vico's work as an emphasis on historical cycles. Most influentially, William York Tindall found, in *The New Science*, an interesting circularity of history, a replay of cycles that were at once "same" and different.[40] Periods were separated into the Divine Age, the Heroic Age, the human, the primitive, and so on, but all were charted on a rise and fall thematic that fits with Joyce's interest in the Fall in *Finnegans Wake*. As Bishop points out, however, this is merely a synopsis of book IV of *The New Science*, comprising less than a quarter of Vico's work.[41] While Tindall's application is in many ways helpful and relevant, a near avalanche of implications have taken Joyce's last work into these archetypal modes of reading. The question remains: if Joyce in some portion partook of the cyclical notion of history, what else was there in Vico that he had to appropriate—and perhaps radically question—in his own work?

In response to questions of "Why Joyce and Vico?" one can just as readily ask, "Why Jung?" Other than the times—the 1950s when Jung's work was being brought into literary studies, supporting the drive to be able to control and interpret the world with a wary eye toward chaos—there is only the possible affinity with aspects of Vico that Joyce arguably works against. Indeed, one might suspect a retaliatory appropriation, in that Joyce refused with annoyance one patroness's insistence that he should try analysis with Jung.[42] Archetypes are invoked in the *Wake*, much as stereotypes are, in the crude and sometimes aggressive service of recognition and assessment. As HCE's transgressions are judged in light of Parnell's, his minor infractions meet with greater offense. Etymologically, the term "archetype" breaks down into two components: the "arche," which defines a point of origin, a ruler, or law (definition itself), and "type," which connotes a copy or imprint of a repetition. Archetypes are thus repeated types governed by predetermined laws, and as such they suppress repetition's more unruly side. Jung surmises that, with its inborn assembly of archetypes, the collective unconscious is "more or less the same everywhere in all individuals."[43]

In dealing with such archetypes, he claims that "we are dealing with the archais or . . . primorial types, that is with universal images that have existed since the remotest times."[44] This may seem benign, providing an important connection between disparate communities. And yet it is also the source of stereotypes, which are, in a sense, "empirically based archetypes," which Jung sees as coming alive in social or individual projections.[45]

Jung, like Vico, was keenly aware of the powers of archetypal universalizations; he saw archetypology as a system that could fill the gap left by religion in the modern era. Although he did not imagine archetypes that work like traditional religious ones (emanating from the mind of a deity), Jung venerated and emulated religion's use of universal symbols and images in order to "attract, to convince, to fascinate, and to overpower."[46] Critics began to suspect Jung's beliefs of a detrimental political edge in the 1930s when Jung, as president of the International Medical Society of Psychiatry, defended National Socialism. Intellectuals have since become acutely aware of the affinities between his rigidly predetermined system and the Third Reich's reliance on racial and sexual stereotypes.[47] Jung in fact works to define the psychology of race and nationalism through a notion of predisposition, a notion demonstrably opposed to Joyce's treatment of race in the *Wake*.[48] Jung himself grapples with the problem of determinism, so latent in his archetypal system. While he begins with a notion of transcendental (or *a priori*) forms that remain unchanged throughout history, he occasionally takes recourse to a more Aristotelian notion of change effected through experience. In analyzing the relationship between archetype and experience, Andrew Samuels suggests that it is a kind of "feedback system," in which "repeated experiences leave residual psychic structures which become archetypal structures. But these structures exert an influence on experience, tending to organise it according to the pre-existing pattern."[49] Samuels sidesteps Jung's early insistence on the hereditary nature of the archetype, however, whereby such "experiences" as are under discussion predate the subject and thereby are more likely to "grip" the individual and "hold him." To be "healthy," according to Jung, an individual must make these unconscious patterns conscious and accept them.

Jung changes his definition of archetype over the course of his career, but most influentially he formulated archetypes as a prehistorically determined possibility handed down through the collective unconscious with which all individuals are born.[50] While Jung does not claim recourse to the consciousness of any deity, the past still controls the present and history predetermines the future. This history of predestination finds a comical echo in Joyce's doubled chronology, which reaches back as it springs forward. In *Finnegans Wake*, such oscillating temporality is defined by the influences of gossip and rumor, effecting only communal amusement and fanciful assessment, thus undermining its mythological and universalizing force. Moreover, in contradistinction to the Wake's transgressive language, which overflows boundaries, archetypology works to maintain an *equilibrious* state between the conscious and the unconscious parts of the mind, enabling the mind to stabilize identity. This is necessary, according to Jung, because the individual's identity is jeopardized whenever the conscious part of the mind dips down into the waters of the unconscious, where chaotic dissolution inevitably occurs. Just as rite and dogma function on the level of consciousness to hold man's identity in place—bracing it against the dissembling waters of the unconscious—so archetype pulls the mind into a stabilizing structure, an organization of the unconscious's chaos.[51] The appeal of this for a first time reader of the *Wake* would be hard to miss.

Despite the slide toward determinism and authoritarian forms of containment implicit in archetypal systems, Joyce's proximity to Vico— and in some quarters Jung—suggests that this system is being parodically and dialectically invoked. The crucial question here is the extent to which Joyce's parody is complicitous with the controlling impulses present in Vico and Jung. Vicki Mahaffey is one of many who view the *Wake* as "an immensely subtle critique, or 'reading,' of the limitations of monological authority that anticipates many of the arguments advanced on different theoretical and political fronts over the last twenty years."[52] Indeed, in the children's school lesson (FW II, i), the archetypal father is tipped over by the uncertainty encoded in (Wakean) words. The lecturer begins by navigating the space, only to focus on "fahr, be fear!" (FW 260.15). This may be an invective to drive on ("fahr" is to ride or travel, in German), but also sounds vaguely like "Father!" This provisional paternal citing is then followed by a discourse on the naughty "marriage of Montan" to a "hoyden" or ill-bred girl (FW 260.16–18). After focusing on the ills and identificatory elisions of H.C.E. ("him, a chump of the evums" FW 261.13–14), he is, once again, waked (mourned and awakened). As "the babbers ply the pen" (FW 262.27), we get a rough attempt to recreate history, soon abandoned with "Pastimes are past times. Now let bygones be bei Gunne's" (FW 263.17–18). Here, Joyce lets the lecturer's voice plunge into a brief invocation of archetypology:

> Saaleddies er it in this warken werden, mine boerne, and it vild need olderwise since primal made alter in garden of Idem. The tasks above are as the flasks below, saith the emerald canticle of Hermes and all's loth and pleasetir, are we told, on excellent inkbottle authority, solarsystemised, seriolcosmically, in a more and more almightily

expanding universe under one, there is rhymeless reason to believe, original sun. Securely judges orb terrestrial. *Haud certo ergo.* But O felicitious culpability, sweet bad cess to you for an archetypt! (FW 263.18–30)

With pompous authority, the lecturer holds forth the image of timeless truth—that of original sin (and—comically—sun). The first line draws off a shrug and explanation, that the world is just like that.[53] It has always been wild, ever since the first altar was erected in Eden. This transtemporal sameness is emphasized, however, in the misspelling of Eden as "Idem" (Latin for sameness). A reversed H.C.E. (emerald canticle of Hermes) is cited as an authority, declaring all as love (and loathing) and pleasure (or please-tear). H.C.E.'s "excellent inkbottle authority" is universalized, "solarsystemised" and set up as a serial truth of the cosmos (seriocomically). *Haud certo ergo* undermines the assertion, claiming, "not at all certainly, therefore," after which we get an interesting outburst, a curse on the "archetypt," who has shamefully (apparently) sexually transgressed. The archetypal letters (H.C.E.) are elsewhere tipped over as ɯ (FW 6.32), and frustration with the language's failure emerges. In a sense then, the malaise of the letter unsettles the universal rootedness of truth and judgment, its sexual parapraxes and sensate seductions operating as a repeated troubling to archetypal power in the text, a reminder of how particularity—in alphabetic bits or patriarchal transgressions—can disrupt definitional categories and far-reaching claims.

Joyce uses verbal slips and puns as a way of taunting authoritarian judgments. In the scenario of Yawn's refusal to reify for the Four magistrates, verbal slips fissure identity and the "tactile O" distracts us from our own interpretive judgments. Toward the middle of *Finnegans Wake*, Jaun bemoans our "crass, hairy and evergrim life" amidst the chaos of eternal change. Looking forward to the Judgment Day, he foresees a time when "the Royal Revolver of these real globoes lets regally fire of his *mio colpo*" and then begins "Putting Allspace in a Notshall" (FW 455.26–29). It was Hamlet who complained that he might be "bounded in a nutshell and count myself a king of infinite space—were it not that I have bad dreams" (I, ii, lns. 254–56). Bad dreams, for Jaun, are full of constant change, shifting identities, and a barrage of particulars. Such chaos inspires him to press for some tidy containment, some reduction into moralism. "Nutshells" and "Notshalls" are not entirely different when the act of judgment requires reduction and containment, and the suppression of future possibilities.

If Joyce enacts this slippage constantly in his gestural language, thematically he repeatedly recasts the destructive nature of polarized aggressions. In the "Shem the Penman" passage (FW I, vii), the speaker

(Shaun) uses identity in order to denigrate and condemn his brother Shem's character. He treats consolidated identity as a means to aggression, using social codes and dictates for a personal end. This is, in Joyce, a model of how broad social codes can be brutally wrought into an act of negative stereotyping. Shem first attacks Shem's origins, his pretense at "respectable stemming," complaining that his origins "will not stand being written about in black and white" (FW 169.3, 7–8). Thus he dismisses one method of establishing identity by tracing ancestral origins. Still, taking a "shot" at describing "what this hybrid actually was like to look at," the speaker decides to use external appearances as indicators of character. The list of items begins technically, with a counting of the "fortytwo hairs off his uncrown," and "eighteen to his mock lip" (FW 169.9–10, 13). But then Shaun turns increasingly toward clichés of character. Shem has "not a foot to stand on," "a deaf heart," and "a manroot of all evil" (FW 169.16–19). He is next taken down even further: "Shem was a sham and a low sham and his lowness creeped out first via foodstuffs. So low was he that he preferred Gibsen's tea-time salmon tinned, as inexpensive as pleasing, to the plumpest roeheavy lax or the friskiest parr or smolt troutlet that ever was gaffed between Leixlip and Island Bridge" (FW 170.25–29). Shem, in his eating habits, seems to be the unfortunate victim of advertisers and prepackaged food of the modern era. If the adage "you are what you eat" can be applied to Shem, Shaun has identified his brother again only to degrade him further. The speaker criticizes Shem's shunning of "fried-at-belief-stakes" and other dogmatic "beefs"—"Rosbif of Old Zealand! he could not attouch it" (FW 171.1–2). Shem, we are told, is not only a "virgitarian" but a pacifist who "even ran away with hunself and became a farsoonerite, saying he would far sooner muddle through the hash of lentils in Europe than meddle with Irrland's split little pea" (FW 171.3–6). Low loathsome Shem is next judged by his alcohol preference, and since he unfortunately drinks "a rhubarbarous maundarin yella-green funkleblue windigut diodying applejack squeezed from sour grapefruice" (FW 171.16–18), he is again dismissed as loathsome.

In the rivalrous process of polarization, identity plays the key role. As twins, Shem and Shaun resist their identificatory aspects. Shaun, especially, repeats scenarios of judgmental denigration of Shem, exaggerating (one suspects) his brother's negative difference. Analyzing the problem of the agonism of identification, Lacoue-Labarthe demonstrates how the desire for stable mimetic identification creates the form of aggression, described by René Girard as a kind of Oepidal violence. Asking if there is an alternative to this violence, Lacoue-Labarthe poses the possibility of "désistence," an oscillation of the self between a variety of identifications.[54] This multiplicity of options reduces the tempta-

tion to lock into an oppositional identification with one; it also complicates the act of taking a moral position—while it does *not* actually dis-
pense with ethical concerns. A reader of the *Wake* might well adopt a
similar gesture of "désistence" or parodic oscillation between moments
of identification with and critical differentiations from Joyce's texts, for
Joyce's own critique of stark identification and polarized aggression suggests that we pull away from such insistences.

Previously, many critics believed Joyce softened polarization through
synthesis, using Giordano Bruno's theory of the coincidence of contraries. Joyce cites Bruno in "The Day of the Rabblement," and, as
Atherton suggests, he seems to have encountered Bruno's work in
school, later reviewing him in translations in Coleridge's *The Friend*.[55]
According to Coleridge, opposition is a force in conceptual formation:
"EVERY POWER IN NATURE AND IN SPIRIT *must evolve an opposite, as the
sole means and condition of its manifestation*: AND ALL OPPOSITION IS A
TENDENCY TO RE-UNION. . . . The *Identity* of Thesis and Antithesis is the
substance of all *Being*; their *Opposition* the condition of all *Existence*,
or Being manifested; and every *Thing* or Phænomenon is the Exponent
of a Synthesis as long as the opposite energies are retained in the Synthesis."[56] Synthesis is termed "Indifference," and indeed it would seem
to put an end to the oscillation Joyce so comically repeats in the *Wake*.
Coleridge explains synthesis with the example of H_2O. Water combines
its elements, attaining a *copula* that is more than the collection of two
bodies; it is a synthesis. In this way, Coleridge determines the emergence
of an essential identity. In Joyce's work, split identities cannot be so easily resolved. He allows characters to be subsumed into one another on
occasion, but this does not function as a full dissolution of differences,
as in consolidated identity. Oppositions are not rigidified but are forever
transforming within the associative process of dreaming. As Margot
Norris approaches the question of Anna Livia's various transformations
in the *Wake*, for example, she asks, "How then do we account for these
diverse forms and functions of Anna Livia Plurabelle—old, young, ugly,
beautiful, faithful, treacherous, brutalized, manipulative, rejected,
desired, redeeming, tempting? 'Dreams go by contraries' (U 571), we
learn in *Ulysses*, and as the dreamer's wishes turn into their opposite in
dream, so the woman is transformed again and again into her opposite."[57] I wish to suggest that contraries are overcome only when identity
is released from conflict by radical multiplication *beyond* the binaristic
tension. Joyce does not copy Bruno; he expands upon his thesis, multi-
plying contraries to destabilize oppositional engagements. Identification
may therefore slip out of its equilibrium and its contained vacillation

between two poles. Coleridge's H_2O is transformed by Joyce into H_2CE_3 (FW 95.12). Comically, this gaseous identity is an essence thinned to near erasure, as Joyce destroys HCE's primary residence of personal identity, his name, signaling a parodic deflation of universalizations.

HCE: THE MAN, THE SIGLA, THE NAME

Joyce tirelessly and repeatedly destroys HCE's "agnomen." He is often sighted passing through the text under the guise of different words such as "Howth Castle and Environs" (FW 3.3) or "Hush! Caution! Echoland!" (FW 13.5), "He'll Cheat E'erawan" (FW 46.01), and backwards as well: "*Et Cur Heli!*" (FW 73.19). He is even identified by one of his accusers in a long acrostic of HERE COMES EVERYBODY: "*Helmingham Erchenwyne Rutter Egbert*" (FW 88.21).[58] In Shaun's first riddle, in the "Shem the Penman" passage, we are asked: "When is a man not a man?" (FW 170.5). The reader eventually finds out that it is "when he is a . . . sham!" (FW 170.23–4). A fake, but also when his name is not spelled right—Sham for Shem. Joyce destroys the proper name by misspelling it, inverting it, reducing it to initials, and then replacing it altogether with sigla. We are given a whole list of abusive names HCE has been called—names like Old Fruit, York's Porker, Hoary Hairy Hoax, Woolworth's Worst, or—simply—Dirt (FW 71–72). But most abusive and decentering is the text's constant rewriting of the name behind the initials.

In the *Wake*, Joyce explains the sigla, marks he initially invented to indicate character appearances in his notes:

> the meant to be baffling chrismon trilithon sign ⋔, finally called after some his hes hecitency Hec, which, moved contrawatchwise, represents his title in sigla as the smaller Δ, fontly called following a certain change of state of grace of nature alp or delta, when single, stands for or tautologically stands beside the consort. (FW 119.17–22)

These signs are thus "meant to be baffling" even as they *do* "represent" characters' changing natures. In a footnote, Joyce later lists the whole "Doodles family ⋔, Δ, ⊣, ×, □, ∧, ⊏. Hoodle doodle, fam.?" (FW 299n4). Joyce's sigla allow characterizations to hang as loosely as possible around an almost non-existent essence, while leaving some tensional connection. Farther from language than nouns, pronouns, initials, or proper names, the sigla are almost pure blank sign. Not satisfied even with this level of dis-identification, Joyce moves one step farther from reference, listing possible descriptions of the sigla's visual image and using these descriptions in the text. X, for instance, is the sigla that marks the presence of the four old men, but the text of the *Wake* at one point indicates this not with an "X" but by mentioning "a multiplication marking for crossroads ahead" (FW 119.28–29). And so character identity, which is normally indicated by a given name, must rise and fall among a multitude of references, while the name thins down to a bare trace. It is as though Joyce has taken characterization and, punning on "character" as a visual mark, reduced character types to alphabetic bits that work, as mere letters do, by circulating their constantly recombinable elements. Just as Joyce's mis- and respellings challenge normative clichés and stereotypic definitions, so his introduction of the sigla takes verbal representation beyond the reach of archetype. The constant defamiliarization of language may be thinly held back from the uninterpretable by HCE and the sigla's persistent associations, but any law of language (particularly the Word of the Father) will dissipate in the face of Joyce's verbal experiment.[59]

MARCEL JOUSSE AND GESTURAL LANGUAGE

Early in *Finnegans Wake*, a Giant stands with "one Berlin gauntlet chopstuck in the hough of his ellboge (by ancientest signlore his gesture meaning: ∃!)" (FW 36.15–17). Joyce found humorous appeal in primitive gestures, here one calling for combat, but he also was serious about their importance to language. As I discussed, in chapter 2, Joyce's work was influenced by eurhythmics, the notion that the body should rhythmically enact musical measure, so as to teach students better the nature of music. Language, in Joyce, incorporates other sensate mediums into its own, and in that Joyce discovers the sensate aspects of words. In *Finnegans Wake*, language ripples under the effects of oral (and cultural) pronunciations, personal vocal inflection, homonymic confusions, and the very visibility of letters. If Jaques-Dalcroze's eurhythmics, along with the predominance of street mime and music in Dublin, helped Joyce shape his early notion of gestural art, in the 1920s, when Joyce was already engaged in the early stages of writing *Finnegans Wake*, he encountered another, equally forceful thinker who was reflecting on the collusion between body and speech. Marcel Jousse's work on the Christological notion of gestural meaning captured the imagination of many authors besides Joyce, perhaps being suited to those working after French Symbolism and also interested in the mimic possibilities of art.[60] As Mary Colum recalls, Joyce had joined her in attending one of Jousse's "evangelical pantomimes" in Paris—in or around June of 1928.[61] Colum reports that the pantomime they witnessed included a parable, which was recited by the "Rabbi Jesus" to a group of young girls. In this parable, Jesus pursues the topic of how the word is shaped by gesture. Lorraine Weir traces Joyce's first encounter with Jousse's ideas, in the evangelical pantomime, to his work, some few months later, on The Third Watch of Shem (FW III, iii). As I discussed in chapter five, Yawn there lies beached like a whale, "wailing" or snoring in his sleep (FW 474). He is approached by the four magistrates, who cross-examine him as to his identity (he is now both Ireland and, they are hoping, HCE). But Yawn resists such reifications, and is at one point distracted by "Typette, my tactile O!" (FW 478.27). Desire for the letter seems to detract from consolidating narratives, and, indeed, in this section Joyce works to fuse desire to language. Later, HCE will again defend himself against the accusations of the cad: "The caca cad!" he stutters, "He walked by North Strand with his Thom's towel in hand. Snakeeye! Strangler of soffiacated green parrots! I protest it that he is, by my wipehalf" (FW 534.26–29). Much like Shaun's protest of Shem's behavior—that he is his worse half—HCE identifies the cad as no more than "caca" or shit ("my wipehalf"). Indeed, the cad is fleetingly associated with Joyce, for he "strangles the parrot," an allusion to drinking absinthe (as Joyce did).[62] But more is going on in this comedy of defenses. What falls out of language, in the interpretive excision of meaning, is both the excremental dross and persistent desire that can shape it. So HCE may obsess on the youthful rainbow girls while he is also focusing on their "alpybecca's unwachsibles" (FW 483.19–20), those alphabetic syllables that are unwashable, unclean, and given to naughty slips. How then is this related to a Joussean notion of gesture?

Jousse was especially interested in the moments where bodily instincts and language fused. In the "Law of Bilateral Gesture," he examines the use of gesture in pantomimes and concludes that they derive from Palestinian culture, where bodily rhythms were consciously integrated into ritualistic recitations, like the Mass.[63] If Joyce discovered in Dalcroze the method of linking the body to art, with Jousse he discovers gesture in its *linguistic* experience. Jousse postulated that, when people are trained to recite orally, a residue of living gestures influences their writing.[64] In contemporary body language, Jousse found that this resonated in the manner in which children, learning to mimic words, recite not only with their mouths but physically respond or "play" with their whole bodies. "It isn't that he (the child) wishes to play; he 'is played,'" according to Jousse, so that the body responds in a compulsive manner as the child struggles with his or her recitation.[65] While Jousse may be interested in the body's accompaniment to language, I would suggest that Joyce seems more intrigued by language's circling about the body, in the Third Watch of Shaun. And so, when HCE rants on about the cad's ill nature, he addresses briefly "Barktholed von Hunarig"

(FW 535.2)—possibly Bartholomew Vanhomrigh, the father of Swift's adored Vanessa[66]—lamenting that it was his "Soesown of Furrows" (season of sorrows, furrowing brows, or sexual burrowing? both if his transgression is discovered). In an aside he commends "hourspringlike his joussture, immitiate my chry! as urs now, so yous then!" (FW 535.2–4). The imitation of a noise (a cry, perhaps) will bring on an automatic physical gesture (spring-like, perhaps a regular as a watch, brought forth or held back as the Cad requests the time). This gesture may be repeated, as it is ours now and once was yours. Joyce seems to have been contemplating not archetypes encrusted in a collective unconscious, so much as gestures embedded in language and remembered in the body. If they are excremental and thereby discarded by modern notions of the word, Joyce works to reintegrate them into our sense of speech and writing.

By the late 1920s, Jousse was scrutinizing the parallel constructions used in recitations, noting the ways in which repetition both shores up memory and teaches innovation. In *Les Rabbis d'Israël*, he notes the binaristic construction of several teachings. In the phrase, "La Vérité demeure, le Mensonge point ne demeure" ("the truth lives, the lie does not live"), Jousse identifies parallel "clichés" ("Parallélismes-Clichés") that create a primary balance of logic.[67] The rabbi's recitations, which his followers must memorize and repeat, are made up of a series of oppositions such as truth/lie, poor/rich, simple/prudent, earth/sky. Often, Jousse finds, opposite words will be derived from the same root. This similarity enables rapid memorization. And while these parallelisms are lessons based on clichéd modes of understanding, what fascinates Jousse is the complex play between conscious teaching and unconscious thought. The parallels introduce a *rhythm* that appeals to a "psycho-physical law," providing a balance between the lesson and its renewal. Jousse notes that "all rhythmic schemes that effect a propositional gesture in the muscles of the throat and mouth of the one improvising or reciting acquire from this the inclination to dance anew."[68] This rhythm reaps not dead repetition but a creative energy that encourages renewal. That is, the rhythm compels the player to repeat spontaneously, and Jousse identifies this as a "psycho-physiological phenomenon of stereotypical gestures" that will allow communication among men across ethnic boundaries.[69] These gestures supply a certain body language which Jousse believes to be capable of at least partial comprehension across linguistic and cultural borders. What I find most interesting here is the notion that both the structure of *returning* repetition and of bodily gesture will allow for a bonding recognition, hinting that some thread of similitude—even the thin sigla of Δ, for instance—might enable the reach of memory. Of course, Jousse's use of the terms "stereotype" and "cliché" signals perhaps a more constricted recontainment. After all, the Abbé was interested as well in how liturgical teaching instilled memory and *subscription* in its pupils.

Joyce, however, treats memory as a mass that uses structural returns only to repeatedly overflow the "riverbanks" and disrupt singular narrative. He needs this continuity for meaning to emerge, but takes it farther from stereotype and containment with his oscillations. The sameness he effects is a repetition of movement *between* opposite gestures. In the recourso, a voice asks,

> What has gone? How it ends?
> Begin to forget it. It will remember itself from every sides, with all gestures, in each our word. Today's truth, tomorrow's trend.
> Forget, remember!
> Have we cherished expectations? Are we for liberty of perusiveness? Whyafter what forewhere? A planplanned liffeyism assemblements Eblania's conglomerate horde. By dim delty Deva.
> Forget! (FW 614.19–26)

As the book's narrative draws to a close, Joyce interjects queries about its significance and outcome, while also echoing concerns for history's future. By releasing narrative from its stringent path, we allow it to return (or fear its inevitable repetitions, as well). It will remember itself, including all gestures encoded from past oral histories (and "gestern"s, German for yesterdays). HCE and ALP appear allusively in the questions, "*H*ave we *c*herished *e*xpectations? *A*re we for *l*iberty of *p*erusiveness?" In the tension between character consolidation, which HCE lives out, and the drive for freedom from scrutiny (being perused like a book), which ALP's free flow effects, arises the plan for assembling Eblania's (Dublin's) hoard.[70] Language and history return only in an oscillating play between reification and dissolution. In answer to the imperative to "Forget!" the textual-historical memory of the *Wake* comes its closest to consolidation. A voice declares that "our wholemole millwheeling vicociclometer" will continue "autokinatonetically" taking its "dialytically separate elements of precedent decomposition for the verypetpurpose of subsequent recombination so that heroticisms, catastrophes and eccentricities transmitted by the ancient legacy of the past, type by tope, letter by litter, word at ward." will arise again in "Finnius the old One" (FW 614.27–615.7). The cycles Joyce takes from Vico's inspiration will repeat, taking any variety of "dialytically separate elements" and reworking them into new combinations, scenarios, results. In this autokinetic and tone-effective art, letters may arise from refuse, and words may be "at ward"—at war, under protection, or operating in defense. But eventually, we are told, "Dear. And we go on to Dirtdump.

Reverend." (FW 615.12), suggesting an excremental or at least refuse-laden ending: death of the excess that overflows meaning, death of marginalized material and groups who have been made "litter" by war in any particular cycle. This reconsolidation of Finn is therefore also about recovered marginality. And it is, predictably, not final. Anna Livia's more fluid voice soon takes memory outwards again. So Joyce reclaims the cast-offs of language, recycling the litter of desire and sensate bits back into a form of meaning and then back out to sea, as a reminder of language's materiality.

The gestural art Joyce develops out of Jousse's inspiration is one of a language that repeats familiar scenarios, carrying with it embodiments of moments past. In Joyce, this brings an allusion to sexual exchanges, fusing the sexual gesture with linguistic acts. This occurs through teasing thematics of the text, the verbal slips that clue us in to possible sexual transgressions. But also it occurs within words, so that Joyce's puns may sometimes only replicate the sound of some Irish brogue in the mouth, or merely trill off a list of rivers, places, or historical figures. These puns may point nowhere or toward double and triple meanings, verbal slips being suppressed or multiple histories being written. The verbal gestures thus sometimes take meaning back into a momentarily crystallization, although Joyce then mockingly parallels any attempt to control meaning in Shaun's repeated efforts to seize upon the implications of his language. Joyce seems to forever return to the early linguistic phase of Stephen Dedalus, in *Portrait*, where words are very close to sensate meaning and desire is not yet emptied out of them. In that sense, Joyce himself recycles through his own history to return to a place where his art shares the common bond to the physical enjoyed by mime and song. Personally and artistically, he revitalizes language by opening up its more sensate aspects. Also, however, he is propelled away from an idealistic dwelling on this notion of primeval or natural language, having already discovered words as "conceptual" and abstract, so that the *Wake*'s words play out the tension between this split potential of language.

Gérard Genette, in his schematization of narrative and mimesis, argues that "the very idea of *showing* [in narration] is completely illusory: in contrast to dramatic representation, no narrative can 'show' or 'imitate' the story it tells. All it can do is tell it in a manner which is detailed, precise, 'alive,' and in that way give more or less the *illusion of mimesis*."[71] Yet *Finnegans Wake*'s disruption of language contests this altogether reasonable assertion. Joyce's transmutation of words most often mimics sounds, picking up broad Irish accents in passages laced with language roots varied well beyond Gaelic and English. And his teasing use of the sigla goes so far as to capture the role of visual representation. Their initial mention comes after Macool takes his fall ("Macool, Macool, orra whyi deed ye diie?" FW 6.13), when we are told, "Well, Him a being so on the flounder of his bulk like an over-grown babeling, let wee peep, see, at Hom, well, see peegee ought he ought, platterplate. ш Hum!" (FW 6.30–33). Joyce shows us the sight, requested by the mourners, of HCE laid out for the wake. He is "exten-solies" from head to foot (extolled extensively), and "all the way (a horn!) from fjord [bay] to fjell [mountain] his baywinds' oboboes [cries] shall wail him" (FW 6.35–36).[72] He is waked as a letter (E) that has ceased to function alphabetically and has become a graphic rather than a morpheme. Likewise, the next play with letters (⊓ ace to ⊔ ace) lets the reader see, in alphabetic illustration, the face-off she reads about, the war of "bellicose figurines"—those alpha-bits Joyce contrarily rear-ranges (FW 18.36). After the falling of the "F," the book mourns that, "When a part so ptee [petite] does duty for the holos [whole] we soon grow to use of an allforabit [alphabet]" (FW 18.36–19.02).[73] If one can grow to use the alphabet, one can also grow *too used to* letters, so that Joyce is driven to estrange them from their normal tasks. They become visual again, hieroglyphic or mimeographic—and this becomes *gestural* language. It refuses pure universalization, calling on its "ptee" parts to remind us that it may be "all-for-abit" while also a very resistant par-ticularity. This resides even within the words, as general definitions (types) are invoked for understanding, only then to be disrupted by alphabetic disobedience, tiny mistyped bits.

In the *Wake*, identities dissolve and resurrect at an alarming rate, and Joyce parodies the drive to fix identity by naming and, as well, by asso-ciation:[74]

> Be ownkind. Be kithkinish. Be bloodysibby. Be irish. Be inish. Be offalia. Be hamlet. Be the property plot. Be Yorick and Lankystare. Be cool. Be mackinamucks of yourselves. Be finish. (FW 465.31–34)

Joyce plays on the invective to "be X," to identify oneself with various properties or aspects of character. There could, of course, be almost *any* kind of "ownkind" to associate with; one could be with all of one's "own" sex (all women, for instance) or with one's countrymen (Irish), or with only leaders (Parnell) or martyrs (Christ, Parnell, et al.). Here, the list begins with a reading of "ownkind" as "kithkinish," or familial. To be too devoted to family interests, however, leads to "bloddysibby" behavior, either war within the family or between family tribes. This expands into a broader national identity of being "irish" and then also "inish," islandish ("inis" is Irish for "island") or remaining within internal spaces (innish).[75] To be "offalia," then would be to be offal, the dross or scraps rather than any essence. The word derives, however, from the word "fall," or that which spills over, hinting at Joyce's repeated retellings, in *Finnegans Wake*, of founding figures who fall and are recycled into other tales. The chain of possibilities straggles into role-playing (Hamlet or Ophelia), into conspiracies (the Popish Plot of 1678),[76] place names, attributes, and finally into completion that is non-completion— to "be finish" may be to be finished but also Finnish or like Finn Mac-Cool, who will forever rise again.

Whenever the *Wake* issues a call to *be* something, that *being* immediately slides into a chain of stages and random shifts. The non-meaning of the text often challenges its twin function—the very imperative to identify with one person, thing, or attribute. As Rabaté observes, the *Wake* "cannot . . . be reduced to a 'mimetic' principle, it has to take into account the various emblematic, archetypal, stereotypical and graphological devices through which 'soundsense' and 'sensesound' are made kin again (121.15). The merely decorative tricks and puns are thus justified, and the most arbitrary conjunctions and echoes acquire a cosmological sense—in the double sense of *cosmos*, meaning both 'decoration' and 'world.'"[77] The general and the particular, or the archetype and the distinct attribute, function in tension with one another, so that the *Wake* is not equilibrious realism but a constantly mobile text, shifting between "decoration" as pleasure and "world" as meaning.

Early in the *Wake*, a drunken voice assures one that

> papyr is meed of, made of, hides and hints and misses in prints. Till ye finally (though not yet endlike) meet with the acquaintance of Mister Typus, Mistress Tope and all the little typtopies. Fillstup. So you need hardly spell me how every word will be bound over to carry three score and ten toptypsical readings throughout the book of Doublends Jined (may his forehead be darkened with mud who would sunder!) till Daleth, mahomahouma, who oped it closeth thereof the. Dor. (FW 20.10–18)

This "abcedminded" (FW 18.17) text is woven of "hides and hints and misses in prints" that eventually swirl into characters, but not personal so much as alphabetical characters: "Mister Typus, Mistress Tope and all the little typetopies" may be subjects fleetingly, but they are more clearly typewritten characters (alphabetical) on the page. The tension between typological categories that are laced through the text and the "type" or typeface of letters is heightened, so that the material presence of language disrupts full access to anything we might call meaning. If one hears, "type us"—and the Latin root *typus* as figure or image—this is not an invitation to stereotype or categorize the characters, so much as a request for immortality—put us in print. By inscribing "three score and ten toptypsical readings" in every word, Joyce creates the multiple readings that generate history, but a form of history that is alternately constructive and deconstructive, flowing in a necessary tension between such points. He creates a cosmopolitan consciousness in this refusal to separate the particularity of perspective (and body) from its more general, conceptual reach.

Joyce writes: "In the beginning was the gest he jousstly says" (FW 468.5). Gesture is now written both in the beginning, prior to concept in some dream of a primitive state, but also at the end, where the word is forever leaping toward the *eidos* that claims it. As Joyce's language repeatedly returns to its materiality to disrupt the conceptual abstraction supposed to structure language, he recasts the ways in which we can understand the definitional boundaries of words, voices, and history. This is a redefinition that is forever recommencing, so that in the *Wake* "no geste reveals the unconnouth. They're all odds against him, the beasties. Scratch. Start." (FW 227.27–28). Over and again.

EPILOGUE

Thank you, I feel a little better of the rheumatism and am now
more like a capital S than a capital Z
                                        —James Joyce, Letter to Poppie Joyce

It is amusing to think of Joyce as a letter, a typographical character in
his own text. If he was more than the textual residue he has left, the odd
notion of an embodiment in language remains. Were he less than a
name, might fewer conceptual quarrels have found him? Imagine him as
a letter, or litter, or simply a typographic character (S or Z). It could be
much the same were he a voice, a singer, and so closer to a recognizably
sensate resonance within his chosen medium.

What Joyce leaves us, instead, is a textual gesture, one that points
away from those many fictional scenarios we might more conventionally
recognize as *what* he represents: a young scholar strident in his resistance to church, state, and religion; a middle-aged man sexually excited
by the glimpse of lifted skirts; a young girl practicing her adolescent
wiles before a mirror; two brothers, split out of one, forever at war upon
one another; an older man falling into dreams, nightmares of societal
censure, and the woman who recovers him with an outward flow of love
and memory. These images may be crystallized by bent of recognition,
but what Joyce's aesthetics were bent toward—and his politics encoded
within—was the problem of *how* representations take shape. Progressively, Joyce moved his form away from fixity and aggression. His fluid
mutation of styles has received much critical attention, yet readers interested in literary politics still often search for a politics hidden somehow
behind the textual transmutations of *Ulysses* and *Finnegans Wake*. As if
"politics" were an abstract collection of beliefs rather than a series of
lived and embodied gestures. Politics as action is not here separate from
textual politics, embedded in language. Did Joyce intend this, as some
pious politics for the critics to evaluate? No, it doesn't seem likely. But
the gradual deliverance of his preoccupation with the Word's recovery
and a resistance to the more insistently masterful and oppressive gestures
in society led him into it. A weave of conscious intentions and unconscious developments culminates in concern with gender, sexuality, and
nationalism, leading so surprisingly to this new, gestural art.

I hope here to have fused an understanding of both thematic concerns and linguistic phenomenon, drawing partially on both American-Anglo and French critical approaches to Joyce's oeuvre. In terms of feminist inquiries into Joyce's representation of women, I am suggesting that the figuration of women crucially influenced Joyce's approach to gestural art. The eroticism suppressed by Stephen Dedalus re-emerges in Joyce's aesthetic transformations, moving him progressively closer to a text that encompasses and enacts desire within its very medium. If, in *Portrait*, textual oscillations fail to undermine Stephen Dedalus's stereotypes and controlling gestures toward women, the gradual explosion of stylistic parody, perspectival fissuring, and the release of women's voices in *Ulysses* demonstrates an increasingly conscious effort, on Joyce's part, to incorporate the feminine rather than control and hold it at a distance. Moreover, Joyce writes a metacritique of gender politics in *Finnegans Wake*, mapping that struggle alongside the history of war between nations. He thus interposes domestic politics and that "other" politics, which goes on in the public sphere. When Earwicker, the "father of Izod," launches a campaign upon Anna Liffey, we are told that "he came, he kished, he conquered" her (FW 512.8, 12). The cycling of wars and the rise and fall of nations has often been remarked in the *Wake*, but few have pursued Joyce's fusion of "politics" as both gendered and national. On both fronts, Joyce evades the aggression, likened to war and sexual, physical force, by writing in puns and parapraxes, reminders that language always enacts a meeting between the concept and its embodiment. The domination of nations, of races, and of women occurs most readily when one separates the "political issues" from the reality of their physical effects. Who other than an author would believe in the *physical* force of words? Who better than Joyce, who feared violence and the crack of thunder, could embed his critique in the word?

With respect to Irish nationalism, I have suggested that Joyce's strong attachment to his country was marked by an ambivalence that for him was *itself* Irish. That is, the very perspectival vantage of Irishness is for Joyce marked by betrayal and a duality of opinions, so impressed as he was in his youth by the social rejection of Parnell. This split operation is gradually encoded within the styles of *Ulysses* and the language of *Finnegans Wake*. Joyce finally understands this tensional perspective as a cosmopolitan movement of sympathies that crosses the space between the subject's situated position and his or her curiosity about more worldly culture, history, and events. Taking up an archetypal system from Vico, Joyce shakes the very foundations of such a form, questioning the call for definitional boundaries and categorical constraints. Consequently, he offers atypical typographies and (dis)identifications in characters who operate like so many dashes scattered across the text, drawing on their ever-expanding associative possibilities.

In his reappropriation of lesbian and gay clichés, Joyce takes Freudian and cultural images of narcissism and paranoia, associated with homosexuality, and turns those supposed negatives into a deconstructive form of textuality. Paranoid-aggressive behavior is now linked to homophobic responses to sexual ambivalence, and narcissism is more readily associated with heterosexual pressures than a doubling of the erotic body. Through these clichés, Joyce maps the extremes of textuality, its radical clarity in force and its muted mumblings that can barely be overheard. As the text that most radically replays scenarios of aggression and narcissism, *Finnegans Wake* also uses those gestures in its textualizing process, to ensure both interpretable reach and pleasurable dissipation in the face of any too stringent fixity. So while Joyce deconstructs stereotypes of gays and lesbians, he also uses those types to reconfigure his writing process.

Scholars talk about textual politics. The concerns raised by Joyce's work go beyond the question of whether to affirm realism or break towards the avant-garde. Implicit in such a formulation is the query: is politics always fully conscious—or is it not also a trajectory of thought? Joyce's work both *identifies* the psychological trajectories imbedded within benign and aggressive representations, while also pointing to the *embodiment* of other rhythmic and associative gestures within the language so crucial to art made with the written word. And so we can come to understand Joyce's parody as not only a comic commentary on previous writers; it is also inscribed within his various narrative perspectives and finally within the words themselves. That is, the early split referentially of Joyce's parody gives way to the dual effect of language, fissuring and occasionally reconnecting in Joyce's play on its conceptual and sensate aspects.

While the rationalist emphasis of the Enlightenment presses us, still, to seize on the concepts *behind* the veil of language, Joyce reminds us that meaning emerges from both the reference and the physical nature of the medium itself. He also writes in the dualities of conscious and unconscious motivations, local and worldly views, masculine and feminine perspectives, foreign and familiar experiences, homo- and heteroerotics. Meaning emerges through the combination of nodal points of intensity and the splintering away from such conceptual and experiential capture. Joyce's examination of significance and signification in *Finnegans Wake* might eventually change the way we understand meaning, so often defined as a normative, homogeneous point, consolidated thought, or singular insight. Joyce has inspired philosophers like Jacques

Lacan and Jacques Derrida in their formulations of psychoanalytic and deconstructive interpretation, and his radical *écriture* has been a focal point for thinkers like Hélène Cixous and Julia Kristeva. His experiments with both form and language continue to influence contemporary writers, whose postmodern art constantly reconfigures our approach to society, self, and perception.

NOTES

CHAPTER 1. INTRODUCTION

1. *The Letters of James Joyce*, ed. Richard Ellmann, vol. 2 (New York: Viking Press, 1966), 183.

2. See Richard Ellmann's biography, *James Joyce*, rev. ed. (New York: Oxford University Press, 1982), 98–104 and passim for a position on Joyce's cosmopolitanism. In his essay "Joyce and Nationalism," Seamus Deane takes up previous characterizations of Joyce as apolitical, arguing that rather than repudiating Irish nationalism Joyce understood its history as a lesson in the potency of rhetoric. Joyce, then, figures as "Irish" as his words stage the rebellion lost in parliament and armed rebellion. See Deane, "Joyce and Nationalism," in *James Joyce: New Perspectives*, ed. Colin MacCabe (Sussex: Harvester Press and Bloomington: Indiana University Press, 1982), 168–83.

3. Kristeva, in *Desire in Language: A Semiotic Approach to Literature and Art*, ed. Leo Roudiez, trans. Thomas Gora, Alice Jardine, and Leon S. Roudiez (New York: Columbia University Press, 1980). For a discussion of *écriture féminine* as it relates to *Finnegans Wake*, see Suzette Henke's discussion in the "Ricourso" of *James Joyce and the Politics of Desire* (London: Routledge, 1990). Gilbert and Gubar, *No Man's Land: The Place of the Woman Writer in the Twentieth Century*, vol. 1 (New Haven: Yale University Press, 1988), discussed below.

4. Vicki Mahaffey argues that Joyce represents homosexuality as one of a range of associated "perversions" in his work, and Jean-Michel Rabaté likewise interprets homosexuality in tandem with a repeated triangulation of desire. See their articles, "Père-version and Im-mère-version: Idealized Corruption in *A Portrait of the Artist as a Young Man* and *The Picture of Dorian Gray*" (189–206) and "On Joycean and Wildean Sodomy" (159–66), respectively, in the special issue on "Joyce and Homosexuality" of the *James Joyce Quarterly* 31.3 (Spring 1994). For more on Joyce and (homo)sexuality, see *Quare Joyce*, ed. Joseph Valente (Ann Arbor: University of Michigan Press, 1998).

5. Hayman begins shaping this argument in his first book, *Joyce et Mallarmé*, 2 vols. (Paris: Lettres Modernes, 1956). It is still taking shape in recent works like *The "Wake" in Transit* (Ithaca and London: Cornell University Press, 1990). See my discussion of this in chapters 2 and 6.

6. Soon after *Ulysses* was published, Adrienne Monnier ironically commented that Joyce's emersion of Gerty MacDowell in the world of women's fiction was all too historically accurate: "That devil of a Joyce has left out nothing. The masculine public keenly enjoyed this chapter." ("Joyce's *Ulysses* and the

French Public," in *Les Gazettes d'Adrienne Monnier*, May 1940. Cited in Bonnie Kime Scott, *Joyce and Feminism* [Bloomington: Indiana University Press, 1984], 103.)

7. For an incisive discussion of these camps, see Marianne DeKoven's piece, "The Politics of Modernist Form," in *New Literary History* 23 (1992): 675–90.

8. See Bell, *Jocoserious Joyce: Fate and Folly in Ulysses* (Ithaca, N.Y.: Cornell University Press, 1991). Bell employs David Hayman's early observation that Joyce uses stagetypes in order to discuss the nature of his farce. While Bell is brilliantly sensitive to the laughter that runs through Joyce's work, he at times inadvertently reinforces the stereotypes that Joyce takes up. Bowen, on the other hand, describes Joyce's humor as that of radical and consistent transgression of social norms. Using Bakhtin's notion of the carnivalesque, Bowen casts Joyce's humor in light of the fertility cycle surrounding the myth of Dionysus, illuminating the humor marvelously but likewise marginalizing the relations between humor and stereotypes. See *Ulysses as a Comic Novel* (Syracuse: Syracuse University Press, 1989).

9. Sigmund Freud, *Jokes and Their Relation to the Unconscious*, trans. and ed. James Strachey *The Standard Edition of the Complete Psychological Works of Sigmund Freud* (New York and London: W. W. Norton, 1960), vol. 8:151. Originally published as *Der Witz und seine Beziehung zum Unbewussten* (Leipzig: F. Deuticke, 1905).

10. Henri Bergson, "Le Rire," translated as "Laughter" in *Comedy*, trans. and ed. Wylie Sypher (Baltimore: Johns Hopkins University Press, 1956), 61–190.

11. This ironic consciousness can be traced through the works of Schlegel, Kierkegaard, and Nietzsche, but also appears in English Romanticism as noncomic denial (Wordsworth). Romantic irony received the greatest attention among the literati in France, and Paul de Man finds it most apparent in the writings of Charles Baudelaire and Stéphane Mallarmé. See Paul de Man, "The Rhetoric of Temporality," in *Blindness and Insight: Essays in the Rhetoric of Contemporary Criticism* (Minneapolis: University of Minnesota Press, 1971), 187–228. De Man emphasizes the intrasubjective nature of the ironic division implicit within Romanticism, analyzing it as "a problem that exists within the self," a problem that is in and about self-constitution and identification.

12. James Joyce *A Portrait of the Artist as a Young Man* (New York: Viking Press, 1964) 275. Subsequent references to this work will be marked parenthetically, preceded by "P."

13. Taylor, "The Politics of Recognition," *Multiculturalism: Examining the Politics of Recognition*, ed. Amy Gutmann (Princeton: Princeton University Press, 1994): 25–73 (25).

14. See Lacan, "Aggressivity in Psychoanalysis," in *Écrits: A Selection*, trans. Alan Sheridan (New York and London: W. W. Norton, 1977), 8–29 (11). In his seminars, Lacan distinguishes aggression and aggressivity, arguing that "aggression has got nothing to do with the vital reality, it is an existential act linked to an imaginary relation" (177). See *The Seminar of Jacques Lacan*, vol. 1: *Freud's Papers on Technique, 1953–1954*, trans. John Forrester (New York

and London: W. W. Norton, 1988). In that sense, aggression is more negatively disengaged from the dialectic or the real. In the essay on aggressivity in *Écrits*, however, the terms are much closer.

15. Lacan, *Écrits*, 17.

16. Lacan, *Écrits*, 19.

17. Lacan, *Écrits*, 20.

18. Joyce's strong reaction to the incident with Henry Carr might be one case, but Ellmann seems most curious about his fallout with Frank Budgen over a letter Joyce sent and then wished returned (Ellmann, *James Joyce*, 542 and passim).

19. *Spurs: Nietzsche's Styles//Épersons: Les Styles de Nietzsche*, trans. Barbara Harlow (Chicago: University of Chicago Press, 1978), En face edition, 99–101. "Ce serait faire de la parodie ou du simulacre un instrument de maîtrise au service de la vérité ou de la castration, reconstituer la religion. . . . Non, la parodie suppose toujours quelque part un naïveté, adossée à un inconscient, et la vertige d'une non-maîtrise, une perte de connaissance. La parodie absolument calculée serait une confession ou une table de la loi" (98–100).

20. While contemporary dictionary definitions of parody tend to characterize it as "ridicule," in the seventeenth century, parody was judged to be innocent of such an act. It attained legal definition through the English courts, which proclaimed William Hone "innocent" of charges of that he had blasphemed God by publishing a parody of *The Bible* (Margaret Rose, *Parody//Metafiction: An Analysis of Parody as a Critical Mirror to the Writing and Reception of Fiction* [London: Crown Helm., 1979], 32). Parody eventually lost its innocence in the eighteenth century, when the term was applied to forms of denigrating satire. In the nineteenth century, this definition was refined and raised. Accompanying this change, literary aestheticism postulated a strict division between moral and aesthetic ends, defining the aesthetic impulse as the preservation of wholeness in contrast to the moral impulse, which, it was argued, would split things into their particularities. Although parody best moves between generals and particulars, there it found itself defined with a moral, satiric edge. See David Kiremidjian *A Study of Modern Parody* (New York: Garland Publishing, 1985), 63.

Beyond the dangers of satire, there is always the problem of the plagiarist's impulse potentially masked within the parody. The U.S. Supreme Court recently exempted parodies from such concern, ruling that the rap revision of "Oh, Pretty Woman" was not a violation of the earlier song's copyright. See Joan Biskupic's article, "Court Hands Parody Writers An Oh, So Pretty Ruling: Copyright Law's Fair Use Standard Redefined," in *The Washington Post*, March 8, 1994, A1, A10.

21. Bakhtin, *The Dialogic Imagination* trans. and ed. Carl Emerson and Michael Holquist (Austin: University of Texas Press, 1981), 7, 52, 236–237, and passim. Brandon Kershner has interpreted the concept of dialogism with great circumspection in his work on Joyce and popular culture. See *Joyce, Bakhtin, and Popular Literature: Chronicles of Disorder* (Chapel Hill andLondon: The University of North Carolina Press, 1989). Another good example of work with Bakhtin is Richard Pearce's book, *The Politics of Narration: James Joyce, William Faulkner, and Virginia Woolf* (New Brunswick, N.J.: Rutgers Univer-

sity Press, 1991). These applications are excellent, though philosophically the problem with Bakhtin's work emerges in later essays where he slides into a simpler formulation of intentionalism, so that author and audience may play more active roles and language as brute and disruptive materiality drops out.

22. Butler, *Gender Trouble: Feminism and the Subversion of Identity* (New York and London: Routledge, 1990), 145. Butler's work allowed feminists to negotiate between projects of resisting established social constructs and the utopian reach for some new order that would be radically distinct from the past. By reclaiming repetition, she escapes the dilemma of imagining something that has no foundation in the past. For according to Butler, we have no option but to repeat the past *in some form*. "The task is not whether to repeat," she writes, "but how to repeat or, indeed, to repeat and, through a radical proliferation of gender, *to displace* the very gender norms that enable the repetition itself" (148). In the critical aftermath of Butler's work on parody, questions about the relations between these subversive appropriations of types and the audience's varying receptions have been raised. When Nancy Fraser asks, "Why is resignification good? Can't there be bad (oppressive, reactionary) significations?," the answer from Butler would be in a sense, yes, but that she is trying to direct feminists toward appropriating repetition instead of denying or avoiding it. See "False Antitheses," in *Feminist Contentions: A Philosophical Exchange*, ed. Seyla Benhabib, Judith Butler, Drucilla Cornell, and Nancy Fraser (New York and London: Routledge, 1995), 59–74 (68). Still, Linda Nicholson raises one of the more difficult questions about such a notion, observing that "this kind of appeal . . . provides no means to distinguish or explain those instances of performativity which generate new kinds of signification from those which are merely repetitions of previous performative acts" ("Introduction," in *Feminist Contentions*, 1–16 [11]). Indeed, it is the very nature of this hinge between representation and reappropriation that is so crucial and still so problematic in our understanding of parody and its bearing on more general problems of interpretation.

23. Butler, *The Psychic Life of Power: Theories in Subjection* (Stanford: Stanford University Press, 1997), 9.

24. Butler, *The Psychic Life of Power*, 6, 104.

25. Joyce, *Stephen Hero* (New York: New Directions, 1944), 189. Subsequent references to this work will be marked parenthetically, preceded by "SH."

26. Joyce, *Ulysses: The Corrected Text*, ed. Hans Walter Gabler (New York: Vintage Books, 1986), 254. Subsequent references to this text will be marked parenthetically, preceded by U with a number denoting the episode, followed by the line number: (U 5.245).

27. Joyce, *Finnegans Wake* (New York: Viking Press, 1976), 167. Subsequent references to this work will be cited parenthetically, preceded by FW, followed by the page number and line numbers. So (FW 167.29–31).

28. Homi Bhabha, "The Other Question . . . : Homi Bhabha Reconsiders the Stereotype and Colonial Discourse," in *Screen* 24 (1983): 18–36. Klaus Theweleit, *Male Fantasies*, vol. 2: *Male Bodies: Psychoanalyzing the White Terror*, trans. Erica Carter and Chris Turner (Minneapolis: University of Minnesota Press, 1989).

29. Bhabha, "The Other Question . . ." 29.

30. For a sharp analysis of the juridical in Joyce, see Joseph Valente, *James Joyce and the Problem of Justice: Negotiating Sexual and Colonial Difference* (Cambridge: Cambridge University Press, 1995).

CHAPTER 2. THE ART OF GESTURE

1. James Joyce *Dubliners* (New York: Viking Press, 1967). Subsequent references to this work will be marked parenthetically, preceded by D.

2. Fred W. Householder, "ΠΑΡΩΙΔΙΑ," *Journal of Classical Philology*, 1 (January 1944): 1–9. Cited in Margaret A. Rose, *Parody: Ancient, Modern, Post-Modern* (Cambridge: Cambridge University Press, 1993).

3. Linda Hutcheon, for example, inclines her description of parody toward the ironic mode, emphasizing the ways in which parodic art marks a continuity (rather than a critique), a force that can "transcontextualize" the prior art form by repeating while inscribing difference. See Hutcheon, *A Theory of Parody: The Teachings of Twentieth-Century Art Forms* (New York: Methuen, 1985), 20–21, 32, and passim. Margaret Rose, on the other hand, emphasizes parody's more satiric side and integrates both roots of the term into her analysis of its historical reception and its metafictional aspects. While Hutcheon's and Rose's work differ in various ways, both are invested in discussing parody as a kind of "refunctioning" of social context.

4. Cheryl Herr documents Joyce's integration of street mime scenarios in *Ulysses* and *Finnegans Wake* in *Joyce's Anatomy of Culture* (Urbana and Chicago: University of Illinois Press, 1986).

5. Joyce, *The Critical Writings of James Joyce*, ed. Ellsworth Mason and Richard Ellmann (New York: Viking Press, 1959), 145. Subsequent references to this work will be marked parenthetically, preceded by CW.

6. James William Johnson, "Lyric," in *Princeton Encyclopedia of Poetry and Poetics*, ed. Alex Preminger (Princeton: Princeton University Press, 1965/1974), 460–70 (462).

7. Jo Pennington, *The Importance of Being Rhythmic* (New York and London: The Knickerbocker Press, 1925), v. The method was spread to "Great Britain and 'the colonies'" by Percy Ingham, a student of Jaques-Dalcroze's. See Jaques-Dalcroze's *Eurhythmics, Art and Education* trans. Frederick Rothwell, ed. Cynthia Cox (New York: Arno Press, 1980, first published in 1930), vi.

8. *The Eurhythmics of Jaques-Dalcroze*, trans. P. & E. Ingham (Boston: Small, Maynard and Co., 1918), 36.

9. *The Eurhythmics*, 29.

10. Dalcroze, *Eurhythmics, Art and Education*, 7.

11. Dalcroze, *Eurhythmics, Art and Education*, 54.

12. Theodore Spencer calculates this period of work on *Stephen Hero* in his introduction to that book.

13. Linda Kyle Revkin, "An Historical and Philosophical Inquiry into the Development of Dalcroze Eurhythmic and Its Influence on Music Education in

the French Cantons of Switzerland," dissertation (Ann Arbor: University Micro-forms International, 1984), 163.

14. Revkin, *An Historical and Philosophical Inquiry*, 164.

15. Jaques-Dalcroze's own inspiration comes in part from Greek use of music as accompaniment to the arts of "leaping, walking, running, singing, reg-ulated gymnastic or scenic combats, rhythmic gestures harmonising with the cadences of Greek poetry" (*Eurhythmics, Art and Education*, 39). Carol Shloss has also been presenting work on Lucia's period of study with a dance troupe highly influenced by the Greeks.

16. Parody is a form of textualized ventriloquism—of the self and simulta-neously of some other—and the term applies not only to the process of alluding to published, literary texts but also, according to M. M. Bakhtin, to cultural texts such as stereotypes, various forms of discourse and dialect, and the sounds and sensations taken from other voices and environments. See M. M. Bakhtin, *Problems of Dostoevsky's Poetics*, trans. R. W. Rotsel (Ann Arbor: University of Michigan Press, 1973), 194.

17. While Harold Bloom may be more famous for his use of *clinamen* as a kind of revisionist twist on a famous predecessor's text, I am here using Jacques Derrida's subtle deconstruction of that term in his essay, "My Chances/*Mes Chances*: A Rendezvous with Some Epicurean Stereophonies," trans. Irene Har-vey and Avital Ronell, in *Taking Chances: Derrida, Psychoanalysis, and Litera-ture*, ed. Joseph H. Smith and William Kerrigan (Baltimore and London: Johns Hopkins University Press, 1984), 1–32. In *The Anxiety of Influence: A Theory of Poetry: A Theory of Poetry* (Oxford: Oxford University Press, 1973), Bloom defines *clinamen as* a "strong poet's" creative misreading of his predecessor, a kind of "deliberate misinterpretation" and caricature of the past, which enables the present poet to create himself. Derrida, however, has less a notion of willful control than an allowance for chance. He writes, "The *clinamen* introduces the play of necessity and chance into what could be called, by anachronism, the determinism of the universe. Nonetheless, it does not imply a conscious freedom or will, even if for some of us the principle of indeterminism is what makes the conscious freedom of man fathomable" (8). Derrida defines this term as a tex-tual function in the writings of Lucretius. The *clinamen*, according to Derrida, would link freedom and pleasure.

18. Alexander Melville Bell and David Charles Bell, *Bell's Standard Elocu-tionist* (Belfast: William Mullan, 1871), 26–27. Joyce may well have studied this school handbook, since it was distributed throughout Great Britain and, specif-ically, in Dublin. Thanks to Fritz Senn for drawing my attention to this partic-ular gem, a copy of which can be found at the Zurich James Joyce Foundation.

19. "*ad pulcritudinem tria requiruntur, integritas, consonantia, claritas*" in the text.

20. Samuel Taylor Coleridge, *Shorter Works and Fragments* ed. H. J. Jack-son and J.R. de J. Jackson, in *The Collected Works* (Princeton: Princeton Uni-versity Press, 1995), 11:353–86 (378).

21. Pater, *The Renaissance*, 71–220, in *Walter Pater: Three Major Texts (The Renaissance, Appreciations, and Imaginary Portraits)*, ed. William E. Buckler (New York: New York University Press, 1986), 152.

22. Emile Benveniste establishes this, focusing largely on 985 and 1014 of the *Metaphysics*. See "La notion de 'rythme' dans son expression linguistique," in *Problèmes de linguistic générale*, vol. 1 (Paris: Gallimard, 1966): 327–35. See also Aristotle, *Metaphysics*, trans. Richard Hope (Ann Arbor: University of Michigan Press, 1960).

23. Joyce may have gotten this as much from Shelley as from Coleridge, for Stephen uses Shelley as an exemplar (P 213). M. H. Abrams casts the former poet's essay "Defense of Poetry," as a demonstration of "the tendency of Platonic aesthetic to cancel differences," and so that Shelley heads beyond Plato to Plotonus, "for whom all considerations had been drawn irresistibly into the vortex of the One." See *The Mirror and the Lamp: Romantic Theory and the Critical Tradition* (1953, reprint London: Oxford University Press, 1971), 127–28. This, of course, reapplies Plato to the Romantics rather than deconstructing their differences, but it allows one suggestion for how Stephen might have been drawn into Plato.

24. Arthur Symons, *The Symbolist Movement in Literature* (New York: E. P. Dutton and Col, 1958), 72.

25. James Atherton cites Mary Colum's memory of this from her book, *Life and the Dream* (London: Macmillan, 1947), 121; Atherton, *Books at the Wake* (New York: Paul Appel, 1959), 48.

26. James Atherton argues that Symons' book is all one need read, with regards to Mallarmé's influence on Joyce. At least he is correct in emphasizing its importance to Joyce's work, although he suggests and David Hayman later argues that Joyce did read Mallarmé first hand. And in an epilogue to a collection of essays on Joyce, Symons compares Joyce's style to that of Mallarmé. See Atherton, *The Books at the Wake*, 48–52. See Hayman, *Joyce et Mallarmé*.

27. See Ellmann's introduction in *The Symbolist Movement in Literature* by Arthur Symons, 71.

28. Symons, *The Symbolist Movement in Literature*, 5, 32.

29. In *Joyce et Mallarmé*, Hayman argues for the significance of Mallarmé for Joyce, both as a young man and then later as Joyce was writing *Finnegans Wake*, tracing various references to Mallarmé in the *Wake* that seem to be taken from later readings in Paris. Hayman concludes, however, that Joyce sets up sensate language so as to allow the reader to *transcend* the particular systems and syntax of words, moving toward the general level of understanding and away from the material particularities of the text.

30. Joyce seems to have been influenced by the figuration of language through female archetypes, described by Symons as the artist's "chimerical search after the virginity of language" (Symons, *The Symbolist Movement in Literature*, 71). I discuss the complications of this appropriation in chapter 3.

31. Quoted in Symons, *The Symbolist Movement in Literature*, 73.

32. Jacques Derrida, *Dissemination*, trans. Barbara Johnson (Chicago: University of Chicago Press, 1981), 219. The original French, from *La dissemination* (Paris: Editions du Seuil, 1972), reads: "joue toujours la différence sans référence, ou plutôt sans référent, sans extériorité absolue, c'est-à-dire aussi bien sans dedans. Le Mime mime la référence. Ce n'est pas un imitateur, il mime l'imitation" (248).

33. Stephen Heath, "Joyce in Language," in *James Joyce: New Perspectives*, ed. Colin MacCabe (Brighton and Bloomington: Indiana University Press, 1982): 129–48. As Heath notes, Jousse "specifically distinguishes his project from Mallarmé's modernist attachment to writing, to the enclosure of the world as book"—he will not have it bound by the book, but will have it transform the book into the living world. As Heath points out, however, Joyce follows the notion of the book as a circular containment, and language given not to an origin (or final destination), but to a interminable play, where there is "no break between world and book" (131).

34. Hayman argues that Joyce picked up on the "art of suggestion" gleaned from his readings of the *Crise de verse* and *Un coup de dés* (*Joyce et Mallarmé*, vol. 1, 30). But Hayman interprets this "art" as a struggle for mastery, a desire to make language his "own," which Hayman describes in terms that, if benignly, make Joyce into the very figure critics like Gilbert and Gubar dread. Hayman writes that, "Joyce's effort (in *Finnegans Wake*) was partly to make language obey *his* rules rather than its own, partly to exploit the potential of words and syntax, partly to discover and disclose his quintessential 'givens' everywhere." Hayman argues that the reader must struggle to "assert a self" while interpreting *Finnegans Wake*, much as the author was engaged in "an effort to assert a self (by imposing a pattern or a flux of patterns) or rather to win a self back from the language over which he repeatedly gains and as often loses mastery." See *The "Wake" in Transit*, 55.

35. David Hume, *Enquiries Concerning the Human Understanding and Concerning the Principles of Morals*, 2nd ed., ed. L. A. Selby-Bigge, 1927 impression (1777, Oxford: Clarendon, 1902), 63.

36. John Locke, *An Essay Concerning Human Understanding*, ed. Peter H. Nidditch (1689, Oxford: Oxford University Press, 1975), book III, 402–524.

37. Immanuel Kant, *Critique of Pure Reason* trans. Norman Kemp Smith (New York: St. Martin's Press, 1929) based on the original *Critique*'s 2nd edition, published in German in 1855.

38. Locke, *An Essay concerning Human Understanding*, 508.

39. George Berkeley, *A Treatise Concerning the Principles of Human Knowledge* (1710, Reprint Indianapolis: Hackett, 1982).

40. For more on phenomenology, see the works of Edmund Husserl or Henri Bergson.

41. Kiremidjian, *A Study of Modern Parody*, 136.

42. Michael Groden, *"Ulysses" in Progress* (Princeton: Princeton University Press, 1977). Taking his cue from Walton Litz's discovery of a shift in Joyce's compositional technique and apparent artistic goals during the course of his composition and revision of *Ulysses*, Groden has identified three stages in Joyce's compositional process in *Ulysses*. Agreeing with Litz that the first nine episodes are novelistic, Groden points out that Joyce was there more interested in working on interior monologue and character. See Litz, *The Art of James Joyce: Method and Design in "Ulysses" and "Finnegans Wake"* (New York: Oxford University Press, 1964).

43. Ewa Ziarek, "'Circe': Joyce's *Argumentum ad Feminam*, in *James Joyce Quarterly* 30.1 (Fall 1992): 51–68 (56).

44. Rabaté, *James Joyce, Authorized Reader* (Baltimore and London: Johns Hopkins University Press, 1991), 76.

45. Rabaté, *James Joyce, Authorized Reader*, 77.

46. Daniel Ferrer reads "Circe" as a break from the form of representation deployed in the rest of *Ulysses*: "The laws that obtain on this stage are no longer the same as those which governed the day-time world of *Ulysses* in which we have spent the earlier chapters." See "Circe, regret and regression," 127–28. See Ferrer, "Circe, Regret and Regression," trans. Gilly Lehmann, in *Post-Structuralist Joyce: Essays from the French*, ed. Derek Attridge and Daniel Ferrer (Cambridge: Cambridge University Press, 1984), 127–44.

47. Hugh Kenner, "Circe," in *James Joyce's "Ulysses": Critical Essays*, ed. Clive Hart and David Hayman (Berkeley and London: University of California Press, 1974), 341–62 (346).

48. Hugh Kenner points out that "naturalistic" or actual events make up only 10 percent of what we witness in "Circe." See "Circe," 347.

49. Don Gifford, *"Ulysses" Annotated* (rev. ed. Berkeley: University of California Press, 1988), 120.

50. Cheryl Herr, *Joyce's Anatomy of Culture*, 162.

51. James Atherton has further observed numerous uses of pantomime in various contexts in *Finnegans Wake*. See J. S. Atherton, "*Finnegans Wake*: The Gist of the Pantomime," in *Accent* 15.1 (Winter 1955): 14–26.

52. Herr, *Joyce's Anatomy of Culture*, 104.

53. Herr, *Joyce's Anatomy of Culture*, 96.

54. David Hayman, "Forms of Folly in Joyce: A Study of Clowning in *Ulysses*," in *ELH: English Literary History*, 34 (1967): 260–83.

55. See "Wyndham Lewis on Time in Joyce" (1927), in Robert H. Deming, *James Joyce: The Critical Heritage*, 2 vols. (New York: Barnes and Noble, 1970), 359–65. Ezra Pound answers these charges, comparing Joyce to Flaubert and calling him a "realistic" author: "Each character speaks in his own way, and corresponds to an external reality." See Pound, "Pound on *Ulysses* and Flaubert," in Deming, *James Joyce*, 1:263–67 (266).

56. Kenner, "Circe," 341.

57. Jacques Lacan, *The Seminar of Jacques Lacan*, vol. 2: *The Ego in Freud's Theory and in the Technique of Psychoanalysis, 1954–1955*, trans. Sylvana Tomaselli (New York: Norton, 1988), 223.

58. Aristotle, *Metaphysics* A6.988a and passim. In *On Being and Essence*, Aquinas writes that we cannot say "that the notions of genus and species belong to an essence as a reality existing outside individual things, as the Platonists held, because then the genus and species would not be attributed to the individual" (45). There must be individuation for reality to occur. See Aquinas, *On Being and Essence*, trans. Armand Maurer (Toronto: The Pontifical Institute of Medieval Studies, 1968).

59. Butler, *Bodies that Matter: On the Discursive Limits of "Sex"* (New York and London: Routledge, 1993), 68. In *Bodies That Matter*, Judith Butler most extensively discusses the relations between gender and the body. See also Elizabeth Grosz's study of the relations between biologism and the body in psychoanalysis and feminism, in *Volatile Bodies: Toward a Corporeal Feminism*

(Bloomington and Indianapolis: Indiana University Press, 1994).

60. Vicki Mahaffey reads this episode in terms of Bloom's struggle with stereotyping, arguing that

> Throughout the day, Bloom has betrayed a sadomasochistic desire to divide Molly into her individual roles, only to discover, disquietingly, a counterpart of each of those roles in himself. He discovers that he has been paralyzed, not by Molly herself, but by the stereotypical views of her that Joyce identifies in a letter as Penelope's "apparitions": the immortal nymph, represented by the photograph over his bed (Calypso), the virgin (Nausicaa), and the whore (Circe). In "Circe," Bloom tries to avoid being categorized as he has categorized Molly, constantly changing roles in a protean attempt to avoid the persecution that inevitably dogs those who allow themselves to be "typed." . . . Only gradually does he begin to suspect that by typing his wife, he types and restricts himself. (*Reauthorizing Joyce* [Cambridge: Cambridge University Press, 1988], 166)

Whether Bloom realizes this aspect of typing explicitly, the text of "Circe" manifests its crucial connection to his own "enslavement" and eventual transfiguration, as Mahaffey implies.

61. Butler, *Gender Trouble*, 106–11.

62. Sandra Gilbert, "Costumes of the Mind," in *Critical Inquiry* 7 (Winter 1980): 391–417 (391f.).

63. A few lines earlier, as Bloom phantasmatically watches Blazes Boylan have sex with Molly, Boylan "hangs his hat smartly on a peg of Bloom's antlered head" (U 15.3764). According to Gifford, antlers were used to caricature the cuckold (Gifford, *"Ulysses" Annotated*, 512).

64. Dan Schwarz, *Reading Joyce's "Ulysses"* (New York: St. Martin's, 1987), 215–19.

CHAPTER 3. "THE WORD IS MY WIFE"

1. McHugh, *Annotations to "Finnegans Wake,"* rev. ed. (Baltimore: Johns Hopkins University Press, 1991), 167. Hereafter, referred to as *Annotations*.

2. McHugh, *Annotations*, 167.

3. Irigaray, *This Sex Which Is Not One* trans. Catherine Porter (Ithaca, N.Y.: Cornell University Press, 1985), 30–31 and passim.

4. This figuration of woman is taken up by Derrida, in his interpretation of the *spur* (l'éperon) in the question of woman for Nietzsche, as "her" very image denies the desire for stabile figuration:

> Perhaps woman—a non-identity, a non-figure, a simulacrum—is distance's very chasm, the out-distancing of distance, the interval's cadence, distance itself, if we could still say such a thing, distance *itself*. . . . There is no such thing as the essence of woman because woman averts, she is averted of herself. Out of the depths, endless and

unfathomable, she engulfs and distorts all vestige of essentiality, of identity, of property. And the philosophical discourse, blinded, founders on these shoals and is hurled down these depthless depths to its ruin. There is no such thing as the truth of woman, but it is because of that abyssal divergence of the truth, because that untruth is "truth." Woman is but one name for that untruth of truth. (*Spurs*, 49–50)

In deconstruction, woman as simulacrum, as a double turning toward and away from truth, becomes a problem of representation. She can never be fully given in a steady, realistic mirror to herself, but must be an image that forever slips out of attempts to fix her. In Nietzsche, these attempts fall into (at least) three separate gestures: woman as castrated, as castrating, and as affirming (*Spurs*, 101). Derrida's deconstruction of Nietzsche is so close to ventriloquism of his views that at times the deconstruction of "woman" appears to appropriate more than it critiques in Nietzsche's attitudes toward women. Or, as Diana Fuss points out, his very de-essentialization of woman "as essence" not only subverts while cleverly appropriating the movement of essentialization; it also "risks, in its effects, continually displacing real material women." See *Essentially Speaking: Feminism, Nature and Difference* (New York and London: Routledge, 1989), 14.

One cannot trust that parody will subvert the types it treats, and Joyce may no more disrupt the urge to control women than Derrida challenges the binary that silences, erases, and alternately invokes only to attack the category that is "woman."

5. See "Mimique" in Stephane Mallarmé, *Oeuvres complètes* (Paris: Gallimard, 1945).

6. Kristeva, *Desire in Language*, 133.

7. Kristeva, *Desire in Language*, 133.

8. Henke, *Politics of Desire*, 7. See also Scott on the *Wake* in *Joyce and Feminism* and most recently, Sheldon Brivic's celebration of Joyce's feminism, in *Joyce's Waking Women: An Introduction to Finnegans Wake* (Madison: University of Wisconsin Press, 1995) and Susan Shaw Sailer's *On the Void of to Be: Incoherence and Trope in "Finnegans Wake"* (Ann Arbor: University of Michigan Press, 1993).

9. The quote here comes from a letter from Joyce to Budgen, in Gilbert, *The Letters of James Joyce*, 1:102.

10. Indeed, Christine Froula argues that Joyce's work critically reveals the masculine aspects so often presupposed as the universals of culture, allowing in his critique the possibility of change and a greater integration of the feminine into our contexts. She hopes that this will promote analysis of "the sexual dialectics underlying the social law of gender and its *père*-verse dichotomizing of the human condition into a 'masculine' spirit that always denies and a 'feminine' flesh that always affirms." See *Modernism's Body: Sex, Culture, Joyce* (New York: Columbia University Press, 1996), 252.

11. Friedman, "(Self)Censorship and the Making of Joyce's Modernism," in *Joyce: The Return of the Repressed*, ed. Susan Stanford Friedman (Ithaca, N.Y., and London: Cornell University Press, 1993), 21–57 (34–39).

12. Mary Ann Caws,"The Conception of Engendering The Erotics of Edit-

ing," in *The Poetics of Gender*, ed. Nancy K. Miller (New York: Columbia University Press, 1986), 42–62 (45–46).

13. See Suzette Henke and Elaine Unkeless, eds., *Women in Joyce* (Chicago: University of Illinois Press, 1982), xii.

14. Vincent Cheng explores Stephen's relation to seduction and vampires in "Stephen and the Black Panther Vampire," *James Joyce Quarterly* 24 (Winter 1987): 161–75.

15. As Henke has observed, Stephen's image of the prostitute vacillates between masculine aggression and feminine nurturance (*The Politics of Desire*, 67). In this swoon Stephen appears to be feminized and loses all control.

16. Henke, *The Politics of Desire*, 75.

17. Joyce's work, in *Ulysses*, suggests an ironization of this position, a complex perforation of the distinction between pornographic and aesthetic experiences. Specifically, Joyce mocks the Bird-girl epiphany by rewriting it, as Fritz Senn has noted, in "Nausicaa," where Leopold Bloom experiences a more explicitly kinetic response to another view of woman's drawers on Sandymount Strand (284). See "Nausicaa," in *James Joyce's Ulysses*, ed. Clive Hart and David Hayman (Berkeley, Los Angelos, London: University of California Press, 1974), 277–312. As Senn observes, the language of "Nausicaa" so strongly echoes that of the Bird-girl epiphany that it would be difficult to deny Joyce's intent to parody Stephen's earlier, elative experience. Like the Bird-Girl, Gerty MacDowell does not speak to her voyeur, but she does, of course, "speak" in a narrative directed outward to some fictionalized audience. Moreover, Gerty's acclaimed narcissism is doubled by Bloom's projection of desire onto her, although Bloom's gaze is less "narcissistic" that Stephen's in the sense of being self-enclosed.

18. Irigaray, *This Sex Which Is Not One*, 29.

19. Aron Stavisky, *Shakespeare and the Victorians* (Norman: University of Oklahoma Press, 1969), 54.

20. He is thinking of death and of memories of his mother, which earlier had "beset his brooding brain" (U 1.265–66), recalling "[h]er glazing eyes, staring out of death, to shake and bend my soul" (U 1.273). Stephen has resisted the command to pray, because he lacks full belief.

Richard Peterson argues that Stephen tries to blame his mother for the painful sea of experience he faces upon his return to Ireland. Ann Kimble Loux, more precisely, demonstrates that Stephen feels betrayed by his mother's love for God, which exceeds her love for her own son. See Peterson, "Did Joyce write *Hamlet*?" *James Joyce Quarterly* 29 (Winter 1990): 369. And Loux, "'Am I a father? If I were?' A Trinitarian Analysis of the Growth of Stephen Dedalus in *Ulysses*," *James Joyce Quarterly* 23 (Spring 1985): 288.

21. Ellmann, *The Consciousness of James Joyce* (New York: Oxford University Press, 1977), 62.

22. Berkeley, *A Treatise Concerning the Principles of Human Knowledge*.

23. William Noon, *Joyce and Aquinas* (New Haven: Yale University Press, 1957), 122.

24. Maurice Maeterlinck was a Belgium Symbolist poet. See *Wisdom and Destiny* (New York: Bodd, Mead, 1898). "Nothing happens to us which is not

of the same nature as ourselves." Cf. Gifford, *Annotated "Ulysses,"* 250.

Earlier in the day Stephen has mentally criticized the conflation of author and character. That is, in "Nestor," his thoughts correct a similar move on the part of Mr. Deasy, who believes he is invoking Shakespeare's wisdom when he is quoting Iago. Deasy uses Shakespeare to shore up his own position as he preaches to Stephen about the importance of money:

> —Because you don't save, Mr Deasy said, pointing his finger. You don't know yet what money is. Money is power. When you have lived as long as I have. I know, I know. *If youth but knew.* But what does Shakespeare say? *Put but money in thy purse.*
> —Iago, Stephen murmured. (U 2.236–40)

Ironically, Iago will become yet another "version" of Shakespeare during the course of Stephen's presentation (U 9.911). This echoes, of course, the problem of reading Stephen as Joyce's spokesperson, and may have left a long trajectory of allowance of that practice. As result, many readers accepting the "all-in-all" thesis as Joyce's own.

25. Gilbert, *The Letters of James Joyce*, 1:285.

26. James Joyce, *The Dead*, ed. Daniel R. Schwarz (Boston and New York: St. Martin's Press, 1994, 11 (Schwarz's introduction).

27. Gilbert, *The Letters of James Joyce*, 1:134.

28. Sigmund Freud, "On Narcissism," in *Standard Edition*, trans. and ed. James Strachey (London: The Hogarth Press and the Institute of Psycho-Analysis, 1955), 14:67–102 (88–89). Freud's description of narcissism defines it as self-enrapture that completely severs the subject's relations to the outside world, eliminating any prospect of influence or affection ("On Narcissism," 74). Even later in his observation of this "disease," Freud insists on a separation between self-love and the love of another. "Love for oneself knows only one barrier," he writes, "love for others, love for objects." See "Group Psychology and the Analysis of the Ego," in *Standard Edition* 18:67–144 (34–35). He furthermore sees a distinction between love with sexual aims and a bond formed through identification, although this opposition might well be deconstructed by his own definitions of desire in other moments. With regards to homosexuality, however, Freud maintains these distinctions and the reductions they entail.

29. Jules David Law, "'Pity They Can't See Themselves': Assessing the 'Subject' of Pornography in 'Nausicaa,'" in *James Joyce Quarterly* 27.2 (Winter 1990): 219–39 (235).

30. Virginia Woolf, *A Room of One's Own* (New York: Harcourt, Brace, Jovanovich, 1927).

31. I would like to clarify here that, on my account, the male and female gaze can *by no terms* be collapsed. The different ways in which men and women experience specularity and absorb stereotypes belie any but a utopian claim for such a mutual positioning. There can, however, be an overlap of gendered positions, such that one or the other sex might twist their socially positioned states away from stereotypical behavior or expectations.

32. Norris, *Joyce's Web: The Social Unraveling of Modernism* (Austin: University of Texas Press, 1992), 106 and passim.

33. Kimberly Devlin names this experience of the woman watching the male who is watching her as sexual object, "counter female voyeurism." See Devlin, "The Female Eye: Joyce's Voyeuristic Narcissists," in *New Alliances in Joyce Studies*, ed. Bonnie Kime Scott (Newark: University of Delaware Press, 1988): 135–43 (136). Devlin argues that "in order to present oneself as a voyeuristic object, one must first be aware of a voyeur, and to be secretly aware of a voyeur is to be a voyeur oneself, a furtively viewing subject" (140). This seems to operate only if the counter-voyeur is furtively also objectifying the other, which Gerty may well be doing to Bloom in her mind.

34. See Mark Shechner, *Joyce in Nighttown* (Berkeley: University of California Press, 1974).

35. Christine Van Boheemen-Saaf, "'The Language of Flow': Joyce's Dispossession of the Feminine in *Ulysses*," *European Joyce Studies* 1 (1989): 63–77 (69).

36. Cixous, "Sorties," *The Newly Born Woman* ed. Cixous and Catherine Clement, trans. Betsy Wing (Minnesota: University of Minnesota Press, 1980): 245–64 (92–93 and passim).

37. See Kristeva, *Revolution*, 102; and Cixous, "Sorties."

38. *James Joyce*, 429–30.

39. See Mark Franko's book, *Dancing Modernism/Performing Politics* (Bloomington and Indianapolis: Indiana University Press, 1995), 5. Carol Shloss has been working on Lucia's interest in dance and its influence on Joyce. See her forthcoming biography on Lucia Joyce.

40. Duncan, *The Art of Dance*, ed. Sheldon Cheney (New York: Theatre Arts, 1928), 77.

41. Mark Franko, *Dancing Modernism/Performing Politics*, 2, 10.

42. Adaline Glasheen, *Third Census of "Finnegans Wake": An Index of the Characters and Their Roles* (Berkeley and London: University of California Press, 1977), 138.

43. Although Shari Benstock sensibly suggests that Joyce's pain at Lucia's encroaching madness would be an unlikely source of his own parody, the traces of schizophrenia in this last text are pervasive. As a writing style, schizophrenic prose would belie attempts to recollect it toward one reified meaning, just as characters might elude categorical containments. See Benstock, "The Genuine Christine: Psychodynamics of Issy," in *Women in Joyce*, ed. Suzette Henke and Elaine Unkeless (Urbana and London: University of Illinois Press, 1982), 169–96.

44. Brivic, *Joyce's Waking Women*, 11.

45. McHugh, *Annotations*, 98.

CHAPTER 4. IN THE ORIGINAL SINSE

1. In his discussion of the polymorphous perversity of child sexuality, Freud delineates five "excessive sexual impulses" that society treats as differing from what is taken for normal: "first, by disregarding the barrier of species (the gulf between men and animals), secondly, by overstepping the barrier against disgust, thirdly that against incest (the prohibition against seeking sexual satis-

faction from near blood-relations), fourthly that against members of one's own sex and fifthly the transferring of the part played by the genitals to other organs and areas of the body" ("Introductory Lectures on Psycho-Analysis," in *Standard Edition*, vols. 15–16, 15:208). As Jonathan Dollimore points out, Freud is inconsistent on the inclusion of homosexuality in his list of perversions. He at times declares it to be the most important of perversions. See *Sexual Dissidence: Augustine to Wilde, Freud to Foucault* (Oxford: Clarendon Press, 1991), 174–76n.

2. While I address the narrative tilt of the story as its homophobic factor, I agree with Vicki Mahaffey's qualification. She argues that the double monologue, articulating a desire to whip *both* girls and boys, complicates any reading of homophobia in this piece. "By constructing the story this way," she writes, "Joyce makes it clear that the focus of his implied critique here is *not* a critique of sexual orientation but one of the sexual abuse of children" ("Père-version," 192). My argument, however, is that while the man is engaging in sadomasochistic fantasies about children, reminiscent of pandying in the boarding school in *Portrait*, the narrator's terrified reception seems defined by his sex and therefore tilted toward a response to homosexual elements in his interpretation of this monologue. It is also a conspicuous "gay cliché," this confusion of pederasty and homosexuality. In acknowledging its operation within the narrator's perception, my intention is not to validate its distortion of gay men, but to suggest that the story replays the social anxiety that creates such a stereotype.

3. Henry Abelove has emphasized Freud's more progressive commentary on homosexuality, arguing that those who associate stereotypes of homosexuality with Freud are actually responding to the more repressive elements in American psychology, which Freud explicitly resisted. See Abelove, "Freud, Male Homosexuality, and the Americans," *The Lesbian and Gay Studies Reader*, ed. Abelove, Michèle Aina Barale, and David M. Halperin (New York and London: Routledge, 1993), 381–96. While Abelove's argument relieves the more reductive interpretations of Freud, he too readily leaves aside Freud's work on narcissism. It is more the case, as Dollimore observes, that "what emerges in Freud is a tension between a recognition of actual homosexual diversity and a wish to organize it conceptually within a theory of desire which duplicates the problem, and leads him into inconsistency" (*Sexual Dissidence*, 193).

4. MacCabe, *James Joyce and the Revolution of the Word* (New York: Barnes and Noble, 1979), 111–29. Jean-Michel Rabaté interprets Joyce's use of silences in *Dubliners* as a reversal of moralistic narrative and orthodoxy. Silence produces in narrators and, as a mirror effect, in the reader a struggle to understand unfinished sentences. Joyce employs "perversity" as a play of signification that leaves meaning uncertain, in a reversal of orthodoxy, which presents a position with no "meaning" or explanation. See *James Joyce, Authorized Reader*, 20–26.

5. Dollimore, *Sexual Dissidence*, 174–76n; and Warner, "Homo-Narcissism; or, Heterosexuality," *Engendering Men: The Question of Male Feminist Criticism*, ed. Joseph A. Boone (New York: Routledge, 1990), 190–206.

6. See "Five Lectures on Psycho-Analysis," *Standard Edition*, 11:3. It is published just before Freud's study on Leonardo da Vinci, which also discusses

homosexuality. See also Freud's more extensive discussion: "On Narcissism," *Standard Edition*, vol. 14.

7. Richard Brown demonstrates Joyce's familiarity with Freud's notions of perversion and homosexuality in *Psychopathology of Everyday Life*, Freud's essay on Leonardo da Vinci, and Ernest Jones' interpretation of *Hamlet*. See *James Joyce and Sexuality* (Cambridge and New York: Cambridge University Press, 1985), 83.

8. Freud, "Introductory Lectures on Psycho-Analysis," *Standard Edition*, vol. 16, 424.

9. Lacan, *The Four Fundamental Concepts of Psycho-Analysis*, trans. Alan Sheridan (New York: Norton, 1966), 238.

10. Freud, "Introductory Lectures," *Standard Edition*, vol. 16, 429.

11. See François Roustang, "How Do You Make a Paranoiac Laugh?" in *Modern Language Notes* 102.4 (1987): 707–18 (715).

12. For a good example of a reading of the "jouissance" of Issy's language, see Susan Shaw Sailer, *On the Void of to Be*.

13. Suzette Henke has traced the lesbian innuendos in Molly's memories of Hester Stanhope, and further suggests that Molly seems less engaged by heterosexual sex than her playful desire for the female body (*James Joyce and the Politics of Desire*, 145, 134). See also Colleen Lamos' article, "Signatures of the Invisible: Homosexual Secrecy and Knowledge in *Ulysses*," in the special issue on "Joyce and Homosexuality," ed. Joseph Valente, *The James Joyce Quarterly* 31.3 (Spring 1994): 337–56.

14. Freud, "Group Psychology and the Analysis of the Ego," *Standard Edition*, 18:106–7.

15. Warner, "Homo-Narcissism; or, Heterosexuality," 191.

16. Warner, "Homo-Narcissism; or, Heterosexuality," 196–97.

17. Warner, "Homo-Narcissism; or, Heterosexuality," 198.

18. Rabaté, *Joyce upon the Void: The Genesis of Doubt* (London: Macmillan, 1991), 154f.

19. McHugh, *Annotations*, 279.

20. See Martha Vicinus, *Independent Women: Work and Community for Single Women, 1850–1920* (London: Virago Press, 1985), 34–35.

21. Adeline Glasheen points out that Joyce's early working title for this chapter was "Twilight Games." See *Third Census of Finnegans Wake*, xlvi, n6.

22. Later in "The Mime," Joyce additionally drops an allusion to Freud's study of Dora's affection for Frau K., mentioning a "Dodgesome Dora for hedgehung sheolmastress" (FW 228.16–17). Freud initially believed that Dora displaced her desire for her father to the figure of Herr K. As Jacques Lacan has noted, Freud is misled in this assumption by his own identification along lines of sex; he identifies with the father's desire and cannot see Dora's homosexual attraction (*Écrits*, 92–93). Freud's study of Dora's homosexuality was published in 1905. Dora became attached to a Mrs. K, with whom she read books, and so, in a sense, "studied" with her as well.

23. Joyce drops numerous hints in "The Mime" that he is using Proust's *Remembrance of Things Past* as a subtext. In the description of Hump's role (played by Humphrey Chimpden Earwicker), the patriarch is said to have par-

tially recovered from "recent impeachment"—one of Finn's many falls—and he is "studding sail once more, jibsheets and royals, in the semblance of the substance for the membrance of the umbrance with the remnance of the emblence" (FW 220.31–33). The allusion to *Remembrance of Things Past* emerges here, along with Joyce's play on linguistic rhythms. Further on, when Chuff and Glugg fight, the text shrugs off their aggression with a simple, "We've heard it aye since songdom was gemurrmal." "Sodome et Gomorrhe" was the fourth installment of Proust's novel to appear, and its depictions of homosexuality scandalized Europe in the early 1920s. The allusion of greater weight to the question of lesbian eroticism, however, is Joyce's reference to the rainbow of "Floral" girls as "the youngly delightsome frilles-in-pleyurs," who "are now showen drawen, if bud one, or, if in florileague, drawens up consociately at the hinder sight of their commoner guardia" (FW 224.22–24).

24. Marcel Proust, *Remembrance of Things Past*, vol. 1, trans. C. K. Scott Moncrieff with Terence Kilmartin (New York: Random House, 1981), 845, 846, 848, 856.

25. Proust, *Remembrance of Things Past*, 851.

26. Proust, *Remembrance of Things Past*, 847. French original: "Quoique chacune fût d'un type absolument différent des autres, elles avaient toutes de la beauté; mais, à vrai dire, je les voyais depuis si peu d'instants et sans oser les regarder fixement que je n'avais encore individualisé aucune d'elles . . . et même ces traits, je n'avais encore indissolublement attaché aucun d'entre eux a l'une des jeunes filles plutôt qu'à l'autre; et quand (selon l'ordre dans lequel se déroulait cet ensemble, merveilleux parce qu'y voisinaient les aspects les plus différents, que toutes les gammes de couleurs y étaient rapprochées, mais qui était confus comme une musique où je n'aurais pas su isoler et reconnaître au moment de leur passage les phrases, distinguées mais oubliées aussitôt après) je voyais émerger un ovale blanc, des yeux noirs, des yeux verts, je ne savais pas si c'était les mêmes qui m'avaient déjà apporté du charme tout à l'heure, je ne pouvais pas les rapporter à telle jeune fille que j'eusse séparée des autres et reconnue." Proust, *À la recherche du temps perdu* (Paris: Gallimard, 1954), 789–90.

27. Proust, *Remembrance of Things Past*, 847–48.

28. Proust, *Remembrance of Things Past*, 855.

29. Proust, *Remembrance of Things Past*, 691.

30. McHugh, *Annotations*, 227. The first is archaic English, the second French slang.

31. McHugh identifies this as a reference to the Anglo-Irish word, "acushla," which translates to "my pulse." She might then be referring to a rhythmic identification with Earwicker and any other associations the thought of him brings, whether of former lovers or her own identification with him. See *Annotations to Finnegans Wake*, 626–27.

32. Just a few pages earlier, Issy has been referred to as "Is is" (FW 620.32).

33. If the daughterwife comes from Himilayas, McHugh also finds biblical words: *Imla*, meaning fullness, and *maya*, Sanskrit for "illusion." *Annotations*, 626–27.

34. Freud, "Three Essays on Sexuality," *Standard Edition*, 7:207 and passim.

35. Brown, *James Joyce and Sexuality*, 78–88.

36. Eve Kosofsky Sedgwick, *Epistemology of the Closet* (Berkeley: University of California Press, 1990), 186n.

37. Sedgwick, *Between Men: English Literature and Male Homosocial Desire*, Gender and Culture series, ed. Carolyn G. Heilbrun and Nancy K. Miller (New York: Columbia University Press, 1985), 115–16 and passim. Sedgwick clarifies her point concisely in *Epistemology*:

> The result of men's accession to this double bind [of the basically homosocial and heterosexual codes within mentorship, male friendship, and rivalry] is, first, the acute *manipulability*, through the fear of one's own 'homosexuality,' of acculturated men; and second, a reservoir of potential for *violence* caused by the self-ignorance that this regime constitutively enforces. The historical emphasis on enforcement of homophobic rules in the armed services in, for instance, England and the United States supports this analysis. In these institutions, where both men's manipulability and their potential for violence are at the highest possible premium, the *pre*scription of the most intimate male bonding and the *pro*scription of (the remarkably cognate) 'homosexuality' are both stronger than in civilian society—are, in fact, close to absolute. (186).

38. See Levine, "James Joyce, Tattoo Artist: Tracing the Outlines of Homosocial Desire," in *James Joyce Quarterly* 31.3 (Spring 1994): 227–300 (293). Levine observes that "in a patriarchal society like Joyce's Dublin, in spite of the fact that homosexual relations are utterly proscribed and that heterosexual desire is the norm, it is the bonds between men (what Sedgwick calls homosocial relations) that 'normally' take precedence" (293). Levine particularly describes how "Molly lubricates Bloom's relations with other men," in a parallel, in "Eumeaus," with the tattooed sailor's use of women's images.

39. Eric Partridge, *A Dictionary of Slang and Unconventional English*, ed. Paul Beale (New York: Macmillan, 1984).

40. Lacan, *The Four Fundamental Concepts of Psycho-Analysis*, 238.

41. Freud, "Leonardo da Vinci And a Memory of His Childhood," *Standard Edition*, vol. 11, 99n2.

42. Freud, "Some Neurotic Mechanisms in Jealousy, Paranoia and Homosexuality," *Standard Edition*, 18:221–34 (225 and passim).

43. Patrick McGee interprets this term as "collide or escape. That is, the gazer *either* enters the process of culture and collides with the chain of signifiers that makes it up *or* escapes into the ideal, the *all*, the view from outside." See *Telling the Other: The Question of Value in Modern and Postcolonial Writing* (Ithaca and London: Cornell University Press, 1992), 81. He analyzes the way in which *Finnegans Wake* develops a discourse toward the Other, or here the way the book opens the process of reading so that we are brought "face to face with the alterity of writing, with the wall of language, with the language as litter" (81). McGee's chapter on Joyce here is also an excellent example of a reading of the "jouissance" of the text.

44. Hart, "explications—for the greet glossary of code, Addenda to No 1," in *A Wake Newslitter* 2 (April 1962): 1–5.

45. John Gordon, *Finnegans Wake: A Plot Summary* (Syracuse: Syracuse University Press, 1986), 157.

46. René Girard, whose work on triangulation and desire is important to Sedgwick's, is discussed in the chapter on nationalism that follows.

47. "But!" and also Butt (of Butt and Taff), who likewise have an episode of homosexual panic and ensuing aggression (FW 338–54 and passim). Moreover, Glasheen identifies Burrus with Butt (from Butter) (*Third Census*, 46).

48. McHugh, *Annotations*, 161.

49. Partridge, *A Dictionary of Slang*.

50. Late nineteenth-twentieth century. Partridge, *A Dictionary of Slang*. It is, in fact, the first meaning he lists.

51. McHugh, *Annotations*, 161.

52. Glasheen, *Third Census*, 41.

53. The Oedipal scenario that Joyce employs here may replay Freud's conscious attempt to establish the priority of a heterosexual family romance, but the undercurrent indicates as well the subversive potential of homosexual desires repressed. The Oedipal scenario sets up aggression against the father as a reinforcement of heterosexuality, which is replayed within the sons' competition for the female, so that the family romance generally functions as a suppression of homosexual desire. As J. Laplanche and J-B. Pontalis summarize it, it is "a desire for the death of the rival—the parent of the same sex—and a sexual desire for the parent of the opposite sex." See *The Language of Psychoanalysis*, trans. D. Nicholson-Smith (London: Hogarth Press, 1983), 283. While it can also be cast as desire for the same-sex parent and aggression against the other, they note that this is treated as a "negative" form in Freud. As Dollimore observes, however, "perversion proves the undoing of the theory which contains it" (*Sexual Dissidence*, 197), for the more Freud uses the Oedipal scenario to insist on the "naturalness" of heterosexuality, the more he must work to maintain the line between the object of desire and that of identification. Readings of Freud, like Warner's (above), now use homosexuality as the term that introduces—and necessitates—this subtler understanding of cross-identifications and multiplied roles, such that any simple binary between the parent desired and the one resisted is denied (Dollimore, *Sexual Dissidence*, 198). It is more the very repression of such multiple and ambivalent desires that creates the tensional binary that irrupts into violence. Joyce thus employs Freudian cliché, but the parody in this scenario clues the reader in to the fractures within his binaristic construction of Oedipal relations as purely heterosexual in their "positive" definition.

54. Henry G. Liddell, *A History of Rome: From the Earliest Times to the Establishment of the Empire*, vol. II (London: John Murray, 1855), 475 and passim.

55. Liddell, *A History of Rome*, 475 and passim.

56. Liddell, *A History of Rome*, 69, 72.

57. Glasheen notes that "Butt" in the Taff and Butt exchange seems to be associated with Isaac Butt, whose progress toward Home Rule Parnell overtook when he displaced him as party leader (46). She puzzles over the association, but I am fairly sure that, even with Parnell, Joyce was aware that he inherited the progress of the man he displaced.

58. Gilbert, *The Letters of James Joyce*, 1:224–25.

59. Atherton points out that Bruno also believed that "each thing contained the whole," a popular medieval theory that recurs in Joyce (so that each word supposedly contains the structure of *Finnegans Wake*). Atherton mentions several axioms from Bruno's extended works that seem to have influenced Joyce, noting particularly that in a chain of entities "each entity except the last [God, in effect] was continually changing and not merely by becoming greater or less but by exchanging identities with other entities. This suggests the behavior of characters and words in the *Wake* where every part tends to change its identity all the time" (Atherton, *Books at the Wake*, 36). Browne and Nolan seems to be arbitrary association with Bruno (the Nolan) made by Joyce. Probably first attracted to Bruno as a heretic, burned for his ideas.

60. Lacan, *The Seminar of Jacques Lacan*, 1:170.

61. Partridge, *A Dictionary of Slang*.

62. Scott Klein has also pointed out Wyndham Lewis's own anxious relation to homosexual desire. See Klein's book, *The Fictions of James Joyce and Wyndham Lewis: Monsters of Nature and Design* (Cambridge: Cambridge University Press, 1994), 125, 200.

63. McHugh, *Annotations*, 166.

64. Sedgwick, *Between Men*, 49.

65. McHugh glosses the orange versus green and The Peeler and the Goat (a song) and greengrocers. *Annotations*, 522.

66. Partridge, *A Dictionary of Slang*. *Peeler* is an Irish policeman, from the mid-eighteenth century.

CHAPTER 5. IN THE WAKE OF THE NATION

1. Ellmann, *The Letters of James Joyce*, 2:266.

2. Ellmann, *The Letters of James Joyce*, 2:255.

3. See Deane, ed., *The Field Day Anthology of Irish Writing*, vol. 3 (Derry, Ireland: Field Day Publications, 1991), 2. In "Joyce and Nationalism," Deane identifies this tendency to rebel through art a particularly Irish one. "Since [Irish] history could not yield a politics," Deane writes, "it was compelled to yield an aesthetic. In this process, disaffection became disdain, political reality dissolved into fiction, fiction realised itself purely in terms of its own medium, language. As a consequence, the finite nature of historical fact was supplanted by the infinite, or near infinite, possibilities of language" (168). According to Deane, language allows Joyce to extend the range of significations, opening up a world of possibilities shut down by the Irish history of failure and colonialization. Where politics fails, art becomes the space of the political imaginary. Writing then becomes the supreme form of action in Joyce's later works, which Deane finds "aggressively verbal, insisting on the linkages of words rather than on the illusion of events" (173). Joyce may have abandoned Ireland in various ways, but the returning representation of the Irish in his writings signals a formative attachment, even if it is a heavily mediated one.

Denis Donoghue also suggests that "Irish literature is a story of fracture: the death of one language . . . and the victory of another, both claiming to be Christian; the divergence of one Irishman from another." See *We Irish: Essays on Irish Literature and Society* (New York: Knopf, 1986), 145–46.

4. As Joyce's brother Stanislaus recalls, he made elaborate plans with a neighborhood boy, some two years his senior, to collaborate on an adventure novel, which they never finished; he also composed several sentimental poems "in the style of the drawing room ballads." See *My Brother's Keeper: James Joyce's Early Years* (New York: Viking Press, 1958), 45. Dominic Manganiello similarly invokes "Et Tu, Healy" as a sign of Joyce's interest in Irish nationalism in *Joyce's Politics* (London: Routledge and Kegan Paul, 1980), 3.

5. Parnell met Katharine O'Shea in the summer of 1880. She was then the wife of Captain O'Shea and mother of three children, although she and her husband had been living in separation for several years. Although Captain O'Shea argued, during the divorce proceedings, that he had been deceived for many years, Lyons presents strong evidence that he was fully aware of the affair and only sensitive to public scandal. See F. S. L. Lyons, *The Fall of Parnell, 1890–91* (Toronto: University of Toronto Press, 1960), 35–71.

6. The poem apparently ended with the image of Parnell, who died shortly after his removal from politics. Joyce has him resurrected as an eagle, looking down on a crowd of degenerate Irish politicians. (Stanislaus Joyce, *My Brother's Keeper*, 45–46).

7. Ellmann, *James Joyce*, 33

8. In an essay written for the Trieste paper *Il Piccolo della Sera* in 1912, Joyce bitterly concludes with a description of Parnell's fall: "They [the Irish] did not throw him to the English wolves, they tore him to pieces themselves" (CW 228). In *Finnegans Wake*, Earwicker at one point pleads with the masses railing to depose him, "Do not flingamejig to the twolves" (FW 479.14, CW 228).

9. In 1882, chief secretary Lord Frederick Cavendish and one of his senior officers were murdered in Phoenix Park just a few days after Parnell was released from Kilmainham prison, where he was held as a political prisoner. Parnell was shocked and offered his resignation, although he had no part in the events and an Irish terrorist group (the Invincibles) was credited with the crime. In 1887, however, *The Times* began a series on "Parnell and Crime," attempting to link Parnell to the organization. A series of letters were used as evidence, and Parnell sued for libel, accusing the paper of using forged material. In 1889, Dublin journalist Richard Pigott broke down on the witness stand after being unmasked as the forger. He confessed and later shot himself in Madrid (Lyons, *The Fall of Parnell*, 14, 20–21).

10. Stanislaus Joyce, *My Brother's Keeper*, 68.

11. Suzanne Clark suggests this resistance to the domestic, although she primarily discusses American modernism. Yet her work also speaks to the "revolution of the word" in the British and European literature of that period. Her particular formulation of the sentimental focuses on modernism's adversarial relation to domestic culture, which implicitly discredited much of women's writing from the previous era. See Clark, *Sentimental Modernism: Women Writers and the Revolution of the Word* (Bloomington and Indianapolis: Indiana University Press, 1991). While Joyce's work could be read in concert with this ges-

ture, his wariness of the sentimental is more deeply entrenched in resistance to religious and nationalistic strictures. In Joyce's work, however, these strictures are often imposed by women. This is also often an assumption of his cultural context (manifest, for example, in Yeats' *Countess Ni Houlihan* and *Countess Cathleen* plays and much of his poetry). Ireland is herself a woman to whom male authors are exhorted to be faithful.

12. As Declan Kiberd has argued, the Irish actively assimilated the fractional aspects of their past. However, the documents Joyce had access to, at least, suggest the presence of a movement that did press for racial purity. In contrast, Kiberd elucidates those texts in Irish literature that "far from providing a basis for doctrines of racial purity, they seem to take pleasure in the fact that identity is seldom straightforward and given, more often a matter of negotiation and exchange" (1). Kiberd does, in fact, draw on *Finnegans Wake* as an example of the multi-originated aspect of Irishness. See Kiberd, *Inventing Ireland* (Cambridge: Harvard University Press, 1996).

13. I have in mind here Homi Bhabha, Julia Kristeva, and Giorgio Agamben, but there has been a wealth of discussion on these topics in the last ten years. My reading of Joyce, however, will push toward an intersection with recent discussions of cultural identity in terms of multicultural constructions. See, for instance, the writings of Charles Taylor and Jürgen Habermas in Amy Gutmann, ed., *Multiculturalism*.

14. MacCabe, *James Joyce and the Revolution of the Word*, 152.

15. Joyce answers, according to MacCabe, Lenin's call for a "new kind of party" that, according to MacCabe, will be created by subjects not discretely defined but in a plurality of contradictory modes, constantly engaged in self-critical work (*James Joyce and the Revolution of the Word*, 152–53).

16. And so Manganiello writes: "If by politics we mean campaigning for votes, or for particular candidates, Joyce took no part. If by politics we understand attempting to get new laws passed through legislatures, Joyce never participated in such activity either. He did not make himself a champion of causes, however noble. By refusing to do so Joyce did not discountenance his political awareness, but rather indicated his conviction that an active role in politics would compromise his position as an artist" (*Joyce's Politics*, 2).

17. See Vincent Cheng, *Joyce, Race, and Empire* (Cambridge: Cambridge University Press, 1995); Maria Tymoczko, *The Irish Ulysses* (Berkeley, Los Angeles, and London: University of California Press, 1994); and Seamus Deane, "Joyce and Nationalism."

18. Nolan's work is most interesting as a symptomatic manifestation of desire the sort of which becomes embroiled in so many readings of Joyce's work. See *James Joyce and Nationalism* (London: Routledge, 1995). While she never marshals evidence to establish any sympathy, on Joyce's part, for Irish terrorism, Nolan persistently criticizes American critics who have elucidated the tensions between Joyce's cosmopolitanism and his interest in Ireland, accusing the most skilled deconstructive readers, like Derek Attridge and Colin MacCabe, of "universalizing"—a distinctly *contra*-deconstructive gesture. She concludes her book with a similar dismissal of "all" feminist readings of Joyce.

19. D. George Boyce, *Ireland 1828–1923: From Ascendancy to Democ-

racy (Cambridge, Mass. and Oxford: Blackwell Publishers, 1992), 22–26 and passim.

20. As a young man, Joyce supported W. B. Yeats's and later J. M. Synge's rights to represent the Irish beyond the received, celebratory stereotypes, defending Yeats's play *The Countess of Cathleen* when students circulated a petition against it in 1899 (Ellmann, *James Joyce*, 66–67) and evincing strong interest in Synge's work, *Playboy of the Western World*, as it stirred riots in the Abbey Theater in 1907. Joyce apparently identified his own troubles in publishing *Dubliners* with Synge's ability to "set them by the ears" (Gilbert, *The Letters of James Joyce*, Feb. 11, 1907).

21. Ellmann, *James Joyce*, 98–104, 530, 660, passim.

22. Mary Reynolds, "Davin's Boots: Joyce, Yeats, and Irish History," *Joycean Occasions: Essays for the Milwaukee James Joyce Conference*, ed. Janet E. Dunleavy, Melvin J. Friedman, and Michael Patrick Gillespie (Newark: University of Delaware Press, 1991), 218–34.

23. As Vincent Cheng has argued, this story reads as a critique of the imperialist impulse implicit in Gabriel's patronizing and subtly controlling attitude earlier in the evening (Cheng, *Joyce, Race, Empire*, 134–47). Cheng argues that Gabriel's eventual resistance to the urge to pursue his own sexual agenda in the face of his wife's indifference and, indeed, distracted sadness over the memory of her dead lover, Michael Furey, opens the door to Gabriel's recovery from his own potential for patriarchal aggression. Cheng reads this as a moment of emotional expansiveness and generosity, giving Gabriel a vision that releases him from the ghosts of his own repression, so that the falling snow allows him to "break down the barriers of difference constructed by the patriarchal ego he is so deeply (if unconsciously) implicated in" (Cheng, *Joyce, Race, and Empire*, 146–47).

24. The Christmas dinner scene fixes Stephen's memory of the crisis of Parnell's fall; and yet this nationalistic moment is complicated by later exchanges in school, which show him struggling against the influence of constricted nationalism as it is policed the literary movements at the turn of the century.

25. David Lloyd, *Anomalous States: Irish Writing and the Post-Colonial Movement* (Durham, N.C.: Duke University Press, 1993), 105, 131.

26. Several critics have noted an apparent break after this episode. David Kiremidjian has suggested that Joyce begins to develop his use of parody most fully after the close of "Scylla and Charybdis," (*A Study of Modern Parody*, 136), and Marguerite Harkness argues that there is a shift in Stephen's aesthetics within the episode that indicates a better understanding of parody. See *The Aesthetics of Dedalus and Bloom* (London and Toronto: Associated University Press, 1984), 148.

27. Groden, *"Ulysses" in Progress*, 135–36.

28. Ellmann identifies Michael Cusack, historically, as Joyce's intended referent. *James Joyce*, 61n.

29. Jews are here dirty, "coming over here to Ireland filling the country with bugs" (U 12.1141–42) and "have a sort of a queer odour coming off them" (U 12.453). The publicans seem in accord (but for Bloom) that those "of the bottlenosed fraternity" are all swindlers, as well; those like "an ancient Hebrew

Zaretsky or something" try to get out of legal obligations by complaining of their poverty. One gathers that they, like Bloom, are supposed to have stashed away the winnings from some horse-betting or "trading without a license"; they are only too tight-fisted to buy a round of drinks (U 12.1550f). Bloom's "insider's" knowledge of Throwaway's potential is clearly a myth of misunderstanding. In "Lotus-Eaters," Bloom merely mumbles that he was about to "throw away" a paper he hands to Bantam Lyons, a comment Hynes mishears and later apparently reports as insider's knowledge (U 5.537–41). The pub drinkers believe that Bloom is going to collect his winnings (U 12.1551–52) when in fact he is looking again for Martin Cunningham (and escaping a heated argument about nationalism).

30. With regards to Joyce's own relation to antisemitism and Jewishness, recent scholarship has turned up material that complicates any assumptions. In his book *Joyce and the Jews: Culture and Texts* (London: Macmillan, 1989), Ira Nadel finds ample biographical evidence to support an argument that Joyce in many ways identified his own plight with the Jews'. On the other hand, a variety of antisemitic stereotypes find their way ambivalently into *Ulysses*. Richard Ellmann has argued that Joyce most likely used Otto Weiniger's *Geschlect und Charakter* as a source of stereotypes of women and Jews around the turn-of-the-century. See *James Joyce*, 463. Marilyn Reizbaum finds that Joyce's inscription of the Jewish man as womanly-man in "Circe" suggests that he read Weiniger's work critically, "as an expression of the subconscious." She points out the Weiniger was himself a Jew-hating Jew who internalized this self-hatred so violently that in 1928—the year his book was published in full—he committed suicide. Reizbaum argues that, even if Joyce is using negative stereotypes in *Ulysses*, "he does not exemplify the theories in his work, he exposes them." See Reizbaum, "The Jewish Connection, Continued," in *The Seventh of Joyce*, ed. Bernard Benstock (Bloomington: Indiana University Press, 1982), 229–38 (232).

31. Enda Duffy, *The Subaltern "Ulysses"* (Minneapolis and London: University of Minnesota Press, 1994), 109.

32. Roustang, "How Do You Make a Paranoiac Laugh?" 716.

33. Lacan, *The Four Fundamental Concepts of Psycho-Analysis*, 238.

34. Freud, *Introductory Lectures on Psycho-Analysis*, vol. 16, 428.

35. Jacques Derrida has noticed the visible incorporation of "yes" in "eyes," and one can say that the narrator here gives out not just "ay"s but "ayes."

Derrida finds a paradox within the final "yes" of the book. Joyce's signature (the affirming "yeses" in Molly Bloom's monologue) "simultaneously ruins its model" of affirmation of the subject's location. When one says "yes" (on a telephone, for instance) one affirms that one hears the "other." But simultaneously one always "relaunches" oneself. "I am here," one says, but then is immediately in the process conveying one's words someplace else. Playing on the ambiguities in French of the "ouï-dire" (hearsay) and saying yes ("dire oui"), Derrida is able to highlight the impossibility, in *Ulysses*, of locating "truth" (versus hearsay) even at the moment of complete affirmation. This impossibility emerges as the text laughingly expands ("oui-rire") to include all future possibilities its readers might encounter, and thus *Ulysses* never fails to be a text "about" its reader. Derrida argues, with some irony, that one cannot escape Joyce's system, and so cannot be a *legitimate* Joycean, one judging the text from outside. See "Ulysses Gramophone," trans. Tina Kendall, *James Joyce: The Augmented Nineth*, ed. Bernard Benstock (Syracuse: Syracuse University Press, 1988), 27–76. In French, *Ulysse gramophone: Deux mots pour Joyce* (Paris: Éditions Galilée, 1987).

36. Bhabha, "The Other Question. . . ." 22–26.

37. Boyce, *Ireland 1828–1923*, 1–29, and A. Norman Jeffares, *Anglo-Irish Literature* (New York: Schocken Books, 1982), 5–7.

38. Ellmann, *The Letters of James Joyce*, 2:167.

39. Ellmann, *The Letters of James Joyce*, 2:167.

40. Cheng, *Joyce, Race, and Empire*, 27.

41. "Gigantism" is the term that Michael Groden chooses to apply to the mock-heroic parody passages. He takes it from Joyce's schema, where Joyce uses that term as a label for the technique of "Cyclops" (*"Ulysses" in Progress*, 115).

The parallel between cyclops and the Citizen is reinforced when Bloom, answering the Citizen's anti-semitic remarks, says "Some people can see the mote in others' eyes but they can't see the beam in their own" (U 12.1237–38).

42. Groden calls this the "basic" style, one that Joyce himself identified as *Ulysses'* "initial style" (Gilbert, *The Letters of James Joyce*, 129). According to Groden, "it involved a combination of third-person, past-tense narration and direct first-person, present-tense depiction of the characters' thoughts" (Groden, *"Ulysses" in Progress*, 15).

Karen Lawrence goes a step further, and identifies a few stylistic quirks that seem particularly Joyce's own: "The care in the choice of adjectives ("lank black hair," "open moist mouth"), the heavy use of present and past participial phrases, the placement of the modifying adverb after, rather than before, the transitive verb ("leaned his chin gravely upon them"), the compound word ("blindcord"), the phonetic song played by the changing consonants, all indicate how "scrupulous" and well written the narration is. These characteristics of style, associated with the figure of the artist, are developed further in the early chapters of *Ulysses* and provide the book's initial style" (36). See Lawrence, *The Odyssey of Style in "Ulysses"* (Princeton: Princeton University Press, 1981).

43. Groden, *"Ulysses" in Progress*, 134.

44. Brian Cheyette, "'Jewgreek is greekjew': The Disturbing Ambivalence of Joyce's Semitic Discourse in *Ulysses*," in *Joyce Studies Annual*, ed. Thomas Staley (Austin: University of Texas Press, 1992): 32–56 (38).

45. Gifford, *"Ulysses" Annotated*, 215.

46. *The Jewishness of Mr. Bloom/Das Jüdische an Mr. Bloom* (Frankfurt am Main: Suhrkamp, 1984), 20–21.

47. In particular, Lacoue-Labarthe examines the Oedipal model of identification, desire, and violence as it is reworked in the writings of René Girard. Girard argues that society is founded upon the exclusion and murder of a scapegoat who, as "scapegoat," must be arbitrarily chosen. For Girard, the murder of this scapegoat, this "other" taken from beyond the communal identity, is always unavoidable where political representations are concerned. Lacoue-Labarthe, however, is invested in analyzing and avoiding the violence that Girard sees as

implicit in social representations, and he finds that the scapegoat upon which representation is founded is *not* arbitrarily chosen, but is rather the concept of representation itself—mimesis, imitation, repeatability. See Lacoue-Labarthe, *Typography: Mimesis, Philosophy, Politics*, ed. Christopher Finsk (Cambridge: Harvard University Press, 1989).

48. As Ford Madox Ford noted, the wars disrupted any sense of cultural hegemony or objective relation to facts:

> If, before the war, one had any function it was that of historian. Basing, at it were, one's mortality on the Europe of Charlemagne as modified by the Europe of Napoleon. I once had something to go upon. One could approach with composure the Lex Allemannica, the Feudal System, problems of Aerial Flight, or the price of wheat or the relations of the sexes. But now, it seems to me, we have no method of approach to any of these problems. (From a manuscript in the Firestone Rare Book and Manuscript Library, Princeton University, cited in James Longenbach's book, *Modernist Poetics of History: Pound, Eliot, and the Sense of the Past* [Princeton, N.J.: Princeton University Press, 1987], 9.)

49. *On Heros, Hero-Worship, and the Heroic in History* in *The Works of Thomas Carlyle in Thirty Volumes*, vol. 5 (London: Chapman Hall Ltd, 1898, orig. 1841), 1.

50. Nadel, *Biography: Fiction, Fact and Form* (New York: St. Martin's Press, 1984), 13–38.

51. John Bishop, *Joyce's Book of the Dark: "Finnegans Wake"* (Madison: University of Wisconsin Press, 1986), 132.

52. Bishop, *Joyce's Book of the Dark*, 141.

53. "Growing Up Absurd in Dublin," in *A Conceptual Guide to Finnegans Wake*, ed. Michael H. Begnal and Fritz Senn (University Park and London: The Pennsylvania State University Press, 1974), 173–200 (180).

54. McHugh, *Annotations*, 476.

55. This link hinges on the problem of interpretation that points to history, to social perception of the individual, and the act of reading or hearing language. "Fuming censor" here appears to be a side-reference to the reader, as the narrative voice likewise addresses a "temptive lissomer" (FW 477.18) and "drear writer" (FW 476.21).

56. For a more elaborate explanation of how aggressivity relates to the paranoid's need to externalize all traces of ambivalence, see Jacques Lacan, "Aggressivity in Psychoanalysis," *Écrits*, 8–29.

57. *The Coming Community*, trans. Michael Hardt (Minneapolis and London: The University of Minnesota Press, 1993), 27.

58. Agamben is suspicious of The State as that which is founded not on a bond or social contract but on "the unbinding it prohibits," and understanding language in a way that admits of multiple intentions, voices, and tensions in meaning might then suggest that the nation begin to form itself not around the Word, as a single signifier of identity, but in terms of multiple words, voices, and changing images.

59. McHugh, *Annotations*, 484. The second term is archaic.

60. Anderson, *Imagined Communities: Reflections on the Origin and Spread of Nationalism* (New York and London: Verso, 1983, Reprint 1991), 6.

61. For Habermas's comments, see "Struggles for Recognition in the Democratic Constitutional State," in *Multiculturalism*, ed. Amy Gutmann.

CHAPTER 6. RHYTHMIC IDENTIFICATION
AND COSMOPOLITAN CONSCIOUSNESS

1. See Scott L. Malcomson, "The Varieties of Cosmopolitan Experience," in *Cosmopolitics: Thinking and Feeling beyond the Nation*, ed. Pheng Cheah and Bruce Robbins (London and Minnesota: University of Minnesota Press, 1998), 233–45 (233).

2. See Bhabha, *The Location of Culture* (New York: Routledge, 1994); James Clifford, *The Predicament of Culture: Twentieth-Century Ethnography, Literature, and Art* (Cambridge: Harvard University Press, 1988); Clifford, "Traveling Cultures," in *Cultural Studies*, ed. Lawrence Grossberg, Cary Nelson, and Paula A. Treichler (New York: Routledge, 1992), 92–112; and Robbins, *Secular Vocations: Intellectuals, Professionalism, Culture* (London: Verso, 1993) and "Comparative Cosmopolitanisms," in *Cosmopolitics*, 246–64. Among recent returns to *cosmopolitanism* as a concept, there are of course some positions that tilt closer to Enlightenment breadth and universals. Julia Kirsteva, for example, calls for a *thinned* version of Enlightenment principles, which maintains a normative center, thought much qualified. I would hope to distinguish such unfortunate refusals of multicultural proliferations from the version of cosmopolitanism in the works of Bhabha et. al. For Kristeva's version, see *Nations without Nationalism* trans. Leon S. Roudiez (New York: Columbia University Press, 1993).

3. Cheah, "Given Culture: Rethinking Cosmopolitical Freedom in Transnationalism," in *Cosmopolitics*, 290–328 (295).

4. Bhabha, "Postcolonial Authority and Postmodern Guilt," in *Cultural Studies*, ed. Lawrence Grossberg, Carl Nelson, and Paula A. Treichler (New York: Routledge, 1992), 59. Discussed by Pheng Cheah, "Given Culture," 295.

5. Robbins, "Comparative Cosmopolitanisms," 250.

6. As Robbins explains it: "Instead of renouncing cosmopolitanism as a false universal, one can embrace it as an impulse to knowledge that is shared with others, a striving to transcend particularity that is itself partial, but no more so than the similar cognitive strivings of a many diverse peoples. The world's particulars can now be recorded, in part at least, as the world's *discrepant cosmopolitanisms*" ("Comparative Cosmopolitanisms," 259). He sees this new cosmopolitanism, in his particular version, rooted in the academy and/or its particular place, while also extending anti-imperial and democratic principles abroad (261).

7. Kant's work, *Zum ewigen Frieden: Ein philosophischer Entwurf. Kant's Gesammelte Schriften* (1795), translated as *Toward Perpetual Peace: A Philosophical Project*, formulated one of the most often invoked theories of cos-

mopolitanism. It extends a call for nations to overcome self-interest in the name of international good. Allen Wood provides an astute analysis of this text in "Kant's Project for Perpetual Peace" in *Cosmopolitics*, 59–76. As he observes, history has proven Kant to have been overly optimistic about the *good* that will come from such notions. Enlightenment philosophy and universalism paved the way for imperialism and colonization of other countries and cultures.

8. Cunard, "Thoughts about James Joyce," 10/1/56, in the Harry Ransom Research Center Archives, University of Texas at Austin.

9. "Jacques Lacan: Le Sinthome," Seminaire du 16 Mars 1976, text established by J-A. Miller, *Ornicar?* 32–40 (37). Translations are my own. French original: "À preuve que Joyce, après avoir soigneusement témoigné du sinthome de Dublin, qui ne prend âme que du sien à lui, ne manque pas, chose fabuleuse, de tomber dans le mythe Vico qui soutient le *Finnegans' Wake* [sic]. La seule chose qui l'en préserve, c'est que quand même *Finnegans' Wake* [sic] se présente comme un rêve, et, de plus, désigne que Vico est un rêve tout autant; en fin de compte, que les babochages de Mme Blavatsky, le Mahanvantara et tout ce qui s'en suit, l'idée d'un rythme. . . . On ne retrouve pas, ou bien c'est désigner qu'on ne fait jamais que tourner en rond. On trouve" (37).

10. Lacan, "Jacques Lacan: Le Sinthome," 38.

11. Ellmann, *The Letters of James Joyce*, 1:241.

12. Thomas C. Hofheinz, *Joyce and the Invention of Irish History: "Finnegans Wake" in context* (Cambridge and New York: Cambridge University Press, 1995), 143.

13. Giambattista Vico, *The New Science of Giambattista Vico* (from 1744 edition), trans. Thomas Goddard Bergin and Max Harold Fisch (Ithaca, N.Y.: Cornell University Press, 1984), 73, 104.

14. Bishop, *Joyce's Book of the Dark*, 176.

15. Bernard Benstock, "The Anti-Schematics of *Finnegans Wake*," in *James Joyce Studies Annual* I (Summer 1990): 96–116 (98, 97).

16. McHugh, *Annotations*, 3.

17. Note also that chronology is confused, even inoperable, in the first two paragraphs of the *Wake*. The first sentence refers to a post-seventeenth-century period (when Adam and Eve's church was built), while the second sentence moves back to Sir Tristram's arrival at Howth (in the twelfth century). Synchrony appears on the "river of time," and one cannot locate the narrative(s) in one single historical period. Memory runs simultaneously past Adam and Eve's church and Eve and Adam's home in Eden.

18. McHugh, *Annotations*, 3.

19. They actually both spring from the same period (twelfth century), one historical and one mythological, so one might suspect Joyce was pointing toward an origin of the myth. But their lives seem to be extremely different.

20. Rosa Maria Bosinelli, "'I use his cycles as a trellis': Joyce's Treatment of Vico in Finnegans Wake," in *Vico and Joyce*, ed. Donald Phillip Verene (Albany: State University of New York Press, 1987), 123–31 (127).

21. Joseph Mali, "Mythology and Counter-History: The New Critical Art of Vico and Joyce," *Vico and Joyce*, 32–47 (37).

22. As Hofheinz comments, "Vico's 'cyclical' theory operates uneasily in

conjunction with orthodox Catholic eschatology: the trials and retrials of human history trace a mysterious progress according to a divine agenda that leads humanity toward a final verdict" (*Joyce and the Invention of Irish History*, 143).

23. Gilbert, *The Letters of James Joyce*, 1:165.

24. Ole Vinding, "James Joyce in Copenhagen," trans. Helge Irgens-Moller, in *Portraits of the Artist in Exile: Recollections of James Joyce by Europeans*, ed. Willard Potts (Seattle: University of Washington Press, 1979), 149. Cited in Bishop, *Joyce's Book of the Dark*, 131.

25. He is briefly associated with Myles Joyce, as well, who was given an unsound trial for murder in Maamtrasna in 1882, an "incompatibly framed indictment on both counts" (McHugh, 85). Humorously, this "child of Maam" is of a family "long and honorably associated with the tar and feather industries" (FW 85.23–24). Evidence is also given against HCE by "an eye, ear, nose and throat witness." Biographical reference to Joyce himself is suggested both by association with the name of Myles Joyce, and also by the attack on an eye, ear, nose, and throat specialist whom, perhaps, Joyce knew: Oliver St. John Gogarty.

HCE is also John Joyce. Joyce writes to Budgen, "the encounter between my father and a tramp (the basis of my book) actually took place at that part of the park" (Gilbert, *The Letters of James Joyce*, 1:396). Of his father Joyce writes, "hundreds of pages and scores of characters in my books came from him" (Gilbert, *The Letters of James Joyce*, 1:312).

26. "Mr. Delaney" also sings of "Piggott's purest" note in *The Ballad of Persse O'Reilly*, listing the indictments against HCE, the fallen leader. Piggott, referred to in bits throughout the *Wake*, forged letters from Parnell, "showing" that he conspired toward the murders.

27. See Lyons, *The Fall of Parnell*.

28. Double-ends Joined or Dublin's Ginned, etc.

29. Dor is also Cornish for "earth" and Hebrew for (1) generation and (2) dwelling (McHugh, *Annotations*, 20).

30. Frederick Hoffmann has noted that all devices described by Freud in *The Interpretation of Dreams* are used in the *Wake*. See chapter 7 of *The Interpretation of Dreams* and Hoffmann, "Infroyce," in *James Joyce: Two Decades of Criticism*, ed. Seon Givens (New York: Vanguard Press, 1939), 390–435 (422).

31. Lacan, *Écrits*, 69.

32. See Mark Shechner, *Joyce in Nighttown*.

33. Samuel Beckett, "Dante . . . Bruno. Vico . . . Joyce," in *An Exagmination Round His Factification for Incamination of Work in Progress* (New York: New Directions, 1929/1972), 1–22 (3–4).

34. Joseph Campbell and Henry Morton Robinson, *A Skeleton Key to "Finnegans Wake"* (New York: Harcourt, Brace and Co., 1944).

35. Clive Hart, in *Structure and Motif*, balks at the notion that the *Wake* functions strictly along archetypal lines, arguing that Joyce was "temperamentally incapable of committing himself to any world-view, least of all so pretentious a theory as that of archetypes" (147). Hart is presumably referring to Joyce's anti-institutional temperament, most notably his rebellion against religion.

Arguing that Joyce's correspondences follow neither the pattern of "traditional" correspondences (universal symbols like those of Yeats) nor the surrealists' notion of the unconscious mind, Hart focuses instead on motif in the *Wake*. HCE can be Dublin not by crude analogy, but by motif, since objects are drawn into each new context, are magnetized by certain patterns. So, for example, we find recurring overtones of captivity, exile, and betrayal in HCE's "character" (165). These motifs forbid us to read an individual characterization or correspondence in isolation, but we must somehow read them "when all their occurrences are related together, a part from one version combining with a part from another to build up the sense" (156–57). James Atherton, in *The Books at the Wake* (128f) launches similar objections to archetypology.

36. David Hayman, who has probably made the greatest contribution to recent scholarship on the *Wake*, still explicitly uses the notion of archetype in his work (*The Wake in Transit*, 69 and passim). C. George Sandulescu, in *The Language of the Devil: Texture and Archetype in "Finnegans Wake"* (London: Colin Smythe, 1987), defines archetypes as lexical, rather than conceptual, but he retains the limiting structure.

37. C. G. Jung, *Collected Works of C. G. Jung*, vol. 9, trans. R. F. C. Hull, Bollingen Series XX (New York: Pantheon Books 1959), 4.

38. Discussed in Jung, *Collected Works*, 9:4.

39. Attridge, *Peculiar Language: Literature as Difference from the Renaissance to James Joyce* (Ithaca, N.Y.: Cornell University Press, 1988), 197.

40. Tindall, *A Reader's Guide to "Finnegans Wake"* (New York: Farrar, Straus, and Giroux, 1969).

41. Bishop, *Joyce's Book of the Dark*, 175.

42. Ellmann, *James Joyce*, 466. Joyce did, however, resort to calling on Jung's expertise in the case of Lucia. He was her twentieth doctor (676).

43. Jung, *Collected Works*, 9:4.

44. Jung, *Collected Works*, 9:5.

45. Jung, *Collected Works*, 9:70.

46. Jung, *Collected Works*, 9:7–8.

47. William McGuire and R. F. C. Hull, eds., *C. G. Jung Speaking: Interviews and Encounters* (Princeton: Princeton University Press, 1977).

48. On Joyce's approach to race, see Cheng, *Joyce, Race, and Empire*.

49. Samuels, *Jung and the Post-Jungians* (London and Boston: Routledge and Kegan Paul, 1985), 26.

50. Jolande Jacobi, *Complex/Archetype/Symbol in the Psychological of C. G. Jung*, trans. Ralph Manheim, Bollingen Series LVII (New York: Pantheon Books, 1950), 74–77.

51. Jung, *Collected Works*, 9:21–22.

52. Mahaffey, *Reauthorizing Joyce*, 2.

53. McHugh, *Annotations*, 263, picks this out of Danish, "Saaledes er det i denne vakhre verden, mine børn." It is like that in this beautiful world, my children.

54. Lacoue-Labarthe, *Typographies*, 175f.

55. Atherton, *Books at the Wake*, 37.

56. Coleridge, *The Collected Works of Samuel Taylor Coleridge, The Friend* vol. 1, ed. Barbara E. Rooke (London: Routledge and Kegan Paul, 1969), 94.

57. Margot Norris, "Anna Livia Plurabelle: The Dream Woman," in *Women in Joyce*, 197–213 (211).

58. This consists of a collection of king's names, and HCE thereby is aggressively identified with everybody, as the text exclaims, "Holy Saint Eiffel, the very phoenix!" (FW 88.23–24). Perhaps one bad king may pass away, but another will always rise to take his place: a skeptical reading of Vico's historical cycle.

59. Christine Froula notes that French feminism has invoked Joyce's writing as a means of subverting the Law of the Father, so prominent in Lacan's work: "Cixous celebrates 'Penelope' as an avatar of *écriture féminine* that moves writing in the direction of an imaginary realm beyond the jurisdiction of the father's law." See "The Laugh of the Medusa," by Hélène Cixous, trans. Keith Cohen and Paula Cohen, in *New French Feminisms: An Anthology*, ed. Elaine Marks and Isabelle de Courtivron (Amherst: University of Mass Press, 1980), 245–64, and "Sorties" in Cixous and Catherine Clement, *The Newly Born Woman*, trans. Betsy Wing (Minneapolis: University of Minnesota Press, 1985). Froula also points out that Julia Kristeva, in *Desire in Language*, makes Joyce's style the exemplar of a semiotic play that disrupts the symbolic and subverts the Oedipally constituted law of the father. See Froula, *Modernism's Body*, 291n128.

60. Lorraine Weir points out that Joseph Frank has noticed a similar syntheses between "the sensuous nature of the art medium and the condition of human perception" in modern writings, which resists the traditional separations between content and form. See *Writing Joyce: A Semiotics of the Joyce System* (Bloomington and Indianapolis: Indiana University Press, 1989), 30.

61. Recent critical work has focused on the link between Joyce's later experiments in *Finnegans Wake* and the linguistic theories proposed by Marcel Jousse, whose work Joyce avowedly admired in the late 1920s while he was initiating work on the *Wake*. See Lorraine Weir and Jean Michel Rabaté, both of whom discuss Jousse's influence. See Rabaté, "Joyce: Les lèvres circoncises," *Leçons d'écriture: Ce que disent les manuscrits*, ed. A. Grésillon and M. Werner (Paris: Minard, 1985), 107–28. [Mentioned in Weir, "The Choreography of Gesture: Marcel Jousse and *Finnegans Wake*," in *James Joyce Quarterly* 14:3 (Spring 1977): 313–25. See also Mary and Padriac Colum, *Our Friend James Joyce* (London: Gollancz, 1959), 130–31.] If Joyce apparently did not discover Jousse until after the completion of *Ulysses*, the interest Joyce evinced in the linguist's work on gestures might indicate a trajectory of curiosity about such an art, sparked by the earlier influences of mime, eurhythmics, and Mallarmé.

62. McHugh catches the French allusion to absinthe, *Annotations*, 534.

63. Weir, "The Choreography of Gesture," 314–15. Weir refers to Gabrielle Baron's biography, *Marcel Jousse: Introduction à sa vie et à son oeuvre* (Paris: Casterman, 1965).

64. Weir, "The Choreography of Gesture," 314.

65. Baron, *Marcel Jousse*, 248.

66. McHugh, *Annotations*, 535.

67. Jousse, *Les Rabbis d'Israel: Les Récitatifs rythmiques parallèles* (Paris: Éditions Spes, 1929), xvii, xix. All translations are my own.

68. Jousse, *Les Rabbis d'Israel*, xxiii. Original French: "Tout Schème rythmique qui a fait danser un Geste propositionnel sur les muscles laryngo-buccaux d'un Improvisateur ou d'un Récitateur, acquiert par là une tendance à danser de nouveau."

69. Jousse, *Les Rabbis D'Israel*, xxiii.

70. According to McHugh, Eblana is Ptolemy's name for Dublin, *Annotations*, 614.

71. Genette, *Narrative Discourse: An Essay in Method*, trans. Jane E. Lewin (Ithaca, N.Y.: Cornell University Press, 1980), 163–64.

72. McHugh, *Annotations*, 6.

73. See also FW 121 with its upside down F's. And FW 266 with F's facing off.

74. Christine Van Boheemen-Saaf discusses the "deterioration into chaos" as Joyce plays with concepts of identity and difference in *Ulysses* and *Finnegans Wake*. She remarks that this deterioration brings about an "erosion of identity" in Joyce's writing. See *The Novel as Family Romance: Language, Gender, and Authority from Fielding to Joyce* (Ithaca, N.Y.: Cornell University Press, 1987), 138f.

75. McHugh, *Annotations*, 465.

76. McHugh, *Annotations*, 465.

77. Rabaté, "'Alphybettyformed verbage': the shape of sounds and letters in *Finnegans Wake*," in *Word and Image* 2.3 (July-September 1986): 237–43 (243).

WORKS CITED

Abelove, Henry. "Freud, Male Homosexuality, and the Americans." *The Lesbian and Gay Studies Reader*. Edited by Abelove, Michèle Aina Barale, and David M. Halperin, 381–96. New York and London: Routledge, 1993.

Abrams, M. H. *The Mirror and the Lamp: Romantic Theory and the Critical Tradition*. 1953. Reprint, London: Oxford University Press, 1971

Agamben, Giorgio. *The Coming Community*. Translated by Michael Hardt. Minneapolis and London: The University of Minnesota Press, 1993.

Anderson, Benedict. *Imagined Communities: Reflections on the Origin and Spread of Nationalism*. 1983. Reprint, New York and London: Verso 1991.

Aquinas, Thomas. *On Being and Essence*. Translated by Armand Maurer. Toronto: The Pontifical Institute of Medieval Studies, 1968.

Aristotle. *Metaphysics*. Translated by Richard Hope. Ann Arbor: University of Michigan Press, 1960.

Atherton, James. *Books at the Wake*. New York: Paul Appel, 1959.

———. "*Finnegans Wake*: The Gist of the Pantomime." *Accent* 15.1 (Winter 1955): 14–26.

Attridge, Derek. *Peculiar Language: Literature as Difference from the Renaissance to James Joyce*. Ithaca, N.Y.: Cornell University Press, 1988.

Bakhtin, M. M. *The Dialogic Imagination*. Translated by Carl Emerson and Michael Holquist. Austin: University of Texas Press, 1981.

———. *Problems of Dostoevsky's Poetics*. Translated by R. W. Rotsel. Ann Arbor: University of Michigan Press, 1973.

Baron, Gabrielle. *Marcel Jousse: Introduction à sa vie et à son oeuvre*. Paris: Casterman, 1965.

Beckett, Samuel. "Dante . . . Bruno. Vico . . . Joyce." In *An Exagmination Round His Factification for Incamination of Work in Progress*, 1–22. Edited by Sylvia Beach. 1929. Reprint, New York: New Directions, 1972.

Bell, Alexander Melville and David Charles Bell. *Bell's Standard Elocutionist*. Belfast: William Mullan, 1871.

Bell, Robert. *Jocoserious Joyce: Fate and Folly in Ulysses*. Ithaca, N.Y.: Cornell University Press, 1991.

Benstock, Bernard. "The Anti-Schematics of *Finnegans Wake*." *James Joyce Studies Annual* 1 (Summer 1990): 96–116.

Benstock, Shari. "The Genuine Christine: Psychodynamics of Issy." In *Women in Joyce*. Edited by Suzette Henke and Elaine Unkeless, 169–196. Urbana and London: University of Illinois Press, 1982.

Benveniste, Émile. "La Notion de 'rythme' dans son expression linguistique." *Problèmes de linguistic générale*. Vol. 1, pp. 327–35. Paris: Gallimard, 1966.

Bergson, Henri. "Le Rire." In *Comedy*. Translated and edited by Wylie Sypher. Baltimore: Johns Hopkins University Press, 1956.

Berkeley, George. *A Treatise Concerning the Principles of Human Knowledge*. 1710. Reprint. Indianapolis: Hackett, 1982.

Bhabha, Homi. *The Location of Culture*. New York: Routledge, 1994.

———. "The Other Question . . . : Homi Bhabha Reconsiders the Stereotype and Colonial Discourse." *Screen* 24 (1983): 18–36.

———. "Postcolonial Authority and Postmodern Guilt." In *Cultural Studies*. Edited by Lawrence Grossberg, Carl Nelson, and Paula A. Treichler, 56–68. New York: Routledge, 1992.

Bishop, John. *Joyce's Book of the Dark: "Finnegans Wake."* Madison: University of Wisconsin Press, 1986.

Biskupic, Joan. "Court Hands Parody Writers An Oh, So Pretty Ruling: Copyright Law's Fair Use Standard Redefined." *The Washington Post*, March 8, 1994, A1, A10.

Bloom, Harold. *The Anxiety of Influence: A Theory of Poetry*. Oxford: Oxford University Press, 1973.

Bosinelli, Rosa Maria. "'I use his cycles as a trellis': Joyce's Treatment of Vico in *Finnegans Wake*." In *Vico and Joyce*. Edited by Donald Phillip Verene, 123–31. Albany: State University of New York Press, 1987.

Bowen, Zack. *Ulysses as a Comic Novel*. Syracuse: Syracuse University Press, 1989.

Boyce, D. George. *Ireland 1828–1923: From Ascendancy to Democracy*. Cambridge, Mass. and Oxford: Blackwell Publishers, 1992.

Brivic, Sheldon. *Joyce's Waking Women: An Introduction to Finnegans Wake*. Madison: University of Wisconsin Press, 1995.

Brown, Richard. *James Joyce and Sexuality*. Cambridge and New York: Cambridge University Press, 1985.

Butler, Judith. *Bodies That Matter: On the Discursive Limits of "Sex."* New York and London: Routledge, 1993.

———. *Gender Trouble: Feminism and the Subversion of Identity*. New York and London: Routledge, 1990.

———. *The Psychic Life of Power: Theories in Subjection*. Stanford: Stanford University Press, 1997.

Campbell, Joseph and Henry Morton Robinson. *A Skeleton Key to "Finnegans Wake."* New York: Harcourt, Brace and Co., 1944.

Carlyle, Thomas. *On Heros, Hero-Worship, and the Heroic in History*, in *The Works of Thomas Carlyle in Thirty Volumes*. vol. 5. London: Chapman Hall Ltd., 1898, orig. 1841.

Caws, Mary Ann. "The Conception of Engendering the Erotics of Editing." *The Poetics of Gender*. Edited by Nancy K. Miller, 42–62. New York: Columbia University Press, 1986.

Cheah, Pheng. "Given Culture: Rethinking Cosmopolitical Freedom in Transnationalism." In *Cosmopolitics: Thinking and Feeling beyond the Nation*. Edited by Pheng Cheah and Bruce Robbins, 290–328. London and Minneapolis: University of Minnesota Press, 1998.

Cheng, Vincent. *Joyce, Race, and Empire*. Cambridge: Cambridge University Press, 1995.

———. "Stephen and the Black Panther Vampire." *James Joyce Quarterly* 24 (Winter 1987): 161–75.

Cheyette, Brian. "'Jewgreek is greekjew': The Disturbing Ambivalence of Joyce's Semitic Discourse in *Ulysses*." *Joyce Studies Annual 1992*. Edited by Thomas Staley, 32–56. Austin: University of Texas Press, 1992.

Cixous, Hélène. "The Laugh of the Medusa." Translated by Keith Cohen and Paula Cohen. In *New French Feminisms: An Anthology*. Edited by Elaine Marks and Isabelle de Courtivron, 245–64. Amherst: University of Mass Press, 1980.

———. "Sorties." In *The Newly Born Woman*. Edited by Cixous and Catherine Clement, translated by Betsy Wing. Minneapolis: University of Minnesota Press, 1980.

Clark, Suzanne. *Sentimental Modernism: Women Writers and the Revolution of the Word*. Bloomington and Indianapolis: Indiana University Press, 1991.

Clifford, James. *The Predicament of Culture: Twentieth-Century Ethnography, Literature, and Art*. Cambridge: Harvard University Press, 1988.

———. "Traveling Cultures." In *Cultural Studies*. Edited by Lawrence Grossberg, Cary Nelson, and Paula A. Treichler, 92–112. New York: Routledge, 1992.

Coleridge, Samuel Taylor. *Shorter Works and Fragments* Edited by H. J. Jackson and J. R. de J. Jackson. Vol. II. *The Collected Works*. Princeton: Princeton University Press, 1995.

———. *The Friend*. Vol. I. *The Collected Works of Samuel Taylor Coleridge*. Edited by Barbara E. Rooke. London: Routledge and Kegan Paul, 1969.

Colum, Mary. *Life and the Dream*. London: Macmillan, 1947.

——— and Padric Colum. *Our Friend James Joyce*. London: Gollancz, 1959.

Cunard, Nancy. "Thoughts about James Joyce." Written at the request of Richard Ellmann. 10/1/56. Harry Ransom Research Center Archives, University of Texas, Austin, Texas.

Deane, Seamus, ed. *The Field Day Anthology of Irish Writing*. Vol. III. Derry, Ireland: Field Day Publications, 1991.

———. "Joyce and Nationalism." In *James Joyce: New Perspectives*. Edited by Colin MacCabe, 168–83. Sussex: Harvester Press and Bloomington: Indiana University Press, 1982.

DeKoven, Marianne. "The Politics of Modernist Form." *New Literary History* 23 (1992): 675–90.

De Man, Paul. "The Rhetoric of Temporality." In *Blindness and Insight: Essays in the Rhetoric of Contemporary Criticism*. 187–228. Minneapolis: University of Minnesota Press, 1971.

Deming, Robert H. *James Joyce: The Critical Heritage*. 2 vols. New York: Barnes and Noble, 1970.

Derrida, Jacques. *Dissemination*. Translated by Barbara Johnson. Chicago: University of Chicago Press, 1981.

———. *La dissemination*. Paris: Éditions du Seuil, 1972.

———. "My Chances/*Mes Chances*: A Rendezvous with Some Epicurean Stereophonies." Translated by Irene Harvey and Avital Ronell. In *Taking Chances: Derrida, Psychoanalysis, and Literature*. Edited by Joseph H. Smith and William Kerrigan, 1–32. Baltimore and London: Johns Hopkins University Press, 1984.

———. *Spurs: Nietzsche's Styles//Épersons: Les Styles de Nietszche.* Translated by Barbara Harlow. Chicago: University of Chicago Press, 1978.

———. *Ulysse gramophone: Deux mots pour Joyce.* Paris: Éditions Galilée, 1987.

———. "Ulysses Gramophone." Translated by Tina Kendall. In *James Joyce: The Augmented Nineth.* Edited by Bernard Benstock, 27–76. Syracuse: Syracuse University Press, 1988.

Devlin, Kimberly. "The Female Eye: Joyce's Voyeuristic Narcissists." In *New Alliances in Joyce Studies.* Edited by Bonnie Kime Scott, 135–43. Newark: University of Delaware Press, 1988.

Dollimore, Jonathan. *Sexual Dissidence: Augustine to Wilde, Freud to Foucault.* Oxford: Clarendon Press, 1991.

Donoghue, Denis. *We Irish: Essays on Irish Literature and Society.* New York: Knopf, 1986.

Duffy, Enda. *The Subaltern "Ulysses."* Minneapolis and London: University of Minnesota Press, 1994.

Duncan, Isadora. *The Art of Dance.* Edited by Sheldon Cheney. New York: Theatre Arts, 1928.

Ellmann, Richard. *The Consciousness of James Joyce.* New York: Oxford University Press, 1977.

———. *James Joyce.* Rev. ed. New York: Oxford University Press, 1982.

Ferrer, Daniel. "Circe, Regret and Regression." Translated by Gilly Lehmann. In *Post-Structuralist Joyce: Essays from the French.* Edited by Derek Attridge and Daniel Ferrer, 127–44. Cambridge: Cambridge University Press, 1984.

Franko, Mark. *Dancing Modernism/Performing Politics.* Bloomington and Indianapolis: Indiana University Press, 1995.

Fraser, Nancy. "False Antitheses." In *Feminist Contentions: A Philosophical Exchange.* Edited by Seyla Benhabib, Judith Butler, Drucilla Cornell, and Nancy Fraser. Introduction by Linda Nicholson. New York and London: Routledge, 1995.

Freud, Sigmund. *Der Witz und seine Beziehung zum Unbewussten.* Leipzig: F. Deuticke, 1905.

———. "Five Lectures on Psycho-Analysis." *Standard Edition of the Complete Psychological Works of Sigmund Freud.* Vol. 11. Translated and edited by James Strachey. London: The Hogarth Press and the Institute of Psycho-Analysis, 1955.

———. "Group Psychology and the Analysis of the Ego." *Standard Edition,* 18:67–144.

———. "Introductory Lectures on Psychoanalysis." *Standard Edition.* vols. 15 & 16.

———. *Jokes and Their Relation to the Unconscious. Standard Edition.* vol. 8.

———. "Leonardo da Vinci And a Memory of His Childhood." *Standard Edition.* vol. 11:59–138.

———. "On Narcissism." *Standard Edition.* vol. 14:73–102.

———. "Some Neurotic Mechanisms in Jealousy, Paranoia and Homosexuality." *Standard Edition,* 18:221–34.

———. "Three Essays on Sexuality." *Standard Works*. vol. 7:123–246.

Friedman, Susan Stanford. "(Self)Censorship and the Making of Joyce's Modernism." *Joyce: The Return of the Repressed*. Ithaca, N.Y., and London: Cornell University Press, 1993.

Froula, Christine. *Modernism's Body: Sex, Culture, Joyce*. New York: Columbia University Press, 1996.

Fuss, Diana. *Essentially Speaking: Feminism, Nature and Difference*. New York and London: Routledge, 1989.

Genette, Gerard. *Narrative Discourse: An Essay in Method*. Translated by Jane E. Lewin. Ithaca, N.Y.: Cornell University Press, 1980.

Gifford, Don. *"Ulysses" Annotated*. Rev. ed. Berkeley: University of California Press, 1988.

Gilbert, Sandra. "Costumes of the Mind." *Critical Inquiry* 7 (Winter 1980): 391–417.

Gilbert, Sandra and Susan Gubar. *No Man's Land: The Place of the Woman Writer in the Twentieth Century*. Vol. 1. New Haven: Yale University Press, 1988.

Glasheen, Adaline. *Third Census of "Finnegans Wake": An Index of the Characters and Their Roles*. Berkeley and London: University of California Press, 1977.

Gordon, John. *Finnegans Wake: A Plot Summary*. Syracuse: Syracuse University Press, 1986.

Groden, Michael. *"Ulysses" in Progress*. Princeton: Princeton University Press, 1977.

Grosz, Elizabeth. *Volatile Bodies: Toward a Corporeal Feminism*. Bloomington and Indianapolis: Indiana University Press, 1994.

Gutmann, Amy, ed. *Multiculturalism: Examining the Politics of Recognition*. Princeton: Princeton University Press, 1994.

Habermas, Jürgen. "Struggles for Recognition in the Democratic Constitutional State." Translated by Shierry Weber Nicholsen. In *Multiculturalism*. Edited by Amy Gutmann. 107–148. Princeton: Princeton University Press, 1994.

Harkness, Marguerite. *The Aesthetics of Dedalus and Bloom*. London and Toronto: Associated University Press, 1984.

Hart, Clive. "explications—for the greet glossary of code, Addenda to No 1." *A Wake Newslitter*. no. 2 (April 1962).

———. *Structure and Motif in Finnegans Wake*. Evanston, Ill.: Northwestern University Press, 1962.

Hayman, David. "Forms of Folly in Joyce: A Study of Clowning in *Ulysses*." *ELH: English Literary History* 34 (1967): 260–83.

———. *Joyce et Mallarmé*. 2 vols. Paris: Lettres Modernes, 1956.

———. *The "Wake" in Transit*. Ithaca, N.Y., and London: Cornell University Press, 1990.

Heath, Stephen. "Joyce in Language." In *James Joyce: New Perspectives*. Edited by Colin MacCabe, 129–48. Brighton and Bloomington: Indiana University Press, 1982.

Henke, Suzette. *James Joyce and the Politics of Desire*. London: Routeledge, 1990.

Henke, Suzette and Elaine Unkeless, eds. *Women in Joyce*. Chicago: University of Illinois Press, 1982.

Herr, Cheryl. *Joyce's Anatomy of Culture*. Urbana and Chicago: University of Illinois Press, 1986.

Hildesheimer, Wolfgang. *The Jewishness of Mr. Bloom/Das Jüdische an Mr. Bloom*. Frankfurt am Main: Suhrkamp, 1984.

Hoffmann, Frederick. "Infroyce." In *James Joyce: Two Decades of Criticism*. Edited by Seon Givens, 390–435. New York: Vanguard Press, 1939.

Hofheinz, Thomas C. *Joyce and the Invention of Irish History: "Finnegans Wake" in Context*. Cambridge and New York: Cambridge University Press, 1995.

Householder, Fred W. "ΠΑΡΩΙΔΙΑ." *Journal of Classical Philology* 1 (January 1944): 1–9.

Hume, David. *Enquiries Concerning the Human Understanding and Concerning the Principles of Morals*. 1777. 2nd ed. 1927 impression. Oxford: Clarendon, 1902.

Hutcheon, Linda. *A Theory of Parody: The Teachings of Twentieth-Century Art Forms*. New York: Methuen, 1985.

Irigaray, Luce. *This Sex Which Is Not One*. Translated by Catherine Porter. Ithaca, N.Y.: Cornell University Press, 1985.

Jacobi, Jolande. *Complex/Archetype/Symbol in the Psychological of C.G. Jung*. Translated by Ralph Manheim. Bollingen Series LVII. New York: Pantheon Books, 1950.

Jaques-Dalcroze, Emile. *Eurhythmics, Art and Education*. Translated by Frederick Rothwell. Edited by Cynthia Cox, 1930. Reprint, New York: Arno Press, 1980.

———. The Eurhythmics of Jaques-Dalcroze. Trans. P & E Ingham. Boston: Small, Maynard & Co., 1918.

Jeffares, A. Norman. *Anglo-Irish Literature*. New York: Schocken Books, 1982.

Johnson, James William. "Lyric." *Princeton Encyclopedia of Poetry and Poetics*. Edited by Alex Preminger, 460–70. 1965. Reprint. Princeton: Princeton University Press, 1974.

Jousse, Marcel. *Les Rabbis d'Israel: Les Récitatifs rythmiques parallèles*. Paris: Éditions Spes, 1929.

Joyce, James. *The Critical Writings of James Joyce*. Edited by Ellsworth Mason and Richard Ellmann. New York: Viking Press, 1959.

———. The Dead. Edited by Daniel R. Schwarz. Boston and New York: St. Martin's Press, 1994.

———. Dubliners. New York: Viking Press, 1967.

———. Finnegans Wake. New York: Viking Press, 1976.

———. The Letters of James Joyce. Edited by Stuart Gilbert and Richard Ellmann. 3 vols. New York: Viking Press, 1966.

———. A Portrait of the Artist as a Young Man. New York: Viking Press, 1964.

———. Stephen Hero. New York: New Directions, 1944.

———. Ulysses: The Corrected Text. Edited by Hans Walter Gabler. New York: Vintage Books, 1986.

Joyce, Stanislaus. *My Brother's Keeper: James Joyce's Early Years*. New York: Viking Press, 1958.

Jung, C. G. *Collected Works of C. G. Jung.* Vol. 9. Translated by R. F. C. Hull. Bollingen Series XX. New York: Pantheon Books, 1959.

Kant, Immanuel. *The Critique of Pure Reason.* Edited and translated by Norman Kemp Smith. New York: St. Martin's Press, 1964.

Kenner, Hugh. "Circe." In *James Joyce's "Ulysses": Critical Essays.* Edited by Clive Hart and David Hayman, 341–62. Berkeley and London: University of California Press, 1974.

Kershner, R. B. *Joyce, Bakhtin, and Popular Culture: Chronicles of Disorder.* Chapel Hill and London: University of North Carolina Press, 1989.

Kiberd, Declan. *Inventing Ireland.* Cambridge: Harvard University Press, 1996.

Kiremidjian, David. *A Study of Modern Parody.* New York: Garland Publishing, 1985.

Klein, Scott W. *The Fictions of James Joyce and Wyndham Lewis: Monsters of Nature and Design.* Cambridge: Cambridge University Press, 1994.

Kristeva, Julia. *Desire in Language: A Semiotic Approach to Literature and Art.* Edited by Leo Roudiez. Translated by Thomas Gora, Alice Jardine, and Leon S. Roudiez. New York: Columbia University Press, 1980.

——. *Nations Without Nationalism.* Translated by Leon S. Roudiez. New York: Columbia University Press, 1993.

——. *Revolution in Poetic Language.* Translated by Margaret Walker. New York: Columbia University Press, 1984.

Lacan, Jacques. "Aggressivity in Psychoanalysis." In *Écrits.* Translated by Alan Sheridan, 8–29. New York and London: W. W. Norton, 1977.

——. *Écrits: A Selection.* Translated by Alan Sheridan. New York: W. W. Norton, 1977.

——. *The Four Fundamental Concepts of Psycho-Analysis.* Translated by Alan Sheridan. New York: W. W. Norton, 1966.

——. "Jacques Lacan: Le Sinthome." Seminaire du 16 Mars 1976. Text established by Jacques-Alain Miller. *Ornicar?* 32–40.

——. *The Seminar of Jacques Lacan.* Book 1: *Freud's Papers on Technique 1953–1954.* Translated by John Forrester. New York and London: W. W. Norton, 1988.

——. *The Seminar of Jacques Lacan.* Book 2: *The Ego in Freud's Theory and in the Technique of Psychoanalysis, 1954–1955.* Translated by Sylvana Tomaselli. New York: W. W. Norton, 1988.

Lacoue-Labarthe, Philippe. *Typography: Mimesis, Philosophy, Politics.* Edited by Christopher Finsk. Translators: Eduardo Cadava, Barbara Harlow, Robert Eisenhauer, Judi Olson, Jane Popp, Peter Caws, Christopher Fynsk. Cambridge: Harvard University Press, 1989.

Lamos, Colleen. "Signatures of the Invisible: Homosexual Secrecy and Knowledge in *Ulysses.*" *The James Joyce Quarterly* 31.3 (Spring 1994): 337–56.

LaPlanche, Jean and Pontalis, J. B. *The Language of Psychoanalysis.* Translated by D. Nicholson-Smith. London: Hogarth Press, 1983.

Law, David Jules. "'Pity They Can't See Themselves': Assessing the 'Subject' of Pornography in 'Nausicaa.'" *James Joyce Quarterly.* 27.2 (Winter 1990): 219–39.

Lawrence, Karen. *The Odyssey of Style in "Ulysses."* Princeton: Princeton University Press, 1981.

Levine, Jennifer. "James Joyce, Tattoo Artist: Tracing the Outlines of Homosocial Desire." *James Joyce Quarterly* 31.3 (Spring 1994): 227–300.

Liddell, Henry G. *A History of Rome: From the Earliest Times to the Establishment of the Empire.* Vol. II. London: John Murray, 1855.

Litz, A. Walton. *The Art of James Joyce: Method and Design in "Ulysses" and "Finnegans Wake."* New York: Oxford University Press, 1964.

Lloyd, David. *Anomalous States: Irish Writing and the Post-Colonial Movement.* Durham, N.C.: Duke University Press, 1993.

Locke, John. *An Essay Concerning Human Understanding.* Edited by Peter H. Nidditch. 1689. Reprint, Oxford: Oxford University Press, 1975.

Longenbach, James. *Modernist Poetics of History: Pound, Eliot, and the Sense of the Past.* Princeton, N.J.: Princeton University Press, 1987.

Loux, Ann Kimble. "'Am I a father? If I were?' A Trinitarian Analysis of the Growth of Stephen Dedalus in *Ulysses.*" *James Joyce Quarterly* 23 (Spring 1985).

Lyons, F. S. L. *The Fall of Parnell, 1890–91.* Toronto: University of Toronto Press, 1960.

MacCabe, Colin. *James Joyce and the Revolution of the Word.* New York: Barnes and Noble, 1979.

Maeterlinck, Maurie. *Wisdom and Destiny.* New York: Dodd, Mead, 1898.

Mahaffey, Vicki. "Père-version and Im-mère-sion: Idealized Corruption in *A Portrait of the Artist as a Young Man* and *The Picture of Dorian Gray.*" *James Joyce Quarterly* 31.3 (Spring 1994): 189–206

———. *Reauthorizing Joyce.* Cambridge: Cambridge University Press, 1988.

Malcomson, Scott L. "The Varieties of Cosmopolitan Experience." In *Cosmopolitics: Thinking and Feeling beyond the Nation.* Edited by Pheng Cheah and Bruce Robbins, 233–45. London and Minnesota: University of Minnesota Press, 1998.

Mali, Joseph. "Mythology and Counter-History: The New Critical Art of Vico and Joyce." In *Vico and Joyce.* Edited by Donald Phillip Verene, 32–47. Albany: State University of New York Press, 1987.

Manganiello, Dominic. *Joyce's Politics.* London: Routeledge and Kegan Paul, 1980.

Mallarmé, Stephane. *Oeuvres complètes.* Paris: Gallimard, 1945.

McGee, Patrick. *Telling the Other: The Question of Value in Modern and Postcolonial Writing.* Ithaca, N.Y., and London: Cornell University Press, 1992.

McGuire, William, and R. F. C. Hull, eds. *C.G. Jung Speaking: Interviews and Encounters.* Princeton, N.J.: Princeton University Press, 1977.

McHugh, Roland. *Annotations to "Finnegans Wake."* Rev. ed. Baltimore: Johns Hopkins University Press, 1991.

Nadel, Ira. *Biography: Fiction, Fact and Form.* New York: St. Martin's Press, 1984.

———. *Joyce and the Jews: Culture and Texts.* London: Macmillan, 1989.

Nicholson, Linda. "Introduction." *Feminist Contentions: A Philosophical Exchange.* Edited by Seyla Benhabib, Judith Butler, Drucilla Cornell, and Nancy Fraser. New York and London: Routledge, 1995.

Nolan, Emer. *James Joyce and Nationalism*. London: Routledge, 1995.

Noon, William. *Joyce and Aquinas*. New Haven: Yale University Press, 1957.

Norris, Margot. "Anna Livia Plurabelle: The Dream Woman." In *Women in Joyce*. Edited by Suzette Henke and Elaine Unkeless, 197–214. Chicago: University of Illinois Press, 1982.

———. *Joyce's Web: The Social Unraveling of Modernism*. Austin: University of Texas Press, 1992.

Partridge, Eric. *A Dictionary of Slang and Unconventional English*. Edited by Paul Beale. New York: Macmillan, 1984.

Pater, Walter. *Walter Pater: Three Major Texts (The Renaissance, Appreciations, and Imaginary Portraits)*. Edited by William E. Buckler. New York: New York University Press, 1986.

Pearce, Richard. *The Politics of Narration: James Joyce, William Faulkner, and Virginia Woolf*. New Brunswick, N.J.: Rutgers University Press, 1991.

Pennington, Jo. *The Importance of Being Rhythmic*. New York and London: The Knickerbocker Press, 1925.

Peterson, Richard. "Did Joyce Write *Hamlet*?" *James Joyce Quarterly* 29:2 (Winter 1990): 365-72.

Proust, Marcel. *Remembrance of Things Past*. Vol. 1. Translated by C.K. Scott Moncrieff with Terence Kilmartin. New York: Random House, 1981.

———. *À la recherche du temps perdu*. Paris: Gallimard, 1954.

Rabaté, Jean Michel. "'Alphybettyformed verbage': The Shape of Sounds and Letters in *Finnegans Wake*. *Word and Image* 2.3 (July-September 1986): 237–43.

———. *James Joyce, Authorized Reader*. Baltimore and London: Johns Hopkins University Press, 1991.

———. "Joyce: Les Lèvres circoncises." In *Leçons d'écriture: Ce que disent les manuscrits*. Edited by A. Grésillon and M. Werner, 107–28. Paris: Minard, 1985.

———. *Joyce upon the Void: The Genesis of Doubt*. London: Macmillan, 1991.

———. "On Joycean and Wildean Sodomy." *James Joyce Quarterly* 31.3 (Spring 1994): 159–66.

Reizbaum, Marilyn. "The Jewish Connection, Continued." *The Seventh of Joyce*. Edited by Bernard Benstock, 229–38. Bloomington: Indiana University Press, 1982.

Revkin, Linda Kyle. "An Historical and Philosophical Inquiry into the Development of Dalcroze Eurhythmic and Its Influence on Music Education in the French Cantons of Switzerland" Dissertation. Ann Arbor: University Microforms International, 1984.

Reynolds, Mary. "Davin's Boots: Joyce, Yeats, and Irish History." In *Joycean Occasions: Essays for the Milwaukee James Joyce Conference*. Edited by Janet E. Dunleavy, Melvin J. Friedman, and Michael Patrick Gillespie, 218–34. Newark: University of Delaware Press, 1991.

Robbins, Bruce. *Secular Vocations: Intellectuals, Professionalism, Culture*. London: Verso, 1993.

———. "Comparative Cosmopolitanisms." *Cosmopolitics*. Edited by Pheng Cheah and Bruce Robbins, 246–64. London and Minneapolis: University of Minnesota Press, 1998.

Rose, Margaret A. *Parody//Metafiction: An Analysis of Parody as a Critical Mirror to the Writing and Reception of Fiction*. London: Crown Helm., 1979.

——. *Parody: Ancient, Modern, Post-Modern*. Cambridge: Cambridge University Press, 1993.

Roustang, François. "How Do You Make a Paranoiac Laugh?" *Modern Language Notes* 102.4 (1987): 707–18.

Sailer, Susan Shaw. *On the Void of to Be: Incoherence and Trope in "Finnegans Wake."* Ann Arbor: University of Michigan Press, 1993.

Samuels, Andrew. *Jung and the Post-Jungians*. London and Boston: Routledge and Kegan Paul, 1985.

Sandulescu, C. George. *The Language of the Devil: Texture and Archetype in "Finnegans Wake."* London: Colin Smythe, 1987.

Schwarz, Dan. *Reading Joyce's "Ulysses."* New York: St. Martin's Press, 1987.

Scott, Bonnie Kime. *Joyce and Feminism*. Bloomington: Indiana University Press, 1984.

Sedgwick, Eve Kosofsky. *Between Men: English Literature and Male Homosocial Desire*. Gender and Culture series. Edited by Carolyn G. Heilbrun and Nancy K. Miller. New York: Columbia University Press, 1985.

——. *Epistemology of the Closet*. Berkeley: University of California Press, 1990.

Senn, Fritz. "Nausicaa." In *James Joyce's Ulysses*. Edited by Clive Hart and David Hayman, 277–312. Berkeley, Los Angelos, London: University of California Press, 1974.

Shakespeare, William. *Hamlet*. Arden edition. Edited by Harold Jenkins. New York and London: Methuen, 1982.

Shechner, Mark. *Joyce in Nighttown*. Berkeley: University of California Press, 1974.

Staples, Hugh. "Growing Up Absurd in Dublin." In *A Conceptual Guide to Finnegans Wake*. Edited by Michael H. Begnal and Fritz Senn, 173–200. University Park and London: The Pennsylvania State University Press, 1974.

Stavisky, Aron. *Shakespeare and the Victorians*. Norman: University of Oklahoma Press, 1969.

Symons, Arthur. *The Symbolist Movement in Literature*. New York: E. P. Dutton, 1958.

Taylor, Charles. "The Politics of Recognition." In *Multiculturalism: Examining the Politics of Recognition*. Edited by Amy Gutmann, 25–73. Princeton: Princeton University Press, 1994.

Theweleit, Klaus. *Male Fantasies*. Vol. 2: *Male Bodies: Psychoanalyzing the White Terror*. Translated by Erica Carter and Chris Turner. Minneapolis: University of Minnesota Press, 1989.

Tindall, William York. *A Reader's Guide to "Finnegans Wake."* New York: Farrar, Straus, and Giroux, 1969.

Tymoczko, Maria. *The Irish Ulysses*. Berkeley, Los Angeles, and London: University of California Press, 1994.

Valente, Joseph. *James Joyce and the Problem of Justice: Negotiating Sexual and Colonial Difference*. Cambridge: Cambridge University Press, 1995.

————, ed. *Quare Joyce*. Ann Arbor: University of Michigan Press, 1998.

Van Boheemen-Saaf, Christine. "'The Language of Flow': Joyce's Dispossession of the Feminine in *Ulysses*." *European Joyce Studies* 1 (1989): 63–77.

————. *The Novel as Family Romance: Language, Gender, and Authority from Fielding to Joyce*. Ithaca, N.Y.: Cornell University Press, 1987

Vicinus, Martha. *Independent Women: Work and Community for Single Women, 1850–1920*. London: Virago Press, 1985.

Vico, Giambattista. *The New Science of Giambattista Vico*. Translation of the 1744 edition, by Thomas Goddard Bergin and Max Harold Fisch. Ithaca, N.Y.: Cornell University Press, 1984.

Vinding, Ole. "James Joyce in Copenhagen." Translated by Helge Irgens-Moller. *Portraits of the Artist in Exile: Recollections of James Joyce by Europeans*. Edited by Willard Potts. Seattle: University of Washington Press, 1979.

Warner, Michael. "Homo-Narcissism; or, Heterosexuality." In *Engendering Men: The Question of Male Feminist Criticism*. Edited by Joseph A. Boone, 190–206. New York: Routledge, 1990.

Weir, Lorraine. "The Choreography of Gesture: Marcel Jousse and *Finnegans Wake*." *James Joyce Quarterly* 14.3 (Spring 1977): 313–25.

————. *Writing Joyce: A Semiotics of the Joyce System*. Bloomington and Indianapolis: Indiana University Press, 1989.

Wood, Allen. "Kant's Project for Perpetual Peace." *Cosmopolitics*. Edited by Pheng Cheah and Bruce Robbins. London and Minneapolis: University of Minnesota Press, 1998.

Woolf, Virginia. *A Room of One's Own*. New York: Harcourt, Brace, Jovanovich, 1927.

Ziarek, Ewa. "'Circe': Joyce's *Argumentum ad Feminam*." *James Joyce Quarterly* 30:1 (Fall 1992): 51–68.

INDEX

Abelove, Henry, 187n3
Abrams, M. H., 179n23
advertising, 72, 135, 158
aesthetics, 22–24, 27–29, 32, 56, 61,
    111, 169–72, 192n3, 195n26
    aesthetic transformations, 2, 36,
    37, 44, 53, 55, 63, 120, 180n42
Agamben, Giorgio, 135, 194n13,
    198n58
agency, 66, 71, 123. See also parody,
    mastery, unconscious and
    conscious flux
aggressivity or aggression, 7, 8, 14,
    29, 31–32, 35, 49, 51, 53–55,
    64, 67, 79, 82, 99, 101, 102,
    108, 113, 121, 123, 128, 141,
    154, 158–59, 170, 198n56
    aggressivity versus aggression,
    174n14, 191n53
    representational aggressions
    (gestural), 5, 8, 16, 20, 49, 66,
    108, 138, 143, 158
alienation (subjective), 5, 8, 99, 108,
    120
allusion, 26, 30, 31, 39. See also
    parody
Anderson, Benedict, 137
Anna Livia, 18, 51, 54–57, 78–85,
    192, 98–101, 109, 111, 159
antisemitism, 121, 122, 125–28,
    185n24, 195n29, 196n30
Aquinas, Saint Thomas, 27–28, 135,
    181n58
archetypes, 17, 60, 142, 144, 150,
    152–60, 161, 163, 167, 170,
    201n35, 203n36
Aristotle, 28, 44–45, 63, 155, 179n22
art, social impact, 65

association, 25, 39, 41–49, 55, 60,
    62, 66, 77, 81, 84, 93–98, 117,
    131, 132, 134, 141,145, 147, 152,
    159, 161, 166, 171
Atherton, James, 159, 181n51,
    191n59, 202n35
Attridge, Derek, 154, 194n18
Augustine, Saint, 8
autoeroticism, 75, 89, 100, 101,
    112
avant-garde, 4, 54, 77, 171

Bakhtin, Mikhail, 10
Beckett, Samuel, 153
belief, 19–20, 64, 103, 117, 123, 145,
    169, 184n20
Bell, Robert,4, 174n8
Benjamin, Walter, 4
Benstock, Bernard, 147
Benstock, Shari, 186n43
Benveniste, Emile, 179n22
Bergson, Henri, 5
Berkeley, George, 35, 66
betrayal, 68, 90, 103, 106, 107, 115,
    116, 118, 123, 136–38, 170,
    184n20
Bhabha, Homi, 15, 124, 142–43,
    194n13
binarism, 29, 32, 36, 45, 55, 57,
    59–60, 68–69, 88, 98, 104–6,
    120, 121, 129, 136, 138, 158,
    159, 163
biographical reading, 21, 35, 65–67,
    79, 151, 185n24
bird/bat, 57
bird-girl, 60–61, 184n17
Bishop, John, 132, 146–47, 154
Bloom, Harold, 26, 178n17

217